ALIVE ON THE *ANDREA DORIA*!

ALIVE
ON THE *ANDREA DORIA!*

The Greatest Sea Rescue in History

Pierette Domenica Simpson

A Harbor Hill Book

PURPLE MOUNTAIN PRESS
Fleischmanns, New York

Alive on the Andrea Doria!
The Greatest Sea Rescue in History

First Edition 2006

A Harbor Hill Book
Published by Purple Mountain Press, Ltd.
P.O. Box 309, Fleischmanns, New York 12430-0309
845-254-4062, 845-254-4476 (fax), purple@catskill.net

Copyright © 2006 by Pierette Domenica Simpson

Orders in the United States and Canada:
Purple Mountain Press, Ltd., 1-800-325-2665, www.catskill.net/purple
Distributed in the United Kingdom, Australia, New Zealand for Purple Mountain Press:
Warsash Nautical Books, +44(0) 1489 572384, www.mainmastbooks.co.uk

Published in Italian by Sperling & Kupfer, Milan

Library of Congress Cataloging-in-Publication Data

Simpson, Pierette Domenica, 1947-
  Alive on the Andrea Doria! : the greatest sea rescue in history /
Pierette Domenica Simpson.-- 1st ed.
     p. cm.
  Includes bibliographical references and index.
   ISBN 1-930098-73-1 (cloth : alk. paper) -- ISBN 1-930098-74-X (pbk. : alk. paper)
   1. Andrea Doria (Steamship) 2. Stockholm (Motorship) 3. Shipwrecks--North
Atlantic Ocean. 4. Search and rescue operations--North Atlantic Ocean. I. Title.
   G530.A244S56 2006
   910.9163'46--dc22
                        2006008918

Cover design: Nancy Massa. Cover photos, used by permission:
Andrea Doria sinking: Mariners' Museum, Newport News, VA;
Red Cross nurse and Maria Paladino: Leonardo and Giovanna Paladino;
Stockholm bow: David A. Bright Collection;
Ruth Roman and son: Ted Russell.
Frontispiece and title page illustration courtesy of Captain Robert J. Meurn.

Please note: Chapter 12 on diving to the wreck site is intended to inform and not
inspire. The author and the publisher do not recommend diving to the *Andrea Doria*,
where the risk of death for the diver is very great.

Manufactured in the United States of America on acid-free paper.

Dedication

To my grandparents, who raised me with love and sacrificed all their worldly goods and ways to accompany me to America.

To my mother, who welcomed me to the New World.

To the people in my native Pranzalito, who helped breathe life into many dim memories of my childhood.

To the late Anthony Grillo, who expertly created and maintained our Web site, which became the catalyst for writing this book.

To the captain and crew of the Andrea Doria, who endangered their own lives to keep the passengers safe.

To the rescue ships and their people, whose invaluable assistance helped us survive.

To the personnel of the Red Cross, whose caring mission helped those with physical and psychological needs at our moment of crisis.

To the poor souls of the Andrea Doria *and the* Stockholm, whose lives were sacrificed due to the frailties of their fellow man.

To the survivors of the Andrea Doria *and the* Stockholm, who had the good fortune to escape a calamity.

In memory of my loving husband, Richard,
whose wisdom guided and inspired me.

Contents

FOREWORD   9

ACKNOWLEDGMENTS   13

INTRODUCTION   15

PART ONE   Stories of Survival

CHAPTER 1   Autobiography of a Survivor   21

CHAPTER 2   Officers and Gentlemen   53

CHAPTER 3   Lost and Found   77

CHAPTER 4   Prayers from Vieste   93

CHAPTER 5   When Her Watch Stopped   105

CHAPTER 6   Making Music and Memories   117

CHAPTER 7   Sisters and Priests: Saving Spirits   131

CHAPTER 8   The Rich and the Famous   153

CHAPTER 9   History's Greatest Sea Rescue   187

AN *ANDREA DORIA* PHOTO GALLERY   211

PART TWO   Stories of the Ship

CHAPTER 10   Anatomy of a Collision   217

CHAPTER 11   The Sinking of the Unsinkable   247

CHAPTER 12   Diving the *Doria*   255

EPILOGUE   Passages   265

APPENDIX 1   Passengers and Crew on the *Andrea Doria*   275

APPENDIX 2   In Memoriam   289

NOTES   291

GLOSSARY   299

SOURCES   303

INDEX   307

BOUT A HALF-CENTURY AGO, one of the greatest sea rescues of all time occurred off the Nantucket Shoals during the darkness of the night and through a thick blanket of enveloping fog. The pride of Italy's merchant marine fleet, the beautiful ocean liner *Andrea Doria*, collided with a smaller Swedish American liner named *Stockholm* in an area of the ocean known as "Times Square." What could have become a "second *Titanic*," the event became known, instead, as "the greatest sea rescue in history." In spite of the clearly successful rescue operation, the answer to why the collision occurred has been shrouded in mystery and controversy to this day.

The *Andrea Doria* was the first truly opulent ocean liner that the Italian Line built following the decimation of its merchant fleet in World War II. Although it was not meant to be the largest transatlantic ocean liner, it was almost 700 feet long; not meant to be the fastest, it cruised at more than 24 knots. The *Andrea Doria* was built for beauty. Many people have called this ship the most beautiful ever built, and it was referred to by its builder, Ansaldo, as a floating art museum. For this renaissance of the Italian fleet, the Italian government commissioned its most famous artisans to design and build the various social rooms in a way that chronicled the distinguished history of Italy's contributions to the arts and sciences. The ship embodied the vibrant heart and soul of Italian heritage and its people; and it was loved by all who traveled on its decks.

The collision and sinking of the *Andrea Doria* marked the twilight of the ocean liner as a significant means for passage across the ocean. Within a year of this tragedy, the first transoceanic flights were routinely scheduled and replaced these greyhounds of the Atlantic as the major route of immigration to the New World. The demise of the *Andrea Doria* was also a major milestone in the advent of real-time media coverage of a historic event. The sinking was covered by all the world's leading media firms, and it was the first ocean liner sinking ever captured on film for the new medium called television. The *Stockholm*'s destruction of Italy's maritime crown jewel had ramifications throughout the world and was a devastating loss to the country and its people. Unfortunately, many questions about why the disaster occurred have never been officially addressed, and the reasons have been left up to conjecture. Once limits of liability were placed on the legal proceedings, all evidence gathered to adjudicate the true reasons for the collision and sinking of the *Andrea Doria* were halted, and the contents were never divulged.

Other books, magazine stories, and newspaper articles have offered theories about what may have caused two modern ocean liners to collide in open seas. But these printed works have been authored by journalists with very little, if any, direct knowledge of the sea, and this makes many professional mariners question the validity of their sometimes outlandish theories. Additionally, these journalists have tended to embellish the story of the rescue in such grandiose style that even the survivors have found it hard to recognize their own stories. No commercial books and only a few texts have given a plausible answer that reflects professional mariners' experience.

But now, in this book, *Andrea Doria* survivor Pierette Simpson has compiled the most extensive and factual accounts of the fateful night of July 25, 1956, that have ever been published. She has accumulated rare and historical information from various nautical experts, government bureaucrats, maritime admiralty lawyers, and survivors on two continents. This could not have been done without knowledge of the Italian language and culture. As an immigrant child traveling with her grandparents, Simpson experienced the tragedy with a young girl's innocence, but she has written through the eyes and sensibilities of a brave lady who survived to tell her side of the story and that of many fellow survivors.

The most refreshing aspect of this book is its simplicity in dealing with the facts and details of the event without overselling its dramatic nature. It provides the reader with the actual survivors' stories in detail in their own words, not adulterated by journalistic liberties. Furthermore, the words of the nautical experts are not changed to fit a Hollywood adventure but are given in terms that not only reflect the absolute facts of the collision and the sinking but also make perfect sense to both the professional and the lay reader.

Alive on the Andrea Doria! The Greatest Sea Rescue in History will provide evidence for justice in this cold case—a case that has been buried in the coffers of injustice for a half-century. Much of the latest evidence that Pierette Simpson has uncovered will result in changing the minds of many people who for many years have portrayed the historical account of the *Andrea Doria* tragedy through the distortions of pure journalistic fantasy. It is my strong belief that this information will clarify and correct history. Also setting this book apart from any other on the topic are the autobiographical and biographical survivor profiles painstakingly retold in personal vignettes. These serve as historical documentation of profound human experiences. *Alive on the Andrea Doria!* will become a classic in history.

David A. Bright
Shipwreck historian, deep technical diver,
president of Nautical Research Group, Inc.
January 2006

ACKNOWLEDGMENTS

I OWE MUCH GRATITUDE to world-renowned scientist David Bright and master mariner Captain Robert Meurn for believing in my project and for being my consultants. David Bright contributed many spectacular photographs of the ship, the rescue, and dives on the wreck from his personal archives. The collision chapter would not have been written without the precious documents, books, and Computer Assisted Operational Research Facility presentation of Captain Meurn. All of us are grateful to naval engineer John C. Carrothers, whose initial research into a "cold case" led others to pursue what might have been forgotten.

In Italy, I am indebted to naval architect Francesco Scotto, for his research and publication, *Collisione Andrea Doria-Stockholm— The Round Table,* and for sharing many documents from his archives with me; my cousin Giovanni Del Ponte, whose critiques from an author's point of view were invaluable; Captain Franco Ricci, for his articles and the connections he established for me; and journalist Fabio Pozzo, for sharing information and publicizing my work.

I express my thankfulness to the following people in my life, whose support, assistance, and inspiration were part of the book's creation: my mother, for having saved sentimental photographs, letters, and articles; the survivors and their families, who gave me countless hours of their time for interviews, articles, and photographs; my editors and consultants, Wendy Warren Keebler, Alice Nigoghosian, and Maggie Terry, for their expertise and countless hours of hard work; my dear friends, who spent hours of their time offering support and encouragement: Ida D. Mucciante, Cynthia Zimber, Germaine Strobel, Marge Strobel-Donofrio, Katana Abbott, Karen Kett, Karl-Heinz Baumann, Lynn McCloud, and Alessandro Donini. Also, I am grateful to many friends who expressed their confidence in me.

For their "tech" support, I thank James Kett, Charlene Lilla, Richard Caleal, and my cousins Richard, Ray, and Nancy Massa.

I am grateful to the students, parents, and faculty of the Detroit Country Day Schools. who planted the seeds for this project.

Among my dearest supporters, I count my Siamese cat, Delilas, who sat nearby every single hour of my writing and purred me on.

Finally, I thank Costco and Trader Joe's for their delicious, nutritious foods that I could cook in a jiffy.

"The *Andrea Doria* Sinks," drawing by fourth-grader
Michael Azzopardi, Detroit Country Day School. He drew it
two years after having heard me tell the *Andrea Doria* story.

INTRODUCTION

IT HAS TAKEN ME NEARLY FIFTY YEARS to find the courage to face my memories of the *Andrea Doria* tragedy. For many of those years, I simply wanted to put the unpleasant recollections behind me. As time passed, I figured most people would forget what took place on July 25, 1956. I never realized that this one event, which took "only" fifty-one lives, compared with the hundreds lost on the *Titanic*, would become embedded in the minds of millions for decades to come. After all, it wasn't the greatest disaster in naval history.

When I retold my story from time to time in casual conversations, mostly for interesting chatter, I was amazed to learn that so many people had connections to the *Andrea Doria.* They knew someone who had been on the ship. Or someone they knew should have been on the tragic voyage but had been placed by chance on another liner that sailed before or after the *Andrea Doria.* One person told me that he remembered standing on the seashore on Nantucket Island with his father, watching the dreadful debris from the collision wash up as tangible evidence of the disaster.

Many years of living and growing have taught me that the tragic collision with the Swedish liner *Stockholm* had much more importance than could be guessed from the relatively small number of fatalities. There was much to tell of courage and heroism before, during, and after the voyage from Italy to America.

The real impetus for sharing the story in this book came only when I was assigned to deliver a "socially redeeming" message for an assembly at the private school where I was teaching in 1996. The weekend before the assembly, a friend had invited me to attend an operatic recital by a Russian woman who, I was told, had immigrated to the United States in hopes of launching a singing career. Her story of sacrifice—leaving behind her husband and child, coming to a strange land alone with only a dream of making it big—reminded me of who I was. And who some of my fellow

Andrea Doria passengers were. The ship was transporting mostly Italian immigrants who had packed all of their possessions in trunks and had decided to take a chance, a permanent one, at improving their quality of life. The immigrants were full of hopes, dreams, and excitement, ready to overcome all obstacles: language and cultural barriers, joblessness, loneliness, and separation from all that felt secure in the Old World.

The assembly speech I delivered at the elementary school was received with awe, especially because I was a survivor of a ship that sank in the Atlantic Ocean. These children of affluent families listened intently as I talked about the "immigrant ethic" that built our country. I told them they should not take for granted their privileged lifestyle, because it was a gift made possible by the courage and determination of their immigrant ancestors. The students came to know the plight of immigrants who were traveling to America with trunks full of dreams, only to have them engulfed by the sea, facing survival (if they were the lucky ones) on a new shore with only the clothes they were wearing. By the end of the assembly, the students' and teachers' faces, and later their words, told me that this story needed to be shared.

Shortly after, I began digging into my personal archives of photographs, articles, and letters from the 1950s. As I read through family correspondence, I began to relive my own *Andrea Doria* experience. I felt grateful to be alive. Moreover, the frail, yellowed articles before me, with their emotion-laden photographs, resounded with the voices of other survivors. They imposed on me a sense of duty to transmit their words.

With this renewed sense of gratitude for my own life and the inspiration to tell our stories, I conducted numerous interviews, both in the United States and in Italy. In the process, I was awestruck by the incredible accounts of courage, heroism, and determination—whether told by poor immigrants or wealthy voyagers. In Part One of this book, I present the *Andrea Doria* passengers. Age, social class, and background have been taken into account, and there is a focus on unique experiences and how lives were shaped by them. To offer a complete account of the tragedy, the narratives also involve the captain, officers, and crew of the *Doria*—those who left behind the legacy of what has been called the greatest sea rescue during peacetime. With some trepidation, I have also included my personal story, which reawakens painful memories of difficult life circumstances in Italy, disaster at sea, and a peculiar family situation in a strange land.

After writing up these personal accounts, I remained troubled by a voice that could no longer speak for itself: the voice of the *Andrea Doria*. It seemed to beg for answers: Why did this happen? Who was to blame? What did people learn from this tragedy? The documents at my disposal revealed contradictions of fact, and, surprisingly, all the data seemed inconclusive. Disturbed by this and haunted by the sight of gruesome *Life* magazine photographs of the sinking, I decided to embark on a mission to locate nautical experts who could represent the voice of the ship and give scientific explanations and answers. Armed with data gathered in Italy and the United States, I began the process of analyzing old documents along with newer research findings. Hence, Part Two consists of state-of-the-art technological documentation and conclusions from maritime scientists who welcomed the opportunity to share their findings.

This book represents my quest to ascertain truth, which seems to have been the greatest casualty of the disaster. Whether in the voices of survivors or through the analysis of nautical experts, I have laid out the facts of what has been called the "mystery of the *Andrea Doria*." I hope this will serve to restore some of the honor due to Captain Piero Calamai and Italian maritime brilliance, which, after all, dates back to Christopher Columbus.

I wish to emphasize that it gives me no pleasure to find fault or innocence, especially since there has already been so much suffering by all involved in the collision. In fact, it fills me with great sadness. No one on that fateful night meant to do harm, and all were doing their best under the circumstances. What is important is to uncover the other side of the story, which up to now, astonishingly, has been untold.

PIERETTE DOMENICA SIMPSON

PART ONE

Stories of Survival

CHAPTER 1

Autobiography of a Survivor

It is my conviction that it is the intuitive, spiritual aspects
of us humans—the inner voice—that gives us the knowing,
the peace, and the direction to go through the windstorms of life,
not shattered but whole, joining in love and understanding.
—Elisabeth Kübler-Ross

Dear Pierette,
. . . I tried to tell you this so many times, but instead I always
broke down and cried.
The day I had to leave for America, I did not want to leave. I
had to be pushed into the car. Your godmother, Isa Bonacini, came
to take me to the port of Genova. Everyone in Pranzalito came to
say good-bye. Everyone cried. When I returned to Italy decades
later, everyone asked me, "Why did you leave? We all loved you,
and Piera too." How I wish that I could go back to then! I would
not have come to America for the American Dream. I would have
stayed there and gone to work in the field alongside my parents.
But at that time, raising a child alone was considered a disgrace.
I felt guilty, worthless, and restless . . .

May 1948
Pranzalito, Italy[1]

I WAS FIFTEEN MONTHS OLD when my mother immigrated to the Promised Land, with feelings of doubt and guilt. Vivina realized that postwar Italy offered little in education and job opportunities for a young woman raising a toddler. She didn't see this as a courageous journey—although it was—but as one of necessity. Vivina consoled herself by telling everyone, including herself, that it was part of the short-term plan to establish her roots in the United States and then send for me. But as the best-made plans are meant to change by destiny's will, the strategy became a long-term affair.

My grandparents would often explain to me about my moth-

Clockwise: Piera Domenica Burzio, age nine. My godmother holds me as my mother bids her last good-bye before departing for America. Nonna, Domenica Burzio. Nonno, Pietro Burzio.

er—what she was doing and how she wanted me to come to America. This always frightened me, for I knew that there would be an upheaval in my life one day. I expected the move to be imminent.

When I was about five years old, my great-aunt and uncle came for a visit from Detroit. Uncle Tony had made it big working as a truck driver for Ford Motor Company and had invested his money well. Aunt Theresa worked in a dry-cleaning store owned by Italians. Life was good. They had purchased a new black Ford sedan and had it shipped to Italy so they could travel in luxury— and perhaps in vanity. Being the only car in town, beside Dr. Rovano's, it had an imposing presence. The townspeople liked to prod me for a reaction by asking me if I wanted to go to America with my aunt and uncle. I understood this to mean that my mother had sent the black car to drive me to America. They had come to take me away. And so one day, I hid in a most unlikely place, in a carpenter's cupboard across the village from where I lived. Meanwhile, all the villagers were on a frantic hunt to find me. By evening, Giuseppe, a family friend, had coaxed me out of the cupboard and promised that Aunt Theresa and Uncle Tony would not take me away from my friends Domenica and Gianni—and definitely not from Nonno and Nonna.[2]

All five of the town's children—Domenica, Gianni, Roberto, Assunta, and I—went to a one-room schoolhouse and learned mostly together, although we were a few years apart in age. The room was sparsely furnished, with a teacher's desk, student benches, a brownish map of Italy, and a wood-burning stove. Each day, the teacher filled our inkwells so that we could write entries in our small ruled notebooks. One day, when I was in second grade, we were asked to answer the question "If you were to take a trip, where would you go, and what means of transportation would you take?" My entry read:

I would like to go to America, but I'm still here waiting. To go to America, first I have to take the train and then a ship. The trip is a little long but the trip on board is fun. There are musicians, movies and a lot of people to have fun with. With Nonna and Nonno on board, the trip will not seem long. In America, my

Above: Our family home in Pranzalito. There are two homes under one roof. We lived in the left half, and my great-aunt and great-uncle lived in the right. Below: My one-room schoolhouse, cows going to pasture, and the Alps in the background.

mother is waiting for me and she'll be very happy to see me. On the ship, I'll enjoy the ocean for many days and after I'll be able to hug my mother.

Meanwhile, my grandparents continued to write progress reports to my mother about my childhood. This was no doubt an effort to appease her.

Dear Vivina,

Piera is growing fast. She'll probably become tall and slender like her father. The fact that she has a small appetite and often acts cranky worries me, though. I wonder if she's sick or if she misses not having parents. She insists that she doesn't want to go to America alone and we can't leave our home, farmland and animals behind. You made foolish choices in your youth and now we must deal with them. On a lighter note, Piera's friend, Domenica, asked her if she wants to go to America and this is what she said: "I don't want to leave. My grandmother makes fresh apple fritters for me. My mother doesn't know how to make them!"

The organza skirt and nylon blouse you sent Piera look beautiful with the matching hat—especially over her beautiful brown locks. She'll wear these to the feast of San Maurizio.

Don't worry about your father working so hard in the fields. We have a new ox that pulls the plow. Father is still strong and can guide it through the furrows. We'll have good potatoes and corn. Piera keeps him company by sitting under a tree in the shade, occupying herself by playing with her doll or catching tiny frogs in the brook. In the vineyards, her Nonno makes a toy whistle by tying two vines together. Piera blows whistling sounds into it. She's a very creative child and this makes it easy to keep her occupied.

Your mother

Then my mother would respond—and, of course, always insist that my grandparents make preparations to come to America. And so it went on until I was eight years old and recovering from a case of tuberculosis. I'm not sure which challenge was more exasperat-

ing to me, dealing with the high fever and malaise of tuberculosis
or the idea having to leave everything I knew behind. And what if
I didn't like America? What if I didn't like my new family? Would
I have friends, pets, and a nurturing community as I had in Pranzalito? In my childlike way, I pondered all these mysteries to the
point of frustration. Then, on October 21, 1955, the inevitable came;
my mother sent a letter of ultimatum to my grandparents:

Dearest parents,

*How are you? How is my dear Piera? Has she been happy
and growing since my last letter? I enjoyed seeing the picture
you took of her wearing the green corduroy pinafore I sent. You
told me not to send any more clothes this year, but I can't help
it—I left her eight years ago and didn't get to dress her myself.*

*Now it's time for me to take over my long due responsibility.
Catholic Social Services has finished this long, complicated adoption process. What crazy laws we have—having to put my child
in the custody of others, and then readopt her because she has
your last name and her father is unavailable. It's been a heart-
wrenching procedure that no one should have to bear.*

*But now you must make a difficult decision: whether to let
Piera come alone or whether you want to accompany her. I'll tell
you again: life is easier here. Why do you want to get up at sun-
rise every day to feed the animals, to continue plowing the fields,
and going to the river to scrub clothes on a rock? I have lined up
jobs for you in Detroit; Pa will work in a lumberyard owned by
an Italian and Ma can work as a seamstress in Federals department store.*

*I know you'll be happier here. We can all live in the same
house, as Lino is adding a room upstairs for you. You'll be able to
give Piera the love and support she needs. Otherwise, she might
hate me forever for taking her away from you. As it is, bonding
will be difficult enough. I beg of you, start selling your livestock
and your farm equipment! In America we have grocery stores
that provide food—already in packages!*

By the way, the Italian Line told me that they have a beauti-

ful ship called the Andrea Doria. *You can put our entire family trousseau on board and bring it to America.*

Write to me soon with your answer. You've had Piera as your daughter for years. It's now time for me to enjoy her too.
I send you all my love,
Vivina
P.S. Tell Piera she'll have a cat and a dog here—and who knows, maybe even a sibling!

"Pedrin! Pedrin!"

"What's happened? What's wrong, China?"[3] *Nonna's upset; another letter from America.* My Nonno let go of the rope that was hauling a heavy bale of hay into the loft. Nonna was waving a letter in the air; she was crying hysterically, as she often did when she faced the prospect of changing the family's status quo.

"*Che pazzia!*" Nonna yelled out, indicating that this was madness. "Our daughter insists on taking Cici away from us." Because I meant everything to her, she never ceased inventing sweet nicknames—"Cici" was one of them. "After all the sacrifices we made to raise this child! Who made sure she was safe from the cows while we crossed the river and went to pasture? Who carried her on their backs up the hills for her tonsil surgery? Who put wood in the stove all night long to keep her warm? This is the thanks we get?"

I proudly wear my tailor-made First Communion dress, veil, and purse.

"Calm down, China. Accept it. The adoption is final!"

While listening to this frightening discussion between the only parents I ever knew and loved, I decided to dress up my cat, Carla—against her will, of course. I always liked to pretend she was my baby. Carla and I were very close, but she hated being smothered with this kind of love. I began wrapping fancy rags around her furry gray body. Besides, it gave me a reason to look and feel occupied during these regular outbursts from my grandmother. Even though my grandparents logically expected the inevitable, the idea of losing their surrogate child tormented them; the only way they could respond to it, especially Nonna, was to victimize my mother.

"Adoption, *Cristo!*" Nonna was beside herself, even taking the Lord's name in vain; being a devout Catholic, this was a grievous sin to commit against her Savior.

My poor baby Carla struggled to free herself from her unnatural bondage. She tried to push away from my grasp but had little power with her extremities buried in rags. *I'm going to be adopted by my own mother. Maybe it'll be fun to be adopted. Carla doesn't like me anymore. She wants to leave me. And I dressed her up!* Carla became more and more agitated. She sought freedom from the loving insanity I had forced upon her. She wiggled and pushed with all her might, instinctively knowing that she was a baby that belonged to another mother.

"I'm not leaving my home, my animals, and my fields to go to America. You do what you want, Pedrin, but Cici stays here with me." *Nonno is going to America alone? He wouldn't leave me. Besides, my mother threatened to come get me if Nonno and Nonna don't bring me to America. He'd better stay here with us till we all go to America, together! I'm not going without them, no way! We'll bring Carla and Titti. Titti will bark and howl if I leave him.*

It was Sunday, and Nonna had prepared an abundant holy day meal: one of our rabbits, cooked in a wine sauce and served on top of polenta, the cornmeal puree that is a specialty of the Piedmont. At the table, we ate in brooding silence, as none of us was happy about anything at that moment. Nonno poured me a little wine in a glass of water, saying, "Drink it, Cici, it's good for your blood." *Nonno is drinking more today. It's good for his blood, too.*

July 17, 1956
Pranzalito and Genova, Italy

I'D BETTER GO TELL NONNA APOLLONIA what time we're leaving tomorrow. I want her to come with us to the ship. Sadly, it would be my last visit with my great-grandmother, who had always greeted me with a piece of chocolate and other nurturing. She hugged me even more intensely during this visit, while giving me her words of wisdom about how to act in America. "Be a good girl, Pieretta.[4] Study hard in school, do all your homework, and always help your mother. Your grandparents raised you well. Go forth and love them along with your new family." Nonna Apollonia had a reputation in Pranzalito for being very wise and well educated. In her youth, she had lived in Algeria with her parents, who were experts in the wine industry. I loved her dearly and admired her good judgment.

Nonna Apollonia showed up early for the big event in our small village. The large crowd was unsettling to me. *So many people! Are they coming with us to the port? I wish Carla and Titti would come to Genova. Too much crying here . . . it's making me sad. I want to be happy. Why are Nonno and Nonna crying so much? We're all going to America together!* No one was excited about much of anything, except me, it seemed. It didn't appear to comfort my grandparents to be enveloped with so much goodwill by the townspeople. In fact, it seemed to sadden them even more, standing in their sterile, bleak courtyard, now empty of all the farm implements that had filled it before the auction. *We're going in the shiny black car! Did I pack my doll? How will Nonna prepare my snack today?*

"Don't cry, China. We'll write often. You'll come back to visit," my mother's girlfriend Kety said reassuringly. "Give my love and regards to Vivina. Tell her I miss her and to come visit."

Nonna cried even louder: "Our home, our land, our animals . . . gone . . . our security, gone! Our life is finished! We can't even speak English . . . at our age going to America . . . are we

crazy?" Nonna was sobbing hysterically, while Nonno kept wiping his eyes with a clean white handkerchief. But the shiny sedan
had all its doors open for us to enter, and Giuseppe was anxious to
drive us to Genova.

*WE'RE HERE! I MUST HAVE SLEPT. The band is playing for us. The
ship, wow, it's beautiful, just like they said. It's as big as Pranzalito.* The
Andrea Doria awaited us and many other immigrants who were
wishing to be sheltered from the ocean's perils—until we could
fend for ourselves in the Promised Land. *Where are our trunks?
Hope my First Communion dress is on board.* Our friend Giuseppe
pointed to the band. "Listen to the music that's playing for you!
You're like royalty." If this was supposed to make my family feel
happy, it didn't seem to work. The music was loud, and Nonna
Apollonia's cherished words of affection were nearly inaudible.
"*Ti voglio bene, Pieretta,*" she repeated so that I was certain to hear
it: "I love you very much." *I hope she lets go of me now. I want to get
on that ship. It looks fun. Why is Nonna so worried about the water?
Nothing will happen.*

I ran up the gangplank, pulling on Nonna's hand. She was
trembling from an unfounded fear she always had about water.
Boarding a large ship that was heading across the Atlantic Ocean
must have been the ultimate horror for her. We joined all the other
Tourist Class passengers on the deck and waved white handkerchiefs with wide sweeps. This reassured us that our loved ones on
shore would have a better chance of spotting us among the hundreds. "*Arrivederci, arrivederci!*" everyone shouted, with high
hopes of seeing one another again. We clasped the railing and
leaned way out as the sleek liner pulled away from firm ground.
Tricolored streamers of red, white, and green stretched from ship
to shore—symbolizing the last thread of connection. And tears of
sadness, apprehension, and anticipation flowed freely, plunking
and expanding into the salty water below.

Soon my grandparents took me to our cabin. *I like this! Four
beds. Life jackets. We'll be safe. Nonna's wrong . . . she worries too much
that bad things are going to happen.* It seemed incomprehensible to

**The luxury liner *Andrea Doria* arriving in Genova.
(David A. Bright Collection)**

me that Nonna would be afraid of this luxurious and welcoming "hotel." Everything seemed perfect, including the beautiful Genovese sun of the Italian Riviera.

When we entered the dining room for lunch, I was awestruck by the appetizing smells of various foods—like none I had ever known: meats, cheeses, fruits, wines, all creating a heady blend of flavorful aromas. There were huge flower arrangements and ice sculptures on the long buffet table. White linen and beautiful silverware were quite a contrast from the wood table and dull flatware we were used to. The crystal chandeliers sure looked different from the light bulb that hung from an electric cord above our table—like the one in Vincent van Gogh's *Potato Eaters.* We ate with strangers, something unheard of in Pranzalito. *They're really fun and friendly, like my grandparents said the* Doria *passengers would be.*

"Why don't you bring Piera to the pool later, China? She can swim with my children," proposed Mrs. Mastrincola as she left our table.

"Piera doesn't know how to swim. Besides, I'm afraid to let her go in the water."

"The pool is shallow for the children. My children, Arlene and Pat, will play with her. They're about the same age."

Somehow, this pleasant woman reassured my Nonna, so she unpacked the bathing suit that I'd worn when I took baths in the river outside Pranzalito. It was great fun splashing around the crystal blue pool water and playing with someone new. *I wish Gianni and Domenica could see this pool. There are no frogs to catch here, though . . . smells different from pond water.* Nonna sat at the poolside and enjoyed the distraction offered by Mrs. Mastrincola as she described her son's daring adventures aboard ship.

Each day, Mrs. Mastrincola had a different amusing story to share. I would catch bits of details but did not relate at all to nine-year-old Pat's escapades. "At least he didn't delay the ship's departure on this trip," Pat's mother began. "Several weeks ago, Pat, Arlene, and I were leaving New York to visit my family in Italy. When it was time to leave the dock, he was nowhere to be found. We didn't even know if he was on the ship. So my poor husband, who was already humiliated because someone had ruined his new suit by dropping a slice of pizza on the shoulder, came on board to help find him."

Nonna laughed nervously at the prospect of losing a son in the confusion, but she begged to hear more.

"Pat's name was being paged on the loudspeaker, and finally a crewman spotted him banging on the smokestack and opening windows so he could wave to people on shore. The crewman suspected it was the missing boy, so he brought him up to the bridge to face the captain. Good thing the captain and officials were present, or my husband would have given Pat a good beating!"

By this time, Nonna was holding her stomach, laughing willingly for the first time in months—forgetting momentarily her fear of water.

"But the ship had already left the dock, so my husband had to ride back to shore in a tugboat. That son of mine is a handful," Pat's mother concluded.

The dinners were even fancier and more abundant than the lunches we enjoyed. On the way to the dining room, my grandparents would stop along the corridors and stare at beautiful photographs of Italian coastlines that none of us had ever seen. We sat down at our usual table to experience the new delicacies and to hear more outrageously funny stories, or perhaps lamentations, about Mrs. Mastrincola's daredevil son.

"I'm worried about that boy," the mother shared. "This morning, he climbed up the railing to the Cabin Class. They had to chase him back down to Tourist Class. He's always bored, so he gets into mischief. I just don't want him to get hurt." *How did he know how to climb up the railing? Scary. He could fall into the water.*

Sleeping in the cabin was really fun. Before going to bed, though, I would look at the waves outside our porthole and then look up at the moon. *Is it the same moon that shines in Pranzalito? I wish Nonna would look out and see it with me so I could ask her.*

Sometimes Nonno would stay up late and play cards with other men. The game was more than entertainment for my grandfather; it was about laying all of one's personal cards on the table and shuffling immigrant stories around until they were sure to make an impression. Sometimes I would follow Nonno to daytime card games and listen while we all tried to make sense of this complex phenomenon filled with sacrifices. One day, Nonno began telling his tale, with a somewhat boastful demeanor.

"We sold everything—our farmland, animals, tools—so that we could bring our granddaughter to America to be with her new family. Our priest, Dom Oberto, and a Catholic society offered Piera a free ticket by airplane. But since she was afraid to travel alone and we didn't want to separate ourselves from the child we raised as a daughter, we are all moving to Michigan."

The *paisanos*[5] looked up from their cards and gave an admiring nod to this courageous man who was willing to sacrifice everything for the sake of family.

Next, it was Luciano Grillo's turn to boast a little. "I have a heart problem, and my wife is pregnant. Next month, she's having our baby. Being a machinist, I've got to do heavy labor to support my family. My brother in Connecticut tells me that I can get a good heart operation, and then he has a job lined up for me."

What a revelation for these men used to manual labor! America was the place where doctors could make sick men well.

Gino Chiesa told the card players that he had sold his farm in Piacenza and was leaving behind seven brothers and sisters. "They hired a tailor to make me several suits so I would look good on the ship and in America. They didn't want me to wear American suits." Mr. Chiesa looked dapper and felt it. "I'm heading for New York. My wife has been waiting two months for me, but I wanted to wait for a place on this beautiful ship. I have a job as a dishwasher lined up for me in a New York restaurant. I don't know where I'm going to wear all of these suits." The men didn't have an answer for the would-be dishwasher but smiled at his light-heartedness.

The game of cards and sacrifices was winding down when Pietro Renda told of his sacrifices. "I left my wife and son in Sicily. After I work for a while with my brother in a Chevrolet factory, my family will join us in Flint, Michigan."

Although Pat and Arlene were not immigrants like me, we could still share stories about our lives. One day, I told them how I had learned to ride a bike on a dirt road, using my mother's big bike. I could prove it by showing off the small pebbles that remained embedded in my kneecaps. But of course, Pat had an even better bike story to tell. "My new bike is on this ship. It's a gift from my relatives in Italy. My uncle the jeweler collected $148 from relatives 'cause he got tired of me taking off on his customers' bikes. It's a beige aluminum racing bike." *Sounds like a lot of money. They must be rich, like all American kids. Hope my mother buys me a new bike.* Arlene told me that after passing by the Statue of Liberty, she would see her father. She was going to ask him for a new bike just like Pat's. *My mother told me to look for that statue. It's big. It says hello to immigrants like us.*

For eight days, we were blessed with mostly smooth sailing. Nonna continued to be amused by Pat Mastrincola's antics as the boy kept venturing into scarier and scarier territory—like the grill catwalks surrounding the huge engine room in the bowels of the *Andrea Doria*. He had climbed above generators, pistons, and hydraulic pumps before being discovered. We were assured of one thing: the foolhardy boy would never get lost on that ship. Mrs. Mastrincola was thankful that Pat didn't have much more time to endanger himself, and Nonna was relieved that we were nearing the New York shoreline.

ON JULY 25, 1956, OUR LAST FULL DAY aboard the prized Italian liner, our spirits were covered with a gloomy blanket of fog that even permeated the corridors. For fear of getting lost, passengers spent the day mostly in their cabins packing their suitcases. After we attended our last supper on board, my grandparents took me for a short walk on deck. But the fog's condensation made strolling a slippery affair, and the phantom puffs between us made visibility impossible. So we stopped in one spot just long enough for me to play with the fog; I tried to pack the smoky matter in my hands, like the snowballs I used to make and launch at Gianni and Domenica. Then I decided to taste it by forcing some into my mouth—but each time it eluded me.

Unknown to us, there was a maritime expert on board who had chosen to travel on the *Andrea Doria* for his return to the United States with his wife and two children. Robert Young was a marine engineer and naval architect in charge of Western European operations for the American Bureau of Shipping.[6] He understood the danger of this dense, vertical type of fog that caused ships to play an in-again, out-again game. Mr. Young spent most of the afternoon on the First Class deck, watching the fog, listening to the *Doria* foghorn's rhythmic blasts, and straining to pick up other ships' foghorns. Assuring himself that the ship had every type of modern navigational aid, including two radar sets, and that the captain planned to be on the bridge all night, Mr. Young retired to his cabin.

It was their last evening on board, and neither fog nor rain nor any other importunity could prevent Italians from making merry—and what better event to celebrate than their arrival in America, the Land of Plenty. Tourist Class had no formal plans for celebration on this night, so the passengers created their own festivities in the Social Hall. An impromptu band was formed, and we all joined in special camaraderie with our *paisanos*.

I know this song . . . "Arrivederci Roma." Guess we're saying goodbye to Italy for good. I'm excited; I get to see my mother, new baby sister, and stepfather tomorrow. Nonna finally looks relaxed. I wish Nonno hadn't gone to sleep early . . . he said, "Tomorrow's going to be a big day." What's that noise? I don't like it. I think I'm going to cry.

And cry I did, along with all the astonished passengers who instantly froze into singing and dancing statues of fright. We swayed rigidly from an abrupt jolt accompanied by a thunderous noise. Those who were on the outer deck witnessed startling fireworks created by grinding steel—sparked by an unidentified vessel slamming into our hull at full speed. They watched in horror as the perpetrator tried to withdraw from the hole it had created, slicing through thick walls of steel that had once protected passengers from the dangers of the ocean. In the Social Hall, these gruesome theatrics were magnified by the crashing of hundreds of bottles that landed on the bar floor, as if thrown there by the devil's rage. Every fiber in our spines reacted to the scraping, screeching, and crunching noises from an indefinable source.

The musicians are running away. My friends are crying, too. Everybody's scared of something. I'm scared . . . can't even stand up anymore. The entire floating city began to lean dramatically toward the starboard side, sending all the beautiful furnishings across the floor to crash into the windows. *Where's the light? All the screaming in the dark is scaring me. I want my Nonno . . . hope he can find us.* When the lights finally flickered and stayed on, they revealed a chaotic and frightening scene. Passengers lay on the floor screaming from shock or injury. Shouts of vulgarity and frantic prayers all became part of the pandemonium. The names of loved ones echoed piercingly: "Giovanna!" "Roberto!" "Adelina!" "Antonio!" "Mamma!" "Papà!" Without real purpose, the confused crowd began making a quick dash for the exits. *Glad I'm with Nonna . . . she's brave, not screaming at all. Hold my hand really tight, Nonna.*

It seemed as if time had stopped—as had our fluid ocean liner—as the first few minutes stretched across the waves to eternity. But when the initial shock finally subsided, what followed made eternity seem brief.

What are we going to do? Nowhere to go. . . . What's the Titanic *I keep hearing about? Where's Nonno?* "Nonno!"

To my great relief, my Nonno came through the Social Hall door. I had never seen him this scared. His blue eyes were glossed over in panic, his pants were rolled up to the knees, exposing bare feet, and his hands clasped his briefcase against his chest. The three of us ran toward one another, desperately seeking strength and comfort. "Pedrin, what's happening?" Nonna asked.

"I don't know, but I heard a loud crashing sound. It woke me up from my sleep. There's water in the corridors . . . and the smell of smoke. It was hard to find the stairwell . . . the stairs, *Cristo*, there was an awful-smelling oil on them. I kept slipping with everyone pushing and trying to get past me to reach the deck." My grandfather tried to catch his breath while he told us about the panic in the corridors of Tourist Class. *I don't understand. Why run? . . . Where do we go?*

"*O Dio, aiutaci!*" I could feel my Nonna's hand squeeze mine tighter as she invoked God's help. The three of us huddled together, pressing hard against a wall so we could remain standing. We listened for some guidance, some understanding of this incredible dilemma. The silence was not reassuring. We wondered where the white-uniformed officers were, the ones who always smiled around groups of people. Once in a while, we would spot them running back and forth, their faces tense with expressions of horror, their pristine suits splattered with blotches of grease and soot.

"Listen, China! There's something on the loudspeaker." We strained to hear an official announcement, blaring yet still inaudible above the screams of hysteria that permeated that first half-hour.

"*Calmi . . . salvagenti . . . punti di riunione.*"

The official voice was pleading for calm, life jackets, and something about muster stations. My Nonno let out a vulgar word when he realized we didn't have our life jackets, as they were still neatly stored below our bunks in the cabin now enveloped with smoke and water. Before reporting to the muster station, Nonno felt obliged to help the other men who were boldly pushing heavy objects from the lower side to the higher side of the list—attempting, in vain, to balance the ship. Nonna and I gripped each other even harder with each episode of loud creaking noises, followed by a sudden plunging of the floor bent on descending to some lower depth. A cacophony of mysterious sounds echoed all around us—brief ones, like thuds, bursts, and slams, and longer ones that seemed to resound for several minutes, blasts, bangs, crashes, and other dreadful noises. To make things even worse, the air reeked of hideous fumes, as if concocted by sorcerers of the deep.

"We're going under! We're sinking! We're drowning!" *What is sinking? . . . Drowning? . . . Nonna's not screaming. Nonno will make the ship better. We'll be safe, but I feel like crying.* Nonna was crying and praying, but, amazingly, she did not participate in the madness that surrounded us. Undoubtedly, my grandmother bravely hid her fear—especially her fear of water—so it wouldn't upset me.

Within an hour or so, the bedlam that had unraveled any threads of security wove short outbursts of hysterics through the air. Mrs. Mastrincola did not appreciate the robust woman nearby who was alarming her children with the seemingly obvious: "We're going to die, we're all finished, this is the end!"

"Shh! You're frightening my children," Pat and Arlene's mother admonished. The woman quieted down, allowing others their turn to display sudden outbreaks of despair. *I want to cry, too . . . maybe somebody will hear us and help us.* We heard various versions of what must have happened: a land mine from the war had finally exploded, we had hit rocks, we had hit an iceberg, all the elevators had crashed at once, a boiler had exploded. But people who had gone on deck were now reporting back about what they had seen.

"There's another ship . . . it's trying to pull back from our hull. It hit us. There's a big hole . . . water is pouring into us like a river!"

"*Il* Titanic! *Mamma mia!* How are we going to survive?" *Survive? Titanic? What does it mean? Sounds bad.* Not recognizing the ominous warning was a blessing. But to those who had been less sheltered than I, the conclusion seemed clear, especially since no one was informing us to the contrary: our fate was to be that of the characters in a popular novel of the era, *The Titanic.* Evidence was all around us: the list was worsening steadily, the horrific sounds were becoming amplified, and the revolting smell of smoldering materials was overcoming us. *I want to go back to Pranzalito. I'm really tired. I want to cry.*

My grandparents decided we would feel more protected from looming danger by staying inside the Social Hall, rather than reporting to the deck, which was our muster station. So as best we could, considering the sharp incline, we hung on to whatever would keep us in one place. Meanwhile, we looked helplessly at bloody faces and swollen limbs. A prayer circle recited the rosary for what seemed like forever but was really only four hours. Now and then, "Now and at the hour of our death" was punctuated with doleful wails, not the traditional "Amen."

"THE RESCUE SHIPS HAVE ARRIVED. They're sending lifeboats. We need to abandon ship now!"

These encouraging words from a stranger were exactly what everyone had hoped for. This angel of mercy said he would guide us to the starboard side so that we could be rescued. *Where are we going? What are lifeboats? Please don't make me go on the ocean!* Waiting with nowhere to go had been frightening, but moving from the temporary shelter was more terrifying. I cried dreadful tears, as never before. My grandparents escorted me out of the Social Hall by crawling and groping to reach the door wall. Surprisingly, the moon and stars were shining outside, instead of the earlier opaque vapor. The man who had come to release us from the dirgelike Hail Marys instructed us to hang on tight to the railing and make our way down to the ropes suspended from it.

"*Guardate là! La nave di salvataggio! Sopravvivremo!* Look over there! The rescue ship! We will survive!" Like in the fairy tale where the victim is rescued just in time from everlasting sleep, our rescue ship warmed our souls and awakened us from a ghoulish nightmare. Survival *was* a possibility! But how would we reach the oasis island a mile away—the one that could have been a mirage except that the lights spelled out clearly "ILE DE FRANCE."

A long line of folks with hopeful hearts took small steps along the outer railing, praying that they would not lose their footholds and go careening across the slippery deck—and into the jaws of famished sea creatures lurking not far below. The tense silence was often interrupted by sounds of anguish from someone who had lost his or her balance and was sent slamming into the sides of the pool or into the outer walls of the deck. Their blood-splattered bodies and their wails of fright and pain sent shivers down our spines. We also witnessed impatient people jumping overboard, not wanting to wait in a long line behind those who stood frozen with fear as their turn came to descend the ropes and nets. Only when an elderly gentleman launched his suitcase overboard, hoping it would land in a lifeboat, did we experience a moment of lightheartedness. "The suitcase sank!" someone blurted out, trying to make light of a nonsensical situation.

My grandparents and I finally reached the makeshift debarkation point. It was the lowest part of the severe list, nearing forty degrees. The starboard-side lifeboats had already been launched and were transporting passengers to the rescue ships surrounding us.

Our guardian-angel escort approached me with a very thick rope and began looping it around my waist. I let out a frightful scream at the prospect of being dangled over the black ocean all alone. *I'm not doing this. If I scream, they'll find another way. I want my Nonno and Nonna!* But it was too late. I was twirling through the air, crying, as I looked down to see where I was going. I heard Nonna yelling, "Be brave, Cici. We're coming down, too!" A man grabbed me tight and pulled me toward the lifeboat instead of letting me sway over the water, where I was headed. *What is this boat? These people are scared, too . . .*

Fortunately, Nonna was lowered next, but she had a harder time of it because she lowered herself, scraping her hands on the rope and swinging heavily in the process. *No! Don't go into the water, Nonna!* She struggled to hang on and headed right for the ocean, plunking her legs into the cool water she had always feared. She began kicking the water and shrieking for help. *"Aiuto! Aiutami!"* Before she was immersed completely, two crewmen grabbed her and pulled her into the lifeboat. Nonna and I cried together. Nonno was next, which was fortunate, as women and children had been lowered without male family members and were yelling for them to come down. Because my grandfather was older, he received special consideration. We watched him dangle his way down, clutching his briefcase with one arm.

All of us in the small vessel, bobbing in the shadow of a dreadfully inclined liner, were trembling and crying—wondering if we were really safe as the swell of heavy waves banged us into the hull of the *Doria*. We rowed away slowly but surely, our stomachs retching to the movement of each wave. *I hate to throw up . . . it smells awful in here. Yuck, vomit! I can't stop throwing up.*

As we distanced ourselves from one danger, another was looming before our eyes. My playmate Pat Mastrincola had been lowering himself into a lifeboat when his life jacket hooked onto something on the ship, and he simply hung there waiting for help. We gasped, thinking of the fear he must have felt in this vulnerable perch. *Oh, no, poor Pat. I hope he makes it . . . I know he's used to climbing a lot.* Then we spotted a crewman running down to a lower deck, who proceeded to unhook the boy. We would have cheered, but we were all too busy expunging our innards of trauma and whatever was left of our dinners.

Trying to cross a mile of debris in order to reach the *Ile de France* felt more desolate than the ride of the Ancient Mariner. Leaving the sinking ship should have made us euphoric, but the stupor and shock made people lament ridiculous things: "I'm arriving to safety half naked." "I'm lost without my glasses." "I left my watch on the dresser." "I left my teeth in the bathroom." I admit that I wondered about my First Communion dress and hoped it would be recovered somehow. Moreover, during this ride from hell, we were privy to a sight worse than anything a horror film could conjure: the *Stockholm*, the Swedish ship that had rammed us, stood crippled in the distance, with its bow crumpled like discarded tin foil in a waste basket. On the *Doria*, the area of impact was an enormous black hole, inviting in torrents of water like a river in a raging storm. And its huge funnel was so inclined over the water that it reflected a red-hot glow on the calm sea.

Our pitifully packed lifeboat began circling the *Ile de France*. *I can't stand this anymore. I didn't think this trip would be so hard. I wish I were home, in Pranzalito.* We finally stopped on the starboard side

of the *Ile.* I was very anxious to go on board. *Oh, no, another ladder
. . . it's too high . . . I can't!* With one careful step at a time, I climbed
the steep rope ladder that led to the very top of the rescue ship.
Fortunately, a man was behind me the entire time and tried to keep
me from looking down. It was a surreal experience, feeling as if I
were suspended a mile above the ocean, where I could see all the
rescue ships. The glaring spotlights from these vessels created an
eerie scene, but we were fortunate that the sea was calm and visibility was clear. When I reached the top of the rope, French crewmen pulled me in through a window and stayed with me until my
grandparents also made their death-defying climb.

Finally, a sense of euphoria did take over our very beings.
Although we were exhausted and traumatized, there was indeed
something to rejoice in: safety! We had survived the almost unsur-
vivable; and now I wanted to sleep. My grandparents and I were
escorted to buffet tables, obviously set up for our arrival, covered
with brioches, coffee, and sandwiches. *I'm not hungry. I'm tired.
Why is everybody still crying? Where are Pat and Arlene?*

We collapsed our tired bodies into lounge chairs, which would
be our beds until we arrived in New York. French passengers and
crew alike came around with blankets and soothing words to calm
our agitated souls. Many survivors needed sedation, such as a
woman who began bellowing something from the opera *Aida* from
across the Social Hall. A doctor arrived quickly to tranquilize her.
Nonna spotted the Mastrincolas—Pat seemed angry about something. We were relieved that they were safe. Nonno spotted Gino
Chiesa, the farmer from Piacenza; his new tailored suit made to be
proudly worn in America was stained with oil blotches. Nonna
tried to get my mind off the pathetic theatrics going on all around
us. "Soon we'll see the Statue of Liberty, Cici. Be sure to wave to
her when you see her."

My grandparents were walking around among the deck chairs
when I woke up. "We're almost in America, Cici." I felt as though
I had awakened from a long nightmare that had happened to
someone else. But the promised reality of getting to America and
finally meeting my new family canceled out the details of a disastrous night.

"Will we see the big statue?" I asked excitedly.

"No, Cici. You were fast asleep when she waved at us. We didn't want to wake you." *Darn. I bet Arlene saw it. Who will meet us in New York? Maybe I'll ask my new dad for a bike.*

July 26
New York, New York

OUR ARRIVAL IN NEW YORK HARBOR was met with fanfare. We squeezed onto the deck, along with other survivors and *Ile de France* passengers, to get a glimpse of the frenzy on shore. A squadron of tugboats and media boats escorted us to the shoreline. Cameras flashed and clicked, and microphones on poles strained to reach our voices on the deck.

"Where were you during the collision? How did you get off the *Andrea Doria?* Did the crew help you? Did you see the crew abandon ship?" The significance of these questions eluded me, as did the epic importance of our arrival. But I could see that the reporters were insistent in getting responses, especially about the *Andrea Doria*'s crew.

The closer we came to shore, the louder the cheers all around us. *Wow! I didn't know we were so important. They really do know how to welcome immigrants, just like my mother said.* At this point, we were all unaware that we had just participated in history's greatest peacetime sea rescue.

"Why is everyone cheering, Nonna?"

"We made big news yesterday. We were brave, and we were really lucky because people saved our lives, Cici!" We left it at that, as my grandparents' relieved faces told a story that no words could say.

The three of us descended the gangplank holding on tightly to one another for fear of being separated among the throng. Nonno held his briefcase tightly, too—the only remains from our past. He looked anxious, as he did during those tense moments when he was about to roll a *bocce* ball on a court full of competitive men. The euphoria that had been present on Nonna's face on the *Ile* was also turning into stress. We were about to embark on one of the biggest steps of our lives: immigrating to a strange land and leaving behind everything that had ever felt secure.

"Who's going to meet us, Nonna?"

"I don't know, Cici. Maybe your father or your mother."

All the survivors gathered in a very large hall, with a lot of windows near the high ceiling. The loudspeakers were blaring: "Please move away from the doors. Make room for others to enter." *What are they saying? That must be English. I'm going to learn it at school.* Then they created more pandemonium as they began announcing a long list of names. American families waited nervously, straining to hear the names of their loved ones—the fortunate ones who had been rescued by the *Ile de France.*

"*Ciao, Pedrin! Ciao, China and Piera!*" someone called out excitedly. I recognized my great-aunt Theresa. "Thank God you're alive!" There were joyful hugs and kisses and many, many tears of relief. "Piera, this is your father." *Father . . . what about my Nonno? He's my father, too.*

"Hi, Piera," the handsome stranger said to me, shaking my hand.

He continued, "Your mother wants to say something to you on the telephone. Let's go call her." *A telephone? Wow, I've never used one before.* We located a phone booth, where my new father dialed a number. At the same time, my grandmother was coaching me about what to say. "Tell your mother she's beautiful. Say BE-A-U-TI-FUL." She broke the word up into parts, but it ended up sounding just like Italian. I enunciated the flattering word to the stranger on the phone, and I heard sobs in return.

"You must be hungry," my aunt suggested. So we all pushed our way to the cafeteria. *These foods smell different.* I studied the choices displayed behind glass and saw foods I didn't recognize. But my eyes were drawn to one item that looked like blocks of ice in various colors: green, red, yellow, and orange. *That looks fun to eat!*

"I'll take the green one of those."

"Piera, that's Jell-O. It's just sugar. You need something more nutritious. It's a long plane ride to Detroit.

I don't want anything else, just that pretty food. As I wistfully stared at the crystal-like food, my caring aunt gave in and bought me some Jell-O—in my favorite color, green.

July 27, 1956
Detroit, Michigan

ANOTHER STRANGE PLACE! Big! Everything is big in America, like everybody said. No sooner had we stepped off the airplane than a woman I recognized from my photo album ran toward me and wrapped her arms tightly around me. I hugged back tightly this stranger who was sobbing uncontrollably and asking me, "Pierette, *come stai?" Why is she calling me by that name? Must be Piera in English.* After I told my mother I was fine, she grabbed me by the hand and led me to the rest of my family in the waiting area. *I want to hold hands with my Nonna. Where is she?* Nonna's hands were freely waving in the air, as she began relating the horrific event we had endured. She had the grease stains all over her clothes as proof. Nonno was tearfully responding to questions from my new grandfather, Celeste, and my great-uncle Tony. All the while, a photographer, who I later learned was our neighbor, busily focused on interesting angles of all the commotion and emotion in the waiting room. Years later, my mother recorded these moments of our family history in her diary:

> *I have tried so many times for the past ten years to put this all together for you. Invariably, I will break down and sob uncontrollably. The sinking of the* Andrea Doria *was another test of survival for our family. It was four in the morning on July 26 when Grandpa Celeste phoned and informed me that the* Andrea Doria *was sinking. MY WORLD HAD SUDDENLY COME TO AN END! I asked Daddy and Aunt Theresa to leave immediately for New York to look for you. In no time, the house became full of people attempting to console me. Reporters covered the yard.*
>
> *It was the longest day of my life. Words alone cannot convey the tortured moments; the memories, the guilt, despair, hopelessness, and helplessness. I felt as if I had set in motion the avalanche of mistakes that perhaps would bury you all. Finally, the good news came; the telegram from the* Ile de France *read* "TUTTI SALVI." *I knew you were saved. We went to the airport*

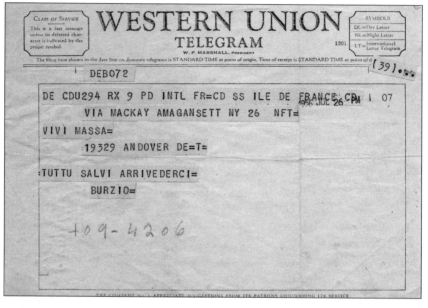

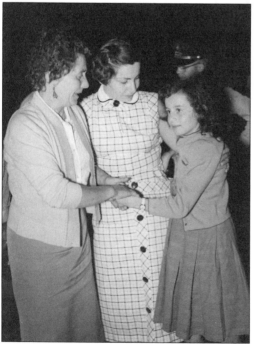

Above: Telegram to my new American family: "ALL SAVED SEE YOU SOON BURZIO."

Left: Happy to be in America at last—and loved by "two mothers."

Facing page, top left: The long-awaited embrace with my mother, as my new father looks on.

Right: My mother, my great-uncle Tony, and my tearful grandfather surround me.

Below: *Where is my Nonna?* I wonder as my new grandfather follows us home.

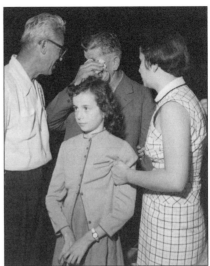

to wait for you. You can see from the pictures that I am still in my housedress; could not put myself together. You were here with me, finally.

The next morning, I woke up in a strange home, with family members who were also strangers. For the first time in my life, I hadn't slept in the same bed with my grandmother; I had slept in my own bed, next to my new sister Marisa's crib. I awakened to the smell of another new food: bacon. We all sat together around a small table in a very small kitchen—even smaller than the one we had in Pranzalito. The telephone rang constantly, while reporters were installing equipment in the yard for their heyday. My mother told us that neighbors had brought boxes of clothes for us.

"Put this white blouse on, Pierette. It will look nice with this flowered skirt when the photographers take your picture." I looked at the old, starched blouse, which had obviously been patched many times from overuse. *It's not pretty. I'm embarrassed. Why is she telling me to wear it?*

"I don't want to wear that blouse. It's ugly!" I exclaimed.

"That's what you're wearing today. Put this on."

I began to cry and make a fuss. I didn't like this new person telling me what to do. Nonna always let me wear what I wanted. My mother slapped me. I suppose it was her way of asserting her own authority in front of my grandmother; or perhaps all the stress of the shipwreck was too much strain on her. My grandmother, who had only ever slapped me once, began yelling horrible things at my mother. And this set a familiar scene for a few years to come—until my grandparents moved across the street to their own home.

Meanwhile, the reporters were waiting with their litany of questions. We were to look happy and smile for the cameras, my mother explained. *I'm not happy . . . I'm going to pout.*

"Stand here, please, and wave," the photographer instructed us. "Now, sit here, and point to the picture of the sinking ship." We went through the motions of becoming famous for being the first *Andrea Doria* survivors to reach Detroit.

"What was the accident like?" the questioning began.

My mother translated as Nonna spoke excitedly. "I was in the ballroom with Pierette. Suddenly, the ship seemed to go up in the air, and we heard a tremendous crashing noise. And just when I thought things couldn't get worse . . ."

"What did you lose on the boat?"

Nonna, the keeper of family heirlooms, was anxious to respond. "We lost four trunks containing thirty handmade sweaters, twenty hand-woven linens, fourteen Persian rugs, Pierette's First Communion dress, a lot of cash . . ."

"Would you ever travel by sea again?"

Even the question was enough to provoke outrage from my grandmother. She made sure to explain just how horrific the ordeal had been: "During the war, our family hid four English soldiers who had escaped from the Nazis. Later, we housed a Jewish family from Turin. And my sister's home was the headquarters for the Partigiani Generals.[7] We always lived in danger and fear—but nothing in comparison to the shipwreck!" Nonna let out a yowl to enhance her account.

Life for us in Detroit took on its own "normalcy"—although nothing ever seemed normal again in my life. Nonna began her job as a seamstress and finally learned to use a washing machine—after much resistance. Nonno worked very hard in a lumberyard, but he was treated poorly by his Italian boss. I learned English quickly, thanks to being young. When I entered school in September, I was temporarily placed in second grade (although I should have been in fourth) until I became proficient in English. This proved to be a humiliating experience—I was much taller and more mature than my classmates. Immersing ourselves in a new culture meant adjusting to the New World and abandoning the Old. We missed our friends, our home, and our way of life. Like all immigrants, we always felt (and continue to do so) like *trapiantati*, a perfect word to describe an uprooting and a transplanting.

As for the uprooting of families from their established gardens so that they can all be planted together in a new one, the act is full of challenges. The blending of my family, although an admirable concept, caused more strain than could have been foreseen. My mother later documented some of the challenges in a letter to me:

> *A small home for five people, an unreasonable husband, and my mother, who had suffered great mental distress from the ordeal, made for a bad outcome. Marisa was just a baby and needed constant care. I had to walk on eggshells not to reveal any of this to the adoption agency, who came by regularly for inspections. You had to get adjusted to the American schools and you did so marvelously. After two years, I was entitled by law to adopt you. You were finally legally my daughter—after 11 years of tribulations, obstacles and trials.*

If only this could have been the beginning of a great new life. Ironically, the ocean journey that was supposed to unite a family stranded us islands apart. Family tribulations continued and resulted in two divorces: that of my grandparents and, later, that of my parents. For decades, I was truly drifting, not only between continents but also unhappily between fidelities. In trying to make sense of it all, I've asked myself many questions to place the pieces of this bizarre puzzle together. Was it the strain of the *Andrea Doria* tragedy? Was it old family wounds that were stirred up in a new world full of insecurities? Was it just my family members' odd quirks that threw a curve ball into bonding on a new playing field? Or was it all of the above, as multiple-choice tests say? I don't have the answer to this test question. But I have learned that life is truly a test of character, and if it is true that obstacles don't change character, they reveal it, I can only hope I have discovered a character that is able to survive and transcend the obstacles in my life's journey.

THE MASTRINCOLA FAMILY went back to life as usual in Wanaque, New York. Pat is still a charming character, and as he did on the *Doria*, he continues to defy near-death experiences: a parachuting accident and the battle of Tet in Vietnam, an explosion of a tanker trailer filled with gasoline, rifle shots through his windshield, a tour-bus accident that broke his neck, and a half-dozen car accidents. In keeping with his quirkish disposition, Pat insists that it all began with a jinx cast on him when he was nine. "Before leaving for Italy on the *Andrea Doria*, I got into a fight with a friend my age. He was mad at me for beating him up, so he said, 'I hope your ship sinks!' Well, you see, it did!"

Undeniably, Pat was born to survive—and to help others survive as well. Thanks to all his escapades on our ship, he could find his way under even dire circumstances. It was this daring spirit that saved his sister Arlene's life. Pat remembers, "My eight-year-old sister, Arlene, was sleeping in the cabin. I was in the dining room with my mother. When we felt the crash, my mother began yelling, 'My baby, my baby!' I told her, 'Mom, I'm all right!' She said, 'Not you, your sister.' So I ran down the dark stairwells. Luckily, I recognized a Red Cross box on the wall, and I knew where to go. When I opened the cabin door, the ceiling was on the floor, and Arlene was sleeping on one of the inclined walls. Then I saw the tip of the *Stockholm*'s bow—it had barely penetrated the wall. One split second later, and my sister would have been killed!"

What Pat regrets most about the collision is that he sacrificed his racing bike to the sharks. It was the last thing he saw as he hung dangling on a rope over the ocean. He explained to reporters who hounded him after the accident, forcing him to take refuge in the trees nearby, "I don't care if that ship sank. I just want my racing bike—and my thirteen *Dennis the Menace* comic books!"

Original drawing by Eugenio Giannini, which depicts what the third officer saw just seconds before the collision: the *Stockholm*'s appearance from out of the fog, heading straight for the *Doria*.
(Courtesy of Captain Eugenio Giannini)

CHAPTER 2

Officers and Gentlemen

Real valor consists not in being insensible to danger;
but in being prompt to confront and disarm it.
—Sir Walter Scott

REAKING THE LULL of a peaceful, foggy night of bridge watch came the bloodcurdling cry: "She's bearing down on us! . . . She's coming straight at us!"

Captain Piero Calamai had only seconds to respond to Third Officer Eugenio Giannini's announcement. He, too, had spotted the red, hazy glow of a nautical stranger's mast a few hundred yards away. This proximity required an immediate decision—a desperate attempt to prevent a head-on collision that could assault his prized ocean princess, the *Andrea Doria*.

"Hard a-port!" the captain shouted to Seaman Giulio Visciano, gambling with time that his ship would not be desecrated by another.

As a drama of calamitous proportions was unfolding on the navigation deck, the slumber of a tired deck officer, who had finished his bridge duty only one hour earlier, was rudely interrupted by the shrill of two whistle blasts. Second Officer Guido Badano identified the signal as that of a sharp left turn. *Why did the captain order this?* he wondered, surprised to feel his bed incline to the left. Seconds later, the officer was hurled to the floor of his cabin by a violent blow. As the ship swayed erratically and sounds of crunching metal echoed, the tall, burly twenty-nine-year-old wrestled to bring his body to an upright position. Although perplexed, he responded alertly. Badano picked himself up, quickly dressed, grabbed his flashlight and master key, and threw on his life jacket. Heading for the bridge, the young officer felt his heart pound as he heard Officer Giannini's announcement imploring all navigational crew members to report on deck.

"Che cosa è successo?" Badano implored his captain for some explanation, squaring himself for news of his ravaged and moaning ship. As there was no time for anything short of desperate measures to save the liner, Badano collected word of its dire condition in fragments from the bridge officers—now engaged in a pitched battle and working as smoothly as the oiled parts of a Swiss watch beating in time to the waves pounding the wounded ship. And as in an intricate timepiece, each crew member assumed a part in the imperative mission of saving the entire group as they worked desperately to stay afloat.

At 11:10 p.m. on July 25, 1956, a silent voyager rapidly ripped through a curtain of fog on the night waters of the Atlantic, deftly slicing the *Andrea Doria*'s starboard flank. Its jagged steel-reinforced bow easily punctured a giant tear through the pristine hull. Resounding screeches, groans, and crackling sparks emanated from the friction of the massive impact, transforming the calm silence of the night into a cacophony of garish sounds. This interlocking between the stranger, named *Stockholm*, and the hull of the *Andrea Doria* resulted in a flood of ocean water and oily substances swelling into the gaping hole occupied by passengers. An immediate, severe list left no doubt that the Italian liner's integrity of seaworthiness had been instantly, and perhaps irrevocably, compromised.

Officer Badano was overcome with rage as he realized the implications of this event: not only was every passenger on board in imminent danger of perishing, but if they survived and the crew was found to be at fault for the collision, his chances of promotion to senior second officer would be thwarted. *Why did this have to happen? Who made this terrible mistake?* But thoughts of his own misfortunes quickly slipped from his mind as he recognized the danger of the perilous list. The inclinometer read 19 degrees—an angle beyond what nautical engineers had ever imagined could befall the pride of the Italian Line.

Facing page: Captain Piero Calamai and the *Andrea Doria*'s gyrocompass, a precise compass repeater to take hazimuthal bearings. (Courtesy of Captain Robert Meurn)

Badano focused his attention on the crisis at hand and on the cool demeanor of the ship's captain. The officer had served thirteen months with Calamai aboard the *Andrea Doria* and was in great awe of the man for his sense of duty to passengers and crew, his wisdom and prudence, and, above all, his composed manner as a true leader and authority figure on a ship seemingly crafted with him in mind. Working in this captain's shadow, the young officer felt the inexperience of his twenty-nine years, but he also felt great comfort and safety. Calamai's father, Oreste, was the founder of the prestigious publication *The Italian Navy*. His brother Paolo was an admiral in the Italian Navy during World War I and World War II. During the latter, Lieutenant Commander Piero Calamai had won the Italian War Cross for saving his torpedoed battleship by running it aground.

Officer Badano followed his master's order to join him and Officer Curzio Franchini in the chart room to take a loran fix. This would establish the exact location of the halted liner so the captain could send out a distress message to radio operators around the world and advise them of the need for immediate assistance.

Minutes later, Captain Calamai ordered "vessel not under control" signals, followed by a request for a report on the engine-room situation. Realizing that the vessel was in danger of capsizing, he also ordered the outboard lights to illuminate the lifeboats. As he was in charge of the port-side lifeboats, Badano ordered the release of the winch brakes holding the davits from their launching position. But because the ship was listing so steeply, the davits would not allow the lifeboats to slide down to the promenade deck, where panicked passengers were already clamoring to board them. Finally, Calamai ordered Badano, fluent in English and Italian, to make a bilingual announcement alerting all on board about how to proceed. Badano quickly took the microphone: *"Personale ai posti di abbandono nave. I passegeri devono recarsi ai punti di riunione, indossando la cintura di salvataggio e mantenersi calmi.*[1] Personnel to their abandon-ship stations. Passengers are to go to their mustering stations, wearing life jackets, and keep calm."

Although Badano made the announcement twice in each language, pausing between broadcasts, he underestimated the chaos on board. His impassioned pleas over the din of chilling screams were mostly unheard as passengers battled through jagged debris, smoke fumes, and seawater mixed with oil in order to reach the nearest exits. Even those near loudspeakers were denied information by broken cables leading to some areas.

Unaware of the extent of the turmoil in the corridors of his liner, Captain Calamai balanced his orders between staying afloat and abandoning ship. First, he ordered the starboard-side lifeboats to be launched immediately, but the incline of the ship—now 20 degrees—made it impossible for passengers to disembark from the Promenade Deck. Seeing the dilemma, Calamai ordered the lifeboats to be lowered directly into the ocean. Badano, who as safety officer was in charge of the lifeboats, feared that the *Doria* was no longer seaworthy and humbly asked the captain, "Shall I give the order to abandon ship now?" Captain Calamai had to make one of the most difficult decisions of his career. He concluded that hastening the rescue of half of his passengers would create a dangerous level of hysteria and firmly denied Badano's request.

The second officer savored a moment of relative peace, understanding the prudence of the captain's decision. But that acceptance was quickly placed under demanding scrutiny as the government commissioner appeared on deck and demanded an abandon-ship order. The commissioner, second in rank only to the captain, felt this was his duty, but the modest and even shy Calamai had no hesitation in denying his request, explaining patiently that only half of the necessary lifeboats were available. As Badano watched the scene, his mind flashed to the captain's unease at cocktail parties and dances, where Calamai often edged his way to the door and the safety of the bridge. Yet here was the same man holding court with dignity during terrifying circumstances.

Taking matters in hand once more and fearing that failure to stabilize the list would lead to the ship capsizing, Officer Badano transmitted an order to the engine room: *"Bisogna raddrizzare la nave con ogni mezzo!"* he implored. "We must balance the ship by all means possible!" The engine-room officers assured him that every effort was already being made to stabilize the ship, even though their labors appeared futile.

As the dangerous slant toward the sea made moving around the bridge hazardous, Calamai ordered the laying of grab lines to allow the staff to move with more security. Keeping his directions brief, Captain Calamai also ordered a series of operations: *"Preparazione dei razzi e fuochi Very, proiettore Aldis, fanali, proiettore in controplancia, controllo chiusure porte stagne, fermare lo sprinkler!"* The order was accomplished quickly: preparation of Very signals and rockets, Aldis searchlight, lights, and bridge searchlight, plus closure of the watertight doors as well as deactivation of the sprinkling system, which had been activated by various breaks, holes, and fractures during the collision.

**Officer Guido Badano in 1972, serving on the *Leonardo da Vinci.*
(Courtesy of Captain Guido Badano)**

Suddenly, a passenger appeared, wearing a torn piece of curtain around his waist. He was splashed with blood from a blow that had catapulted him into an adjoining cabin. He had struggled to make his way to the bridge, where he pushed through the officers to reach the captain. The tall, distinguished-looking man— even though events had left him swathed in oil and detritus—was Dr. Thure Peterson, a chiropractor whom the captain had met on the bridge earlier in the voyage. He had come to plead for assistance. Breathless from the long climb, he tried to explain. "My wife is trapped in heavy debris from the collapse of two cabins. There is also another woman, Jane Cianfarra. They're in severe pain and entangled in the wreckage. I need a rescue crew with heavy tools— a jack, perhaps. I also need some morphine."

It was a simple request from a man capable of retaining his dignity and civility regardless of the turmoil engulfing him. The captain, overwhelmed with the destiny of the 1,706 passengers and his ship, could not spare a single crew member, but he did respond to the piteous husband, "I'll send the ship's doctor down to you." Dr. Peterson made the long descent into the darkly transformed corridors, where his wife lay trapped under beams and girders.

It was now less than an hour after the collision, yet the ship's list was already 23 degrees. The beautiful architectural marvel of the Italian Line was groaning and shuddering with sounds of distress, and with every wave at its flank, the stress of remaining afloat was becoming unbearable. By this time, the potent *Stockholm* had withdrawn its steel grip, leaving the *Andrea Doria* to inhale seawater to a depth of 30 feet. As if God had a hand in the limits of this breach, the swirling ocean waters stopped at the threshold of the ship's chapel. The corridors were filled with rubble and collapsed cabins, wood, steel beams, girders, and furniture all indistinguishable from one another. Water gushed in ever more freely as smoke from burning electrical wiring replaced the darkness. The ill-fated location where luxury cabins once stood and the tiny quarters that had provided shelter for Italian immigrants became a black void with no bias for social class.

Could the master mariner Calamai maintain seaworthiness in

circumstances that seemed hopeless? This was the question on Badano's and every crew member's minds as they looked for signs of lifeboats promised by the *Stockholm*. The Swedish liner, which now looked more like a helpless witness than the ice-breaking voyageur it once was, had established its own seaworthiness and was prepared to offer assistance. Badano was happy for any help but was becoming increasingly impatient with what rescue efforts were under way: *Was the loran fix from an hour ago wrong? Why isn't the* Stockholm *moving closer? Where are its lifeboats? Why haven't the other rescue ships arrived?* After agonizing over these thoughts, Badano asked Cadet Mario Maracci to return to the chart room with him and take another loran fix. Badano picked up a scrap envelope and jotted down in nautical script: 19 miles west of the Nantucket Lightship and 60 miles south of the U.S. shoreline. The original SOS had relayed the sinking *Doria*'s correct position. Breathing a sigh of relief, he stuffed the envelope into his pocket.

Meanwhile, the embarkation of lifeboats was progressing slowly because of the lack of crafts available, as well as the means by which to reach them. Frantic and desperate passengers had to make their descents to the lifeboats from many stories above sea level using Jacob's ladders, ropes, hoses, and swimming-pool nets. The decks were also seriously inclined and slippery in the fog. Children, the elderly, and the wounded were assisted by crew members who volunteered to make the downward climb with each needy passenger. Many had visions of the *Titanic* tragedy, when women and children were given priority, allowing the men to aid crew members in the rescue efforts. But unlike those on the *Titanic*, the passengers of the *Doria* were not reluctant to disembark. The lifeboats were quickly filled, and overfilled.

Could it be, Badano wondered as he watched the passengers flee the submerging vessel, *that on the night the* Titanic *was sinking, there was an absence of a moon and stars?* On this heroic night of July 26, 1956, the fog was finally clearing, and millions of celestial bodies began casting light on those who felt forsaken. Moreover, as the *Doria*'s refugees rowed away with only hope on their backs, the lights of the first rescue ship, the *Cape Ann*, also shined in the distance. Badano hoped and prayed that the tiny vessels would carry their precious cargo to safety.

Most of the 1,706 passengers, however, were still aboard the perilously listing ship. Officer Badano pondered whether they would find the courage to disembark without panic. Would crew members continue to battle with fleeting precious moments to the point of sacrificing their own safety? Or would the entire scene turn to "every man for himself" as the ugly face of doom lurked ever closer? He let these thoughts drift from his mind as he took hold of himself, duty to his ship and his captain knitting his jangled nerves.

Just as he was reassuring himself, Badano received an update from the engine room: *"Allagamento del locale diesel-dinamo; stanno man mano fermando tutti i generatori; rimangono le turbodinamo in funzione."* The news was disastrous. The generators were stopping one by one in spite of the dogged efforts of Officers Pazzaglia, Colombo, Cordera, Gallo, Mantero, Cama, Manzotti, Ravasio, Pino, and Cogliolo—each a comrade with whom Badano had eaten many a meal aboard ship. The engine-room crew worked incessantly to offset the influx of seawater entering at a thousand tons an hour. Struggling to keep their footing on the slippery, inclined, burning metal walkways, they started and restarted any useful machinery—most of which had stopped because of the level of seawater, generator after generator, pump after pump, room after room. The once vibrant *Doria* was gasping for life as its crew suffered from exhaustion; they worked in an environment overheated by steam leaks and lack of force ventilation—purposely depriving themselves of fresh air to save power. The officers and staff felt fortunate that the pumps were still functioning, as was the ship's emergency lighting.

One half-hour later, the engine-room crew informed the captain that the diesel generator room had to be abandoned because of flooding of the starboard-side engines. With no generator, the crew feared the vessel would not be able to maintain electrical energy, which was badly needed to power lighting and communication mechanisms.

Exasperated by the worsening conditions, Calamai turned to Badano, whom he had also come to see as a good and trusted friend, and stated calmly yet resolutely, "If you are saved, go to Genova, and tell my daughters that I did my duty."

"If you are saved, tell my daughters that I did my duty"? What does he mean? Badano pondered. The words ran through his head like an unrelenting tape recording, but he couldn't make sense of them. *Does he think I'll get to Genova first? No, the master must simply be asking for reassurance that his maiden will survive, too,* the young officer concluded. Or, God forbid, had the captain's confidence been eroded along with the hull of his ship? Badano knew that Calamai, well read in the classics, believed a wise man should be free of passion. This stoicism would allow him to tap freely into inner resources, even under the direst circumstances. Was Calamai now viewing himself as a character in a Greek tragedy, with no recourse but to accept death stoically? Badano could not accept that; his master was not just a character but indeed a friend. So the dutiful officer turned to his captain and declared, "Captain, we will all be returning to Genova!"

Captain Calamai's gaze drifted for a moment. Rocking on his heels, he cleared his throat and returned his eyes to Badano just for a second before grasping the ship-to-ship radio microphone and dispassionately appealing to the *Stockholm* to contact the Coast Guard with a towing request. Minutes later, the *Stockholm* replied that the cutter *Evergreen,* along with other similar ships, would arrive with towing hooks within four to five hours. Calamai was visibly reassured by the news that there was yet hope to salvage the liner that he had loved for three years.

As all of this was happening, Officer Badano and the other crew members realized that passengers were panicking and taking matters into their own hands. In their zeal to keep the ship afloat, no one had taken time to keep the passengers abreast of what efforts were being made to save them. Moreover, the loudspeakers had ceased to function in certain areas of the liner, and what little information was being exchanged had been conveyed by daring expeditions across dangerously angling decks. Some passengers were attempting to leave the ship any way possible. Unaware of the lifeboats on the starboard side, they were either scaling down the side of the ship or simply leaping into the black, chilling waters of the Atlantic. Badano could only imagine what must be running through their minds: *What's happening to us? Why aren't they telling us what is happening? Why doesn't anyone tell us what we should be doing? Has the bridge been destroyed and personnel killed? How long before the ship overturns?*

In spite of the seeming disregard, crew members were being assigned to groups of passengers at the various muster stations to accompany them to the safest possible disembarkation sites. Nonetheless, even these efforts were falling short, as passengers continued to abandon the ship or fight their way through wreckage to find pathways that might lead to the upper decks and safety with little knowledge of the ship's architecture to aid them.

Two and a half hours had passed since the collision, and nearly one-third of the ship was now submerged in swirling seawater. The inclinometer menacingly registered a list of 30 degrees. Captain Calamai was compelled to leave the bridge for the first time. Feeling a sense of urgency and displeasure, he summoned First Deck Officer Luigi Oneto and Cadet Maracci to accompany him to his cabin. They were to perform a duty of utmost importance, as prescribed by nautical law: to save certain important documents at the prospect of losing one's ship. The captain directed Oneto to hand over to Maracci the vessel's log, as well as its cipher book, NATO instruction manuals (to be followed in case of war), and any other documents the captain deemed useful to save. As a navigational officer, Badano stood by ready to assist. He noted Maracci's rounded girth as the cadet stuffed document after document under his life jacket. Assuming that all papers were being attended to, Badano returned to the bridge, only to remember that part of the ship's log, which was his responsibility, had been left in the captain's sea chest. He cursed himself, taking blame for his oversight. *Why did I assume Maracci had the logbooks? This was my responsibility! I should not have assumed!*

There was not a second to waste on self-pity, as Badano's focus

Officer Eugenio Giannini, a few months after the collision.
(Courtesy of Captain Eugenio Giannini)

was diverted to a scene grander than life. At this wake for the soon-to-be-interred *Andrea Doria,* Captain Calamai; Officers Badano, Giannini, and Oneto; and Staff Captain Osvaldo Magagnini—still wearing his striped pajamas—watched in wonder as the dark horizon was emblazoned with a myriad of bright lights that spelled "ILE DE FRANCE." The awestruck, exhausted crewmen seemed to surrender momentarily to the wonders of the universe, as they watched another seasoned nautical master, Captain Raoul de Beaudéan, maneuver his 44,500-ton ship through sporadic veils of fog, chancing collision with other rescue ships. The French liner *Ile de France* (which had left New York just before the *Stockholm*'s departure that morning) had made a turn-around on the fog-obscured Atlantic and had raced back toward the *Doria,* postponing the arrival of 900 passengers to Le Havre, France. It had been a difficult decision for the French captain, whose main responsibility was to his passengers and to his company. But Captain de Beaudéan was a man born into royal blood, with a pedigree that impelled his leadership qualities. In his decision to forgo secure maritime business practices, the nobleman chose to respond to another captain and his passengers, simply based on moral imperative. It was 2:00 a.m. The fog had amazingly dispersed, allowing the *Ile*'s array of lights to provide much-needed illumination for the rescue. Quickly, the ship lowered its lifeboats, oared by 160 seamen bold enough to risk being sucked into the sinking *Doria*. Badano observed these heroic missions from the bridge while keeping an eye on the inclinometer. He watched in astonishment and pride as the Swedish, French, and Italian seamen transported hundreds of weary passengers to several rescue vessels, including the freighter *Cape Ann,* the tanker *Thomas E. Hopkins,* the Honduran tanker *Manaqui,* and the U.S. Navy destroyer escort *Edward H. Allen.* The Coast Guard, unable to send aircraft because of the imposing fog, sent several cutters, arriving from various ports along the eastern seaboard. A global, humanitarian circle of hope surrounded the passengers and crew, allowing them to feel optimism for the first time since the collision.

DR. THURE PETERSON, the chiropractor who had fought his way to the bridge to secure medical attention for his wife, Martha, and for Jane Cianfarra, was still attempting to free the two women. His wife was pinned under the weight of an elevator shaft that was creating enormous pressure on her spine, while Mrs. Cianfarra was still enmeshed in the coils of bedsprings that were crushing her from the waist down. As the rescue operations took place above, Peterson returned to the collapsed cabins, crawling under the wreckage once more, rubbing against a cold, lifeless body. Determined to free his beloved Martha, he pressed on, to find her losing strength and pleading for him to save himself. With what strength she could muster, she cried, "Darling, how will they ever get me out of here? Why don't you save Mrs. Cianfarra and yourself?"

Peterson would not hear of this and left the cabin to demand morphine once again, finally obtaining the precious medicine he'd been praying for from the ship's doctor, who had found his way to that area of wreckage. He thanked the doctor and then crawled back into cabin 56, where he injected the tranquilizing painkiller into each woman's arm. A slender ship's waiter from Genova, Giovanni Rovelli, had used every ounce of strength and courage he had to fill the gaping hole that was once the hull with wood planks, thereby sheltering the women from being washed out to sea. Nevertheless, the main task of freeing the two women was before them, and they still needed wire cutters and a jack to lift the heavier debris.

Relentlessly, Peterson made his second trek to the bridge. Gasping to speak, he asked the bridge crew for wire cutters. The radioman, who was busily communicating with other ships, pointed to the radio room, where the doctor found two cutters. The desperate husband took notice of the captain, who was also engrossed in prolonging the life of his own beloved. The young Badano watched the devoted men, each willing to sacrifice his life in line of duty to his passions—unaware that he himself exemplified dutiful devotion to his captain and his ship in a similar fashion.

Cabin 56 was still imprisoning two innocent victims of the dreadful collision. Dr. Peterson crawled again over jagged debris while sliding under the collapsed walls; he paid no attention to the lacerations on all of his extremities that added to the blood already gushing from his head. By the amber glow of the emergency light seeping through the floor from one level below, he could see that Mrs. Cianfarra had to be freed first if he wanted to reach his wife. Relentlessly, Rovelli and Peterson took shifts holding up the heavy mattress and cutting away the paneling that imprisoned the two women. At last, Mrs. Cianfarra was released from the grip of heavy rubble. The two men placed her fractured body on a blanket and summoned help to bring her to safety.

Peterson was relieved when the jack he had requested finally arrived by lifeboat from the military transport vessel *Thomas*. Peterson and Rovelli now faced the task of getting the 150-pound jack onto the Promenade Deck and to the cabin, where Martha lay pinned beneath the elevator shaft. Already exhausted, the two men somehow found the strength to drag the jack up the sloping, wet deck, tearing muscles and sinews in the process, only to be faced with getting the jack to the bottom of the stairs. They muscled the jack down the steps, pausing to breathe, until they arrived on the 35-degree-inclined floor of the cabin.

Peterson and Rovelli attempted to lift the elevator shaft, which had broken Martha's back and legs. "Hang on, Marty!" Peterson said aloud, pumping the jack and finally moving the imposing wreckage. Martha, her face ashen except for the blood hemorrhaging from her mouth, seemed to drift quietly to sleep—but not until she could say her last words: "Oh, darling, I think I'm going." Rovelli placed the back of his hand on Martha's cold face as the doctor was still struggling mightily with the wreckage and, grabbing his arm, said gently, "Doctor, I think your wife's dead."

Dr. Peterson knelt next to his wife's body and performed the routine but painful ritual of checking for her pulse and heartbeat. Numbed by the shock of every event leading to this tragic, final blow, he finally muttered simply, "Marty's dead," a look of disbelief and torment etched across his face.

"Why couldn't it have been me?" Rovelli cried out. "I'm nobody!" Class and social rank had spared no one on this ill-fated voyage, yet this Cabin Class waiter, husband, and father of two young children was so naturally endowed with a sense of duty that he still defined himself as "nobody"—even though he had sacrificed his own safety in an attempt to spare the lives of two strangers.

The mournful husband kissed his wife for the last time and placed cushions on Martha's lifeless body in a final gesture of reverence. Every minute counted now, however, if he and Rovelli were to save themselves. At 4:30 a.m., in a state of painful resignation, the pair headed for the next-to-last lifeboat departing the ill-fated Italian liner.

ON THE BRIDGE A HALF-HOUR EARLIER, Captain Calamai had already dictated to Officer Badano an ominous message headed for the Italian Line offices: "Run down in mist by Swedish ship. Passengers transferred to rescue ships. Vessel in danger. Calamai."

Badano watched his fatigued captain, who, incredibly, still had hopes of rescuing his beloved *Doria* in spite of the water spilling over the A Deck. All the facts available pointed to complete loss of the ship, yet he still valiantly discussed with his officers the possibility of having a tug pull the *Doria* to shallow waters, where it could be repaired. The crew realized that denying the severity of the situation could soon cost the lives of the few volunteers who remained on board: a priest, a nurse, a doctor, the engine-room officers, and, of course, the bridge crew. And, many of them wondered, who would want to approach a nearly capsizing vessel now, anyway? Out of enduring respect for this dauntless captain and war hero, no one protested; no one demanded disembarkation of the apparently doomed vessel.

Moving on the inclining deck, now listing at 40 degrees, was extremely hazardous, yet one by one, officers and crew members Carlo Kirn, Magagnini, and Giannini, along with Dr. Bruno Tortori-Donati, Chaplain Sebastian Natta, and others who had been asked to inspect every cabin for possible survivors, returned to the bridge. Covered with perspiration, oil, and salt water, they confirmed that the last passenger, Peterson, had abandoned the ship with Rovelli. They also announced the death of Martha Peterson. Magagnini reported to his commander, "All the passengers who could be saved are saved." He then asserted that it was time to abandon the ship: "There is nothing more to do, Master."

"You all may go. I'm staying," replied Calamai with no hint of hesitation. Since the tugboats had not yet arrived, Magagnini assumed that his captain wished to stay aboard until they did so, as he and every member of the crew were also well aware of the law of the sea: an abandoned ship becomes the possession of those who occupy it. It wasn't that Calamai was martyring himself, Magagnini believed, but rather that the captain's bond with the ship was so strong and inviolate that he could not countenance other seamen handling it. He had been there for her unveiling in Genova just three years earlier. Together they had courted the sea in moonlight and sunshine, had weathered stormy times and sailed in tranquil ones, had entertained the rich and famous and accommodated more humble guests. The two were like lovers, hand in hand on the Promenade Deck, among the tapestries and sculptures, or in the privacy of the master's den. The captain could never fathom strangers courting his grande dame. He would stand firm on her slippery flanks, unwavering in his efforts to stave off strangers who could claim her as their possession simply by occupying her threshold if he did not.

Officer Badano glared upward at the middle-aged captain, who in one day's work had aged a decade. He now unmistakably comprehended his master's earlier words: "If you are saved, tell my daughters that I did my duty." The young officer knew his captain only too well. Calamai was capable of sacrificing his life to save his ship—yes, even to be entombed with her, like the sea masters of bygone centuries. Badano agonizingly concluded that his master was cut from the same material as that of the captain in *The Rime of the Ancient Mariner*—a sea poem well known to all who manned a vessel's deck. He knew in his marrow that Calamai would never leave his ship, and, just as the captain in Coleridge's poem did, he could trade his life for that of his vessel only to be struck dead minutes from rescue. The *Doria* had also dutifully ferried its passengers within hours of landfall when the calamity occurred, and now the ship lay dying just as the Ancient Mariner had. With no one to guide him, the young officer had to make the most difficult decision of his life: to obey his master dutifully or to save his beloved friend.

Unaware of Badano's anguish—and still unaware of the captain's intentions—Magagnini ordered all of the senior officers to abandon ship in reverse order of rank, a process that would allow the captain to leave his vessel last. When all of the haggard officers had reached the lifeboat, Magagnini suddenly realized his master was not descending. "Come down!" he shouted at him from the ladder.

Captain Calamai signaled with a defiant gesture of his hand that the rest should continue boarding the lifeboat and that he was remaining exactly where he was, adding sharply in his native tongue, *"Andate via. Io rimango!* Go away. I'm staying!"

Magagnini was about to do no such thing, shouting again, "Either you come down, or we'll all come up!"

Seeing that his captain was standing firm, Magagnini began climbing back up the swaying rope ladder as the other officers positioned themselves to queue up behind him, again in order of rank, morally prepared to give their lives. Seeing the danger in which he was placing his crew as they reboarded the sinking vessel, the master of the queen of the Italian Line finally relented. He motioned Magagnini to descend, and he, too, abandoned the *Doria* at her most vulnerable moment, 5:30 a.m. on July 26, 1956.

Once Badano was safely aboard Lifeboat 11 and there was time to collect his thoughts, he wondered, *Who are these bold men who are courageous enough to approach the nearly capsizing liner?* Then he realized it was crew member Pasquale Stingi, a fellow sailor and the chief of the cargo hatch, with whom he'd eaten meals in the ship's galley. Stingi had been assigned to man a *Doria* lifeboat early in the rescue and had been ferrying passengers along with his rowing partner for nearly six hours. Although exhausted from these efforts, Stingi had been determined to return to the capsizing vessel one more time to ensure that his captain had safe passage off the sinking ship. Stingi's partner thought he was insane. "We'll all die! What good will that do?" he yelled to no avail as the unshakable Stingi lifted an oar in the air and threatened to persuade his colleague by beating it over his head. Realizing the danger, or having been influenced by such staunch courage, the crewman submitted. The two worn-out men rowed silently in dogged synchronicity in order to reach the heroic survivors still on board, all the while crossing a quagmire of debris: soggy suitcases, broken beams and deck chairs, torn clothing and mattresses, all drifting on the oily sea. These items, which had once comforted their owners, would soon be reclaimed by the inhabitants of the eastern shoreline as souvenirs from the greatest rescue in maritime history.

Officer Badano sat at the rudder tiller, relieving the exhausted Stingi from his duty as he scanned the crew members on Lifeboat 11, hunger and fatigue written on their aching bodies. They sat silently and detached from one another, uncomfortable with their pathetic situation. Calamai sat on the opposite end of the small craft, apart from the others and looking every bit the Ancient Mariner, white-stubbled beard and sunken jowls rendering him both stoic and pitiable. They were all "in the same boat" now, so to speak—mariners without a ship, all simply survivors.

Nearby were two other lifeboats, sheltering more crew members, a doctor, a nurse, and a chaplain. *How will our families know we survived?* they asked one another. *How will our families react if they believe the worst?* They now shared their self-pity with thoughts of compassion for their family and friends.

Silence prevailed on the three tiny vessels as they bobbed in the daylight, which revealed evidence of desperate means of escape: ropes and nets dangling, oil-slicked decks with marks from human hands groping and sliding across them, torn sheets used as makeshift ropes. *How could this have happened?* they wondered. *Master Calamai and his crew have crossed this part of the Atlantic dozens of times, under the same conditions. Whose fault was this?* Somehow, they had to accept that the once vibrant maritime structure was now a crypt for the victims of the tragedy. Had they personally failed the 1,706 hopeful souls, or had they salvaged what they could from what might have been a worse disaster? Just eleven hours after the collision, they knew that only history would provide the answer; their documentation and that of the passengers would provide testimony. For now, their attention remained fixed on only one question. When would the *Andrea Doria* herself admit defeat and relinquish her duty to her master by sinking to her death?

Members of the press pondered the same question as they raced hungrily toward the scene of the disgraced princess of the Italian Line. Reporters traveling in airplanes and helicopters outfitted with sophisticated photographic equipment drooled at the prospect of being the first to snap images of the horrible event; they were assigned to take some of the most sensational photographs in maritime history. But to the occupants of those three remaining lifeboats, the photographers were voyeurs, men taking pleasure in viewing the indecent exposure of a crippled sea maiden who was displaying her vulnerability while gasping for mercy. To some in the crew, mercy meant a quick dropping out of sight, but to its master, it meant his mistress could still be saved as the *Doria* hovered between worlds, not yet ready to slip away.

As the cutter *Hornbeam*, equipped with towing gear,

approached the small vessel of disheveled characters, Captain Calamai awoke from a silent daze and immediately showed his intention to negotiate the salvaging of his ship. He climbed directly into the pilothouse to discuss the technicalities with Lieutenant Roger Erdmann and desperately pleaded into the microphone, "Coast Guard, save my ship!" The young lieutenant wired the Coast Guard in Boston with the request, only to receive the dispiriting response from those who had assessed the situation: "*Hornbeam* should not attempt to tow."

At about 9:45 a.m., planes began circling like buzzards above the gravesite awaiting the burial at sea. It was to be a mass burial for forty-three souls whose God's acre lay below in the currents of the North Atlantic, dashed dreams for prospective immigrants awaited by the Land of Opportunity and crushed aspirations for the others whose loved ones had been anxiously anticipating their return. Captain Calamai had just begun the humiliating yet necessary process of filing an accident report with officers of the *Hornbeam* when the last forty-six survivors of the *Andrea Doria* were summoned to their rescuer's deck. It was the most dreaded moment in a mariner's life: the entombment of his vessel. Calamai and his officers and engineers walked limply to the banister, sensing that the eleven-hour wake was finally over. The once-proud suitors paid their last respects as they watched a shroud of waves envelop the remains of their cherished grande dame; it was a slow decent, and a graceful one even in the *Doria*'s cadaverous state.

Badano's eyes welled with tears as he discreetly glanced over to his beloved captain. As always, he found Calamai to be composed, yet, being his friend, he knew the turmoil of feelings beneath the surface of this honorable and proud master of the sea. As Dr. Peterson had done, Captain Calamai now relinquished a love that was not meant to endure this inconceivable event.

Mercifully, the weight of the water entering the hull met equally with the push of gravity to send the *Andrea Doria* swiftly to her grave. Her careworn mourners watched her keel over, innocently displaying her rudder, splashing debris from her interior into the air and then into the sea. The inscriptions on her stern, which once proudly identified her as a seductress for those seeking beauty and comfort, now served as her epitaph: *"Andrea Doria . . .* Genova."

Still wearing his complete uniform, including his trademark blue beret, Calamai asked to write a message to the Italian Line and succinctly announced the calamity: *"Doria* sank 10:09—Calamai."

HOPING TO ARRIVE IN NEW YORK SOONER, the forty-six survivors aboard the *Hornbeam,* including Captain Calamai and Officer Badano, reboarded the same lifeboats that had rescued them and took them to the destroyer escort *Allen.* The master rejoined his officers, engineers, and even a few members of the orchestra in order to compile an official report for the Italian Line and the Italian government.

By the afternoon of July 26, the media began exposing every detail it had obtained from a myriad of fractured sources. Frenzied reporting via newspapers, radio, and television managed to alert the world to the most catastrophic maritime accident in modern times. Fortunately for the *Doria*'s crew and those of the rescue vessels, the event was also being reported as the greatest peacetime maritime rescue in history. Sensational headlines united Italians in grieving for the loss of their country's masterpiece of technology— which had symbolized triumph over the devastations of World War II—as Pope Pius XII offered a national prayer of mourning for their countrymen. The Italian president, Giovanni Gronchi, said of the disaster, "It plunges the whole Italian nation into sadness." Then his cabinet met to review the official report, which had been written on the *Allen.* They wrote their own report, expressing "complete solidarity" with the comportment of the captain and his crew. Surprisingly, that report would never be published.

Still sheltered from the tragedy by lack of instant communications, Calamai's wife was shopping for her daily meals when she happened upon a newspaper with the banner headline: "Andrea Doria Sinks." Mrs. Calamai left the store in shock, barely recalling if she had all her bags and not knowing if her husband had been killed or had chosen to go down with his ship. She shared the despair with her sixteen-year-old daughter, Silvia, hoping that the older daughter, Marina, would be sheltered from the dreadful news as she was traveling by train to London. As they shared tears of trepidation, they concurred that, if necessary, Piero Calamai would have chosen to sink with his liner. They knew very well that he was a proud and dedicated mariner, one whose journeys at sea gave profound meaning to his life.

At 11:30 p.m., U.S. Navy officers and Italian consular officials escorted Captain Calamai off the destroyer escort vessel *Allen*. Camera bulbs popped, and reporters intruded relentlessly with absurd and inappropriate questions: "How did the accident happen? How did you react? Did the crew abandon the ship? Who was at fault?" Badano watched with repulsion, as no one seemed to care about the depth of the pain endured by the *Doria*'s survivors. *We've just survived a catastrophe! Bodies are lying at the bottom of the sea. We've saved every person who could be saved. Don't they want to know how we survived?* As Badano became enraged, his attention was diverted to his master standing at the microphone, stoically and professionally taking control one last time. Reading from a tattered piece of stationery from the rescue vessel, Captain Calamai spoke with dignity and brevity, knowing that his words would be taken verbatim for news columns and history books in years to come:

> With the absolute certainty that no passengers were still on board, the vessel having reached such a list that to remain longer on board would have meant nothing else but a useless sacrifice of human lives, the Chief Engineer having already confirmed to me that nothing more could be done inasmuch as only emergency dynamo and pump were still working, having consulted the Staff Captain and the Officers present, I gave the order to embark on the last boat. We left in order of rank. When the last officer had left, I too embarked.

Officer Badano listened carefully as his captain explained these administrative details, while omitting any information regarding the collision as well as the desperate conflict that had torn his captain from the bridge of the dying ship. But the captain and his crew knew in their hearts that there had been a transgression of natural law: the needless demise of their vessel. For now, they would suffer in tormented silence.

As more flashbulbs popped and the insensitive questioning continued, Captain Calamai and Officer Badano turned and left the stage. It was just the beginning of a plot that was worthy of a Greek tragedy.

Retired Captain Badano still has the envelope on which he recorded the ship's position in nautical script. The information was used to send an SOS along the Eastern coastline.

Leonardo and Giovanna Paladino with their daughters
(from left), Maria, Felicia, Antonia, ages four, three, two,
at St. Adelbert's Church in Queens, New York.
(Courtesy of Leonardo and Giovanna Paladino)

CHAPTER 3

Lost and Found

*Love is the only force known to man which it is not possible
to vanquish by any threat, however dire, in any ordeal,
however terrible, to which it may be put. In its purity it
inspires to the most wondrous sacrifice.*
—N. Sri Ram

EONARDO PALADINO, a thirty-year-old immigrant from southern Italy, decided to indulge in a
toast of farewell to his former Italian life and a
spirited welcome to a better life in America. For this
occasion, he went to the Tourist Class lounge to meet with his
buddy Salvatore, a *paisano* he had met on the weeklong voyage. It
was nice to have a couple of hours of respite from his family
duties. He and his wife, Giovanna, were traveling with three
young daughters: Maria, Felicia, and Antonia, ages four, three, and
two. Since Giovanna had been terribly seasick for most of the trip,
Leonardo had spent most of his time with the children. Tonight
was to be different; it was the night before they would land on the
shores of the Promised Land. He deserved to treat himself to a little solace, he thought, before tackling the challenges of the New
World.

"Where are you going to settle down?" asked Salvatore.

"In the Queens. You know, New York. My sister Antoinette
lives there with her family. She found me a job in a clothing factory. I'm a tailor. I can sew almost anything," explained the proud
Leonardo.

The two friends continued to sip their beer and make toasts.

"*Salute, prosperità e fortuna!*" declared Salvatore.

"*Grazie, altrettanto.*" Leonardo's eyes sparkled at his companion's wishes of health, prosperity, and luck, and he returned the
wishes in kind. "I'm sure going to miss my brother and sisters,
though! And Giovanna is already homesick for her parents and
seven brothers and sisters," Leonardo added pensively. "Hey,

what am I worried about? I'll have lots of money to take my family back to the old country every year. I know lots of *trapiantati*, like me. They live in America and go back to visit my town of Toritto all the time!" He recalled how a young man had entered his shop and told him he was making big money just being a clerk. "I've got a trade. If that guy can make good money, I'll make a lot more."

Leonardo explained to Salvatore that it was a struggle to "make ends meet" in Toritto. "Sure, I had my own shop, but people didn't have much money." The two *cumpares* agreed that World War II had played havoc with the Italian economy, and the city of Bari, 24 kilometers from Toritto, was especially suffering. The beautiful medieval city had prospered before and during the war—until December 1943, the fateful day when a German air strike destroyed all the Allied ships in the splendid Adriatic harbor. The ships were loaded with munitions, food, and military equipment, and one Liberty ship was carrying mustard gas. The noxious mix was released into the water and into the air. The brutal air raid produced a twofold disaster for this major supply port. First, it paralyzed a strategic Allied position that had brought prosperity to the region. Second, it produced a human-casualty disaster that later became known as the "second Pearl Harbor."

Leonardo shook his head in sadness as he remembered how the revered medieval city had been reduced to rubble along with the economy of the region. "So I decided to sell my shop, my home, and the land I had. I want my daughters to have more opportunities than Giovanna and me." The two young immigrants toasted to new opportunities, reassuring each other that all their plans would become reality. They boasted about becoming the new "big shots" who would make it big in the New World while maintaining their roots in the Old World. They would send money to their loved ones as proof of their success and perhaps sponsor others to follow in their pioneer tracks. Life looked promising.

"I hear there's an American movie tonight. I've never seen one before. I might as well get used to those cowboys, you know what I mean?" Leonardo wasn't quite sure himself what he meant, but he was curious to find out. *"Andiamo!"* Leonardo and Salvatore walked down to the Dining Hall to watch a movie about a triumphant Western hero, *Foxfire*. Amused at all the shooting, the two immigrants nevertheless identified with the pioneer spirit; they, too, would soon be proving their manhood by establishing themselves among other hardy men. About halfway through the showing, however, Leonardo began to feel restless. First he rationalized that this was from not being accustomed to watching movies. But then he began to fear his children might fall out of bed with the slight rocking of the ship. This uneasiness was enough to make the young father abandon the movie for a good night's sleep with his family. He shook his *cumpare*'s hand, assuming they would never cross paths again, and wished him a good night and good luck. *"Buona notte e buona fortuna!"*

As Leonardo undressed in the dark cabin where his family lay fast asleep, his senses were suddenly shocked by a loud, pounding noise; it sounded like when the bricklayers of Toritto were tearing down an old wall with their sledgehammers. *"Ma che cosa è successo?"* he asked loudly enough to wake Giovanna, who lay startled and wondering what had happened. The young father ran into the corridor to find out from others what they knew. The halls were nearly empty, however, as most of the immigrants in Tourist Class were either in their cabins sleeping or in the Social Hall enjoying music and merriment. The hammering noise continued, along with the floor swaying under the couple's feet, creating a sensation that was like trying to balance while standing in a gondola.

"Che facciamo?" They wondered what to do, but their instincts told them to flee. They woke up Maria and Felicia and explained that they would be going upstairs. Then Leonardo lifted the youngest daughter, Antonia, from her cradle and held her tightly against his chest. As they prepared to leave the cabin, the couple heard an announcement on the loudspeaker: *"Stati calmi . . . salvagenti . . . alle stazioni di recarso."* They now were certain that their lives were in danger; otherwise, they wouldn't be asked to put on their life jackets and report to the gathering stations.

The frantic couple put life jackets on their three daughters and then on themselves, over their pajamas. Leonardo desperately wanted to reach for his brown leather briefcase under the bed, but he realized he wouldn't be able to carry it while holding two of his daughters. He had to make a choice: save his family or save his fortune. It wasn't a difficult decision for the proud husband and father. All the money from the sale of the family home and land, the gold jewelry for friends and family, and a folder of important documents would stay behind.

The fear-stricken family abandoned their cabin; it was the one cabin where they all slept together, even though they had reserved another one next door. They ran into the corridor, where the lights were flickering and the air smelled of smoke. *This is the end. We're going to die,* thought the twenty-five-year-old mother as tears streamed down her terrified face. The loudspeakers made the same plea for calm just as before, but the liner was rocking and inclining more with every passing minute, and composure was not an option. Giovanna began to whisper prayers as she inched her way down the hall and up the oil-slicked stairs, carrying Antonia in her arms. Leonardo followed them, holding Felicia in one arm and squeezing the hand of four-and-a-half-year-old Maria as he pulled her along. *It will be all right,* he thought. *They told us this ship is modern and it can't sink.*

Stumbling over the slanted corridor floors, hanging on to the railing to prevent a jolting fall, all the while hanging on to three small children, became too much of a challenge for the fleeing family. Fortunately, Rocco Paladino (no relation to Leonardo and Giovanna), an immigrant heading for California, offered to assist with Maria. "Let me help you with the girl. I'm heading to the deck, too." But the ship's relentless rocking from side to side made the passage upstairs too fatiguing for Rocco, and he gave Maria back to her father.

Panic-stricken, Giovanna clasped Antonia tighter, cupping her head protectively and hoping the sleepy child would remain calm. The noise of grinding steel and collapsed girders sent shivers through the young parents' bodies, but they were relieved that their groggy children were unaware of the upheaval around them.

Finally, the five Paladinos arrived at the Upper Deck, which was really the lowest deck of the liner. Unfortunately, there was pandemonium there, too. *Now what do we do? Will the captain make another announcement? Where is the crew who's supposed to meet us here?* Leonardo's paternal instincts demanded an answer to the dilemma of keeping his family safe. He looked around for clues, but all he saw was the same plight of other families. One father yelled out, "We must have hit rocks!" while his four sons tried to console him. Leonardo thought he heard someone talk about an iceberg. More passengers arrived, and some were in a more desperate state—heads bleeding, clothing soiled with fuel oil, and wails of separation from family members. All Leonardo could do was run his tanned fingers through his jet-black hair and hope for a quick miracle.

He looked at his wife, who by now had seated herself on the wobbly, leaning deck with her offspring beside her. Her lips were quivering from fear, but a familiar prayer managed to come out. *"Ave Maria, piena di grazia, il Signore è con te . . . prega per noi peccatori adesso e nell'ora della nostra morte. Amen."* Giovanna had recited the Hail Mary many times before, especially after confession, but the last line never had the same meaning as it had now: "Now and at the hour of our death." *Can this be the way the Lord will have my family die? My Savior helped me plan for a better life in America, didn't he?* Incredulous at her circumstances, she prayed to her Savior, her name saint, and her guardian angels.

Leonardo joined in and prayed, too, sitting next to his diminutive wife, who looked even smaller curled up with Antonia against her breast. *"Signore, aiutaci a salvarci! Con il tuo aiuto possiamo ancora arrivare in America."* He hoped that his Savior could hear his prayer along with those of the other anguished immigrants who were begging for mercy. From time to time, Leonardo would try to approach others who were huddled in prayer and inquire what they knew about a rescue. But their piteous faces held no answers. Repeatedly, the discouraged father would return to his family and continue a long wait for whatever the Lord had in mind for them.

Hours passed, as did the fog that had probably contributed to the accident that had stranded them on this immense ocean. The hours were punctuated with moments of cracking, grinding, vibrating, and banging that bellowed from the bowels of the beleaguered liner. Each episode of terrifying sounds was followed by an increasing slant toward the ocean—sending shivers up and down every spine on deck. Leonardo had remained awake the entire time, watching as his wife—still wearing curlers in her light brown hair, so she could look pretty for her new life—dozed from exhaustion. He witnessed a young priest careening among the huddled, offering general absolution; he felt some peace, yet at the same time despair, as he listened to the last rites.

"Are you sorry for your sins?"

"Yes, Father."

"You are now in a state of grace, my child," he repeated to several groups. Sitting in stupor, the exhausted Leonardo began to notice that the inert masses on the now steeply inclined deck were beginning to stir. In fact, passengers who had been hanging on to railings on the high port side of the deck were letting go and sliding uncontrollably across the slippery floor, as if descending a freaky amusement-park slide, built to torment the most daring thrill seekers. In bewilderment, Leonardo watched them crash onto the guardrail, which was now only about 30 feet from the ocean waves.

"Madonna! Ma cosa stanno facendo? Why would they do such a thing?" Leonardo's words awakened Giovanna from her dazed state.

"Another ship!" someone announced. "Look, it's called the *Ile de France!"*

Giovanna and Leonardo looked over the railing and saw the name of the vessel spelled out in twinkling lights strung across the black sea. They resembled the beckoning lights of amusement rides that dazzled young children in Toritto.

"Grazie a Dio. Sono arrivati per salvarci!" Giovanna was right: God had heard her prayers. The French liner *Ile de France* had arrived as part of a rescue of gigantic proportions. Finally, her family would be saved. On this miraculous day of July 26, the Paladinos would resume their American Dream. All would be well—or

so they thought—on the feast day honoring Saint Anne, the mother of the Blessed Virgin Mary. Giovanna continued to pray to Mary as she moved with her flock cautiously along the guardrail.

The couple watched as other parents lowered their daughters' playmates onto lifeboats below—Piera, Pat, Arlene, Anthony, and others. But some parents didn't want to risk waiting, afraid the ship was sinking. Mr. Di Sandro was one of them. Panicked, he hurled his four-year-old Norma into the lifeboat below, but no one caught her, and she screamed in agony as her little head hit the lifeboat gunnel. Little Norma soon fell into a coma. Hearing of this tragedy from other immigrants, Leonardo and Giovanna decided to work together to lower their children. Leonardo had found a rope lying on the deck, but he thought it looked frayed and weak, so he doubled it. Then the frantic couple tied it securely around four-year-old Maria's body and dangled her slowly into the unsteady lifeboat below. To their dismay, as they were preparing to lower Felicia, Maria's lifeboat took off in a mad dash to reach safety. *It's OK. At least we know she's safe,* thought the baffled parents. Thank God, Felicia and their toddler, Antonia, also reached a lifeboat, but again, the vessel sped away for safer territory. The couple did not yet realize that their daughters might reach different rescue ships.

Courageously, Leonardo and Giovanna grasped the frayed rope and inched their strained bodies down into another lifeboat. Shortly after riding away from the terrifying black hole of the *Andrea Doria,* which greedily gulped each wave, their lifeboat's motor unexpectedly failed. The seventeen hopeful survivors looked at the French sailor at the helm in disbelief, wishing for words of encouragement. But his futile efforts to restart the motor spoke for themselves. *Are we far enough from the hole so the waves won't drift us into that cavern? If the* Doria *goes under, will we be swallowed in its whirlpool? Will another lifeboat see us and come help us? Oh, God, will someone find us before the rescue ships leave?* On a warm summer evening, cold sweat poured down Leonardo's forehead. By now, Giovanna was crying inconsolably. *"Dove sono le bambine? E se nessuno ci trova nel buio?"*

Leonardo tried to ease his wife's panicky fears of not being found in the dark and never seeing their daughters again. *"Non piangere, Giovanna. Stai tranquilla."* His words of comfort were as much for himself as for his wife. Nevertheless, neither could remain calm as moments turned to hours of aimless drifting. Moreover, the swell of the sea, caused by the *Ile de France,* bobbed the lifeboat like a discarded piece of cork. This caused violent sea-sickness among all the occupants of the forlorn vessel, including the French sailor. For nearly three hours, their stomachs retched in the upheaval of an uncontrollable situation; mercifully, this served as a distraction from the torment of witnessing their life fortunes being deposited slowly into a permanent salty crypt. At one point, an occupant of the lifeboat realized he had a cigarette lighter in his pocket. He tried repeatedly to send rhythmic flickers in the hope of being recognized as a Morse-code type of message. Astonishingly, an officer on board the *Ile de France* finally did notice the small flicker against a backdrop of black ocean. A final lifeboat was launched from the *Ile,* and it headed straight for the stranded one. "They saw the flame!" someone yelled out. "They're coming toward us!"

Two French sailors used all their might to hurl a nautical rope toward the helpless vessel. With barely enough strength to raise their bodies, the limp limbs of a few men groped for the rope and managed to tie it to their lifeboat. Slowly, the occupants, smelling of vomit, were pulled toward the safety of a viable liner awaiting them. With incredible daring, the spent bodies of seventeen *Doria* survivors and a French sailor would now become part of a small rescue within a larger one. As the moon faded into the light of day, these hopeful ones made a precarious leap over the shark-infested water to reach the swaying Jacob's ladder that led to the summit of the French liner. This was an act for only brave, desperate souls who were anxious to reunite with loved ones.

At about 5:00 a.m., nearly six hours after the collision, the traumatized Leonardo and Giovanna were able to face a new day knowing that a reunion with their daughters was imminent. *I know they're safe,* Leonardo reassured himself, pausing to assess his surroundings on the deck of the *Ile de France*. But Giovanna simply ran from one group of people to another asking for the girls. Finally, someone recalled seeing two little girls on the other side of the swimming pool. As the frantic couple dashed toward the pool, they spotted Felicia and Antonia in the company of other survivors. Giovanna squealed cries of joy, especially when she saw that the two girls were still asleep. In fact, the pacifier that Giovanna had placed in Antonia's mouth on the *Andrea Doria* was still comforting her. *"Le nostre bambine!"* the mother exclaimed as she cuddled her daughters against her body. Leonardo stood by and wiped his teary eyes with the sleeve of his filthy pajamas.

"Avete visto la nostra Maria?" The father repeated his anxious question to several immigrants, hoping someone knew the whereabouts of Maria. They all shook their heads. Meanwhile, others had already gone to their cabins in search of clothes for the family still in their pajamas.

A new dawn came for the survivors who had never gone to bed. Those who had kept vigil over the dying *Doria* realized that her agony would be prolonged for a while longer—perhaps just long enough for the light of day to illuminate the stage of an agonizing drama. Survivors of the "pride of the Italian Line," along with their courageous rescuers, lined the railing of the *Ile de France*. Curiosity drove them there, to witness the demise of their loved ones, acquaintances, fortunes or small treasures, and their dreams. *At least we are safe; all else doesn't matter now*, Giovanna reflected as she held on tightly to her daughters. Then she remembered the stupidity of an elderly man who would not leave the *Doria* without his suitcase. Selfishly, he had launched his belongings into a lifeboat, delaying his own rescue and compromising the safety of those below. *I wonder if he thought about saving himself.*

Giovanna had been missing her large family from the moment she left for America. But now she felt overwhelmingly lost and alone on this vast sea of disaster. *Dear God, please don't let my family find out about the sinking until we can reach them and tell them we're safe! But what if we can't find Maria? They will all be devastated. Signore in Cielo, portaci a New York in fretta.* Giovanna's prayer that they would arrive in New York quickly was approaching reality. She heard the loud, deep whistle of the *Ile*, as it announced its departure. But she never expected the French liner to circle the *Andrea Doria* three times, forcing them to witness her mortality from every angle: the descending bow, the raised port-side rudder, the useless port-side lifeboats, and the disappearing starboard side. Each time the *Ile* made another surveillance trip, it blew its bugle of steam and lowered the French tricolored flag, all in reverence for its wounded maritime colleague. It was after 6:00 a.m. when the *Ile de France* headed west, in the direction of the Statue of Liberty and the pier.

MEANWHILE, IN ITALY, it was past noon—just a half-hour before the main meal of the day. Giovanna's twenty-nine-year-old brother, Franco, was enjoying some camaraderie with friends in a café in Toritto's town square. As in every café, there was music provided by a three-foot-tall radio. All of a sudden, Franco's attention was diverted by an emergency news flash, something highly unusual. "We interrupt this broadcast to bring you the news of the sinking in progress of the beloved Italian liner *Andrea Doria*." The aperitif Franco was sipping stuck in his throat as he sat momentarily in shock. *"Madonna, questa è la nave che trasporta mia sorella e la sua famiglia!"* Before listening to any more details, Franco announced to his friends that his sister and her family were on the *Andrea Doria* and ran home. He found his parents and all of his siblings sobbing in front of the radio, exclaiming that their American-bound family might have perished.

Hungry but too distressed to eat, they went to the church to pray. Their neighbors and friends all joined them in a solemn rosary vigil. They waited many more hours in unbearable apprehension before receiving any specific details about the Paladino family.

ON THE ATLANTIC, the *Ile de France* became the heroine for 759 *Andrea Doria* passengers desperate to reach New York City. Sadly for Leonardo and Giovanna, their beautiful first daughter was not on board. When the four Paladinos reached New York, Leonardo's nephews and nieces, his sister's children, met them at the pier. The family from the Old World and the one from the New World met for the first time under dispirited circumstances, as they all grieved for the missing child. As is typical of Italian families, they expressed their emotions with embraces, kisses, and an abundance of tears. "This isn't how we were supposed to meet each other and meet America!" exclaimed the forlorn Leonardo. "Look at us! No suitcases, no money, nothing! All the new suits I made to wear in America, gone! We're like refugees, not immigrants!" he sobbed.

After a brief sharing of grief, exhaustion, and frustration, the entire family ran to another dock to meet another rescue ship. It was the *Cape Ann,* carrying 153 survivors. Waiting anxiously while hoping Maria would walk down the gangplank, they became impatient at the fruit cargo ship's slow debarkation. Instead, they went to two other docks, where the *Private William Thomas* and the *Edward Allen* were arriving. The Paladinos ran to ship officers and asked to see the passenger list. Dumbfounded, they did not find Maria's name on the list. Faced with more insurmountable odds of finding his daughter, the devastated Leonardo exclaimed, "I lowered her onto the lifeboat with my own hands. I saw her in the boat. They were supposed to bring her to safety. Where is she? Who can help us find Maria?"

Making an unbearable situation even worse, the Paladino family witnessed the arrival of the Di Sandro family, whose grief was beyond description. The young parents were in shock after their four-year-old daughter Norma's horrific accident. Tullio Di Sandro was inconsolable as the family listened to his story. They tried to relieve him of the guilt he felt knowing that his little girl's head was hemorrhaging severely because he had impulsively thrown her into one of the first lifeboats. Paralyzed in empathy for the Di Sandros, Leonardo and Giovanna recounted seeing a helicopter with a cot dangling beneath it, rushing the little girl to an American hospital. "She played at the *Doria*'s swimming pool with our Maria!" Leonardo said, wiping a swell of tears from his eyes. *Dear Lord, please help little Norma recover,* Giovanna prayed silently.

The Paladinos' anguish over Maria continued. Close by, a police officer heard the commotion of the family. In an amazing coincidence, he had watched a news alert put on the air by the Red Cross in an effort to locate Maria's family. He told the family that their daughter was safe in the protection of a Bronx Red Cross center. *"Grazie a Dio!"* exclaimed Leonardo. Giovanna accepted the family's suggestion that she and her two daughters be taken to Elmhurst, where the Paladino family would reside temporarily.

It was nearly midnight. The hungry and exhausted Leonardo, who had not eaten or slept for nearly thirty-six hours, continued to cry all the way to the Red Cross center. When he and his nieces and nephews arrived, they were told that Maria had been taken to the Children's Center under the protection of Catholic nuns. Finally arriving at the Children's Center at nearly 2:00 a.m., the young father unleashed the remainder of his waning energy by waving his arms and hurling out an explanation in Italian to the baffled nun. Leonardo's family translated his predicament, but the nun hesitated to hand over Maria, asking for proof of identity, which was by now lying at the bottom of the Atlantic.

Leonardo felt helpless: he was out of his culture and language, he couldn't prove anything, and he was dead tired. But his nieces and nephews were relentless in demanding Maria's release. Finally, the nun succumbed to their pleas and handed the sleepy child into her father's arms. Awakening briefly, Maria smiled trustingly, something she hadn't done for nearly two days in the company of strangers.

"She never cried while she was with us," the nun explained reassuringly. The young father was overwhelmed with joy. He smiled proudly at his brave little girl, who already looked more American than Italian. Maria had been dressed in new clothing: blue dungarees, a white blouse, and an oversized blue sweater. "She's never worn pants before!" her father exclaimed.

Meanwhile, at the Elmhurst family home, Giovanna was watching the midnight news on television with her new family: sister-in-law Antoinette Misciagna, her husband, and their five children. Miraculously, Maria's face flashed on the screen. *"È la nostra figlia! È salva nel rifugio!"* Giovanna cried out ecstatically. Maria was indeed alive and on her way home, in her father's arms. Giovanna smiled when she recognized a young immigrant named Antonio Regina, a family friend who had eaten many meals with the Paladinos in Toritto. When Antonio had recognized little Maria on television, he had gone to the Red Cross to console and identify his little friend to officials before Leonardo arrived.

Throughout the night, and for weeks to come, the Red Cross, police, steamship officials, and children's agencies worked to reunite separated families of the *Andrea Doria* disaster. Antonio was indeed proud to be aiding this benevolent institution, now involved in the greatest maritime survivor operation since the sinking of the *Titanic* in 1912. The Paladinos were grateful beneficiaries of their good deeds.

Giovanna continued to watch the news in hope of recognizing other survivors. She saw the agonizing drama of little Norma Di Sandro, who had been transported to a Boston hospital. *"Signore, che hai salvato nostra figlia, salva anche questa piccola bambina."* She prayed to the Lord for young Norma, the girl who had earlier been identified only by a note

Maria Paladino, age four, is comforted in the arms of a Red Cross nurse while awaiting the arrival of her father. Maria was separated from the rest of her family during the rescue. The Red Cross fed and clothed her and said the brave little girl never cried. (Courtesy of Leonardo and Giovanna Paladino)

pinned to her nightgown saying "This is a little Italian girl." Later, her parents identified her to the Red Cross, who described the child as wearing a gold ram's horn charm—worn by Italians as a symbol of good luck. Giovanna, Leonardo, and their American family learned the next day that the little girl's luck had expired. She died only hours after her parents' arrival at the hospital. *"Grazie a Dio, nostra figlia è salva. Signore, porta Norma nel tuo regno."* Giovanna faithfully thanked the Lord for saving her Maria and prayed for Norma's soul in heaven.

Finally, Giovanna felt she had some good news to share with her own family in Italy. Nervously, she phoned the town café in Toritto, where the only telephone was located. Giovanna's mother was summoned to speak with her daughter. But it was difficult to console the distressed grandmother, who did not believe that little Maria had been found. *"Mandami una foto di Maria. Voglio vedere con i miei occhi che è viva!"* Only by seeing a photograph of Maria would she feel reassured, and she begged her daughter to send one immediately.

Feeling deep sorrow for so many circumstances—the loss of Maria's little friend Norma, homesickness, and her deep loneliness among strangers—Giovanna went with her family to the local parish church to pray. But she did not experience the consolation of faithful worship that she had felt when she prayed among family and neighbors in Toritto. *"Signore, grazie per avere salvato la nostra famiglia. Putroppo mi sento sola, e sei tu l'unico fra questi stranieri che possa capire la mia solitudine. Dammi il coraggio di continuare questa vita in un paese straniero. Amen.* Dear Lord, thank you for saving our family. Unfortunately, I feel alone, and you are the only one who can understand my aloneness among these strangers. Give me the strength to continue my life in this strange land. Amen."

QUICKLY, THE TRAGIC NEWS regarding many needy *Andrea Doria* families reached the headquarters of a popular television show called *Strike It Rich.* The program prided itself on aiding families whose economic situations had hit rock bottom. Leonardo's sister, Antoinette, called the program to explain the Paladinos' desperate circumstances, how they had lost all their money and literally the shirts off their backs. By Monday, July 30, the family was on the air and struck it rich, so to speak. Mr. Paladino and the entire family were given new wardrobes and spending money. *How ironic,* he thought. *I once bragged about striking it rich on my own. Instead, we have to depend on charity!* Although he was grateful, the proud family man found the experience demeaning.

Fortunately, within a month of their arrival, the Paladinos were able to move out on their own, renting an apartment in Brooklyn. They furnished it with a laminate kitchen table and two mattresses on the floor. The tailor from Toritto worked long hours in a clothing factory, making military uniforms along with 300 other employees. But it was the beginning of their journey toward an American Dream.

Meanwhile, the family waited patiently while court hearings on the collision continued for three months. They were hopeful that the insurance company, Lloyd's of London, would reimburse them fairly for their losses: the newly tailored clothes, the jewelry they had bought in Rome for family and friends, and the cash from their life's savings left in the briefcase inside their cabin. The reimbursement from the insurance company arrived earlier than they had expected, but the amount was extremely disappointing, only about one-twelfth of the value they had declared.

Leonardo's mission to provide a good life for his family kept him focused on succeeding financially. After one year of grueling factory work, he found a better job as a tailor in a department store, where he stayed for many years. Unfortunately, he was never able to be his own boss again, as he had been in Italy, but he was able to provide for his family's needs. And those needs grew as the family grew to seven children, with six daughters and one son.

When reflecting on the *Andrea Doria* tragedy and a new life in America, Leonardo remembers how initially he would have nightmares; he saw people dying in the water as they tried to swim toward the lifeboats. Then he developed a fear of water, even the water in his bathtub. "In Italy, my wife and I would often take our daughters to the Santo Spirito beach and swim together. On Long Island, when our children wanted to go to the beach, I would take them. But I would never enter the water, because I felt like a child full of fear. I was always afraid something would happen!" This *trapiantato* wishes he could have returned to Italy more often to visit his family, but flying was expensive for a wage earner supporting nine people. He managed to visit Toritto twice, both times by air. As for making a living, Leonardo thanks God that he was able to do what was necessary to raise seven children. "All of them finished high school and had good grades. They never got into trouble," he proudly says.

Giovanna has made five transatlantic crossings to Italy, always by air. Her seven brothers and sisters and all of their children live in Italy, and she misses them terribly. Like most immigrants who transplanted their roots in new soil, her experience is bittersweet, never again having a sense of fully belonging anywhere. Giovanna states this succinctly: "When I'm in Italy, I get homesick for America. When I return to New York, I miss Italy."

Having established their own little colony on Long Island has helped Giovanna and Leonardo feel more grounded; their seven children, eighteen grandchildren, and five great-grandchildren all live nearby. They all chose to cultivate their lives in the New World, where the harvest can be shared during frequent family gatherings at the beautiful Paladino ranch home. "I feel bad sometimes that our children couldn't grow up with their cousins to play with, but we felt there were more opportunities in America at that time. Now Italy is prosperous. In some ways, people live better there than in the New World. Our American Dream now is for our family to be able to make a lot of trips to Italy."

As for the health, wealth, and good luck that Salvatore wished for Leonardo nearly five decades ago on the *Andrea Doria*: "Our wealth was invested in raising a family that brings us good luck and good health every day. This is more valuable than making a lot of money." And a lot more precious than the small fortune in a brown briefcase repossessed by the ocean floor.

CHAPTER 4

Prayers from Vieste

*It is God's kindness to terrify you
in order to lead you to safety.*
—Mevlana Rumi

ERMINA D'ONOFRIO MUTTERED TO HER-
SELF as she sat on the deck of the wounded and
listing ship along with a crowd of other *Andrea
Doria* passengers. "How can this be happening?"
Traumatized, she stared at her outstretched legs, gripping the
guardrail with both hands, hoping that this would keep her from
sliding into the black ocean.

Germina could not grasp the reason for her predicament. She
had crossed the Atlantic twice before, the first time in the safety of
her mother's womb as her parents were immigrating to America.
The second time, she had voyaged to Italy just four months ago,
along with her mother, Antonietta, and her two younger brothers,
twelve-year-old Michael and three-year-old Joseph, to connect
with her Italian roots on the beautiful Adriatic coast of Apuglia.
And now, Germina was returning to America to attend a friend's
wedding. She was traveling with Celeste Caputo, who was her
mother's girlhood friend and a former native of Vieste, where Germina's family had originally lived. Germina's mother had asked
Celeste, who was forty-one, to chaperone her daughter on the
return trip, since a beautiful young maiden of nineteen should not
travel alone if she valued her good reputation. Never could the
two women have imagined that they would be thrust into a part-
nership of survival on what should have been a routine crossing of
the Atlantic.

Earlier that evening, Germina and Celeste had been watching
the film *Foxfire* in the large, beautiful Dining Hall, living vicari-
ously through the adventures of a triumphant Western hero. All of
a sudden, they heard a loud crunching sound, the lights flickered,

Germina Donofrio, passport photo.

and the mighty ship swayed and tilted to the starboard side. Empty chairs slid across the room, and passengers held on to tables to steady themselves.

Not terribly alarmed yet, the two women assumed that the ship must have hit a large buoy in its approach to New York Harbor; the liner was on the last leg of its nine-day journey and scheduled to reach port the next morning. Within minutes, the film adventure—with its own explosions—was replaced by a real-life adventure. Celeste could barely distinguish the noises in the movie from the crashing sounds around her.

The movie spectators headed for the exit door of the Dining Hall in a frenzy to inquire about the condition of the listing ship. To their surprise, on their way out, Germina and Celeste were confronted by a dazed and bewildered pack of passengers, some still in their nightclothes, urgently pushing their way up the stairs amid a cloud of steam.

Germina remembered from the routine naval drill at the beginning of the journey that in an emergency, she would have to retrieve her personal life jacket from under the bunk bed. The two traveling companions realized that going down the stairwell would mean taking the risk of being trampled to death by the frightened horde of people. "Celeste, we will just have to do without our life jackets! Everyone is heading for the Outer Deck. We'd better follow them."

Suddenly, Celeste felt her heartbeats swell in her throat. *Dear*

Lord, please tell me this fright is not about the premonition I had about Germina and me having an accident on the Ohio Turnpike on the way home! Could this be why I have felt uneasy on this trip? Is this the real danger that I've been sensing? Feeling clammy and faint, she held to the hope that her fears were unfounded.

An announcement blared from the loudspeakers encouraging the passengers to stay calm—"*State calmi!*"—but mayhem prevailed, not just among the passengers but among the liner's crew as well. The same crewman who had pleaded for calm had also inadvertently left the microphone on, allowing the frantic passengers to hear all of the confusion at the helm. They heard experienced sailors making suggestions, inquiries, and demands in utter chaos. This small glitch of technology revealed to all that the luxury liner's advanced maritime equipment had failed to prevent a calamity—a collision with another ship!

How can this nightmare be happening? Germina asked herself, crawling on her hands and knees on a deck so sharply inclined that standing was no longer an option. The merry souls who had been celebrating the last night of their journey to America, the Promised Land to many, were now scrambling just to stay on the ship. Many tied themselves to fixed objects—beams, stools, railings—so that they would not slide into the black sea off the starboard side. These souls in peril resigned themselves to staying put, praying silently for salvation.

Time seemed to stand still and gave way to random thoughts. Germina remembered her family going to see a film on the *Titanic*, just a few weeks before their trip to Italy. The self-assured young lady had told her mother, who felt quite agitated by the film, that there was nothing to fear. "Don't worry, Mom! This kind of thing doesn't happen anymore. Ships are equipped with advanced radar equipment. They know what's ahead so that they won't crash into anything. There are rarely any kinds of sea accidents these days."

Germina turned to her faithful companion and exclaimed, "Thank God my whole family is not here to die."

Tears streamed down her face as she thought about how her

family in Italy would react to the news of her death by drowning on a sinking luxury liner. She thought about the reaction of the people of Vieste, where she had spent the last four glorious months. She also thought of how her father and brother and friends in Michigan would be confronted with the horrific news via the media. The devoted daughter sobbed. "My life is over, and if that's God's will, fine. But I can't bear the thought of having my family go through this!"

The brutal reality was that the ship was sinking, with no signs of being rescued, no one to console the people whose haggard faces revealed their bewilderment and despair. There was no point in pondering the future, which might last only minutes or hours—no one knew. In fact, incredible as it seemed, there were no more announcements, no explanations, and no directions from the crew. Passengers were left on their own to deal with the illogical and traumatic circumstances.

Germina's mind wandered off in a timeless space. *How much time has passed—two hours, six hours?* She began to take stock of her regrets. She had had several suitors, but the young lady had never been truly in love. She would never have her own family. Being the eldest of four and the only daughter, Germina regretted not having the opportunity to nurture and be nurtured as her own mother had done. She recalled the fairy tale about how her mother had met her Prince Charming, a dashing and talented shoe designer who came to her parents' house to fit her with new shoes. The shoes fit, and the smitten couple fell deeply in love. The new fiancé designed and made by hand the beautiful shoes for the wedding of his life's sweetheart. Why couldn't something like this have happened to her? Then maybe she wouldn't be here with an assigned female companion, on this ship, going home to take part in her girlfriend's wedding instead of her own.

Caught up in this anguished stream of consciousness, Germina, a Catholic, remembered going to confession in the ship's beautiful chapel earlier that day. This act of confessing one's sins assures the faithful that if they should die, they will do so in a state of grace. Germina felt a tremendous sense of consolation knowing this. She had also picked up a prayer card at the confessional, and on it was a special prayer to protect and comfort passengers at sea. The faithful maiden prayed to Mary, Star of the Sea, in the repetitive and lugubrious tone that mourners use to pray over the bodies of their loved ones. Meanwhile, bits of logic would surface, and she and Celeste would both wonder, *Will we be saved? Who will save us? How can we leave this sinking ship?*

"Listen, Celeste!" Germina suddenly exclaimed. "I hear noises coming from down below!"

Germina crawled to the sinking starboard side, thankful that the lights had remained on during these frightful hours. As she leaned over the railing, still on all fours and afraid of slipping off the wet deck, she saw a thick rope leading to the ocean several stories below. A lifeboat was bobbing on the black waves like a toy in a dark lagoon. As she looked overboard, Germina witnessed a desperate scene. Passengers were jumping or falling into the lifeboat. Some attempted to climb down the rope. Then she saw something that made her panic. There appeared to be crew members among those abandoning the ship! She recognized them because they wore gray life vests instead of the orange ones reserved for passengers. "That's it! We have to leave the ship now, Celeste!" Germina exclaimed. "Even some of the staff is leaving. You go down first, and I'll follow you."

Celeste could not accept the option as she watched others falling and crashing into the small vessels below. "This is not a rope ladder, it's only a single line. How can we do this?" Frozen with fear, she declared, "I don't want to go down. My poor Diana has already been orphaned once. I can't let her be abandoned again!" Celeste was thinking of her adopted daughter.

"Then I'll have to leave you!" Germina threatened, hoping to change her friend's mind.

Celeste's assignment had been to accompany Germina and assist her during the voyage. Now there seemed to be an exchange of roles taking place between the two women. Celeste mustered every ounce of courage she could and began her descent on a rope dangling off the side of what looked like a tilting skyscraper. Nervous, exhausted, and in excruciating pain, she descended. With each new grip, she felt more agony in her arms as ligaments tore; a burning and throbbing sensation made the descent almost unbearable.

Meanwhile, Germina was assessing her own vulnerability. With no life jacket, with limited athletic ability, and weakened from exhaustion, how would she reach the small lifeboat many stories below? There was no time to ponder. The ship could capsize at any time. The adrenaline rush from the thought of danger served Germina well. She decided to loop her white stole through the handles of her white purse and tie it around her waist. She lowered her trembling body a few inches at a time as the rope wound between her legs. Germina's burning hands clung so tightly to the rope that it was hard to release it, even when she felt others grasp her legs and her waist and heard voices imploring her to let go. The daring young woman had arrived safely on the crowded vessel.

Germina and Celeste had reached their target, a fragile one at that, which floated in spite of the heavy cargo of dazed passengers and crew. Most were vomiting as they rode the waves while banging against the wounded liner, fearing it would roll over onto them at any moment. The brave sailors who were manning the lifeboat had come from the *Stockholm*, the ship that had collided with the *Andrea Doria*. With each stroke of the paddle, Germina and Celeste rode closer to the giant lit up in the distance. They were approaching the very ship that had created the deep, jagged hole in the side of their beautiful luxury liner. Even though they were headed for the *Stockholm*, they could not stop staring back, transfixed, at the crippled *Doria*.

As they passed the twisted bow of the *Stockholm*, Germina was appalled. "I can't believe it, Celeste. This is what hit us. Look at the bow! You can see chunks of furniture hanging from it!" Bits and pieces of cabin furnishings dangled from the heap of mangled wreckage, like prey dangling from a voracious ogre's jowls. The 300-ton serrated bow of the *Stockholm* had originally been constructed to rip through the ice of the North Sea without sustaining damage. Instead, its sharp lathe had incapacitated another ocean liner whose beauty was unrivaled and whose seaworthiness was unchallenged—until now. The fortified bow that once served as a protective shield was now nothing more than mangled, gutless entrails of steel, pushed 40 feet within itself. Germina thought it was ironic that even steel could appear fragile and useless as it sat tottering over the water without a mission.

Germina and Celeste prepared themselves for the next humbling event: being raised along the side of this foreign invader. As the lifeboat climbed, Germina noticed the letters "STOCKHOLM" amid flashing emergency lights. *How can we be safe on a ship that has been damaged by a horrible accident?* she wondered. No one had an answer, and no one had another option to offer.

The *Stockholm* was crowded. Its deck was occupied mainly by crew members directing the newly arrived passengers to resting areas. Since there were no deck chairs available, the two women made do by sitting on the floor and resting their weary backs against the railing. These were meager accommodations for passengers who had been spoiled by the *Doria's* luxurious quarters, even in Tourist Class. Germina and Celeste were grateful for being rescued but too weary to rejoice at being alive.

The two women were safe for now—safe enough to drift into a surrendered state of shock and disbelief. Germina hoped she'd be able to sleep but instead found her eyes fixed on the *Andrea Doria*. *What about the passengers? Have they all been rescued? That can't possibly be. A lot of water must have been taken on to incline a ship like that,* she surmised, but she did not have the strength to utter her ideas to Celeste. By now, the sight of the corpselike vessel seemed like a mirage. And the scene vividly reminded her of the movie about the *Titanic* that she had watched with her family just a few months before.

In the early dawn, the passengers awakened to the clanking of dishes and the smell of boiled potatoes. Germina ate a small amount, but she felt nauseated, even though the ocean was calm and the *Stockholm* was not moving. She overheard other passengers explaining why the ship was not proceeding to New York.

"The law of the sea is keeping us here. We can't leave until the *Doria* completely sinks!"

Hungry but queasy, sleepy but awake, Germina was shaken into reality by the most horrific sight of her life. "Wake up, Celeste! Look, the *Doria* is rolling over!"

She pointed to the once majestic liner, which now resembled a wounded sea mammal, revealing its mortality in the morning light. Germina and Celeste bore witness to the sinking of their ship, which lay hopelessly on its side and disappeared with each inch of water it inhaled into its cavernous hull. As the swirling water and debris followed the ship beneath the waves in a downward spiral, there were no dry eyes among the *Doria* and *Stockholm* survivors. Many had kept a deathwatch on deck through the night and the dawn. Men and women wept without shame. Within moments, the *Andrea Doria* was gone. The sea, like a ravenous animal, had swallowed its wounded prey whole and was now satiated and calm again.

What a dreadful thought, and what a dreadful sight! Germina thought. Under a clear morning sky, too clear for some, the rescued passengers, of all means and importance, watched their prized personal belongings find their way to a permanent locker owned by all and by no one at all: the ocean floor. Celeste thought for a moment about the handcrafted new rosaries she had lost and that she would never be able to offer them to her friends as religious keepsakes from Italy.

The shocked survivors were soon offered a distraction from their weary staring at the floating debris. They heard amid the chaos that they could send messages to their loved ones. Germina and Celeste both mustered enough energy to write the most essential of words: "SAVED."

After a day and a half, the *Stockholm* limped into New York Harbor like a wounded warship returning from a humiliating defeat. The passengers' tears flowed again as the Statue of Liberty came into view. The *Doria*'s immigrants were grateful to witness— at last—this welcoming symbol, but they felt much sorrow for those who were deprived of the glorious sight. The people on shore could now be spotted in the distance as the bowless ship approached the dock. Onlookers appeared awestruck. Germina felt as though spectators and passengers alike were taking part in a funeral procession. No one spoke. Penetrating silence accompanied the docking of the *Stockholm.* Then, suddenly, the media descended on disembarking survivors—cameras, microphones, reporters.

A television reporter interviewed Germina. "Did the crew abandon the ship, leaving the passengers? Were you given instructions on what to do? How were you treated on the *Stockholm?"*

In a daze, she answered briefly. Her attention was diverted when she heard the loudspeaker. "Celeste, I hear my name being paged! Someone knows we're alive. Good Lord, let it be my mother or father!"

Celeste accompanied her to the office, where Germina was greeted by a representative from the J. L. Hudson Company, her employer. "Hello, Miss Donofrio. I'm here to escort you on a flight to Detroit. In the meantime, is there anything I can get for you right now—clothes, food, anything you need?"

Germina was struck by the gesture of human kindness that the large department store was offering. She pondered and, after taking a quick survey of her condition, could think of only one request. "A pair of hose," she answered meekly. She had been taught that a young lady should never show herself in public with runs in her hose, under any circumstances.

ALL OF HER DUTIFUL UPBRINGING could never have prepared Germina for surviving one horrific event only to be followed by another. The day after she arrived in Detroit, her beloved father, daunted by his daughter's ordeal, suffered a massive heart attack. Germina could not have imagined that she would be accompanying her father by ambulance to the hospital in the aftermath of her own tribulations. Hoping for words of consolation from the doctor at her father's bedside, she was stunned instead to hear, "Call your mother immediately, and tell her to come to the hospital as soon as possible; he may not make it."

Germina Donofrio, still wearing the dress she wore on the night of July 25, enjoys a happy reunion with her father. That evening, he suffered a serious heart attack.

Desperate thoughts ran though her mind. *How can I call my mother in Italy without shocking her into thinking that Daddy is dead? No one makes an overseas call unless it's to report a death. She'll never believe me! Besides, what can she do? She can't afford to take a flight with two boys, and taking a ship might be too late.* Yet the call had to be made. Sure enough, Germina's frantic mother uttered what her wretched gut instincts guided her to say: "He's dead, isn't he? You don't want to tell me, but I know he must be dead!"

Germina delicately but firmly tried to reassure her distraught mother. "No, he's not dead, but he's very sick. You need to return as soon as you can."

In a daze, Antonietta could only surmise that her beloved Giuseppe had died suddenly from the shock of the *Andrea Doria* accident. Being so far away and helpless, she felt that prayer was the only solution. With faith in her heart, Antonietta headed directly for the cathedral up the hill. She walked through the town, where all the residents knew her father's family and the granddaughter who was on the *Andrea Doria*. It had been the talk of the small community. Yes, she needed to thank the Lord for sparing her daughter's life and to pray for her husband's recovery, if he hadn't already died. With bowed head and swollen eyes, Antonietta walked the narrow streets, whose doorways were adorned with long strings of beads, not unlike the sparkling rosary that was wrapped around her hand. Looking up, she noticed that she was not alone. People began to come out of their homes and join her. She began to lead, unintentionally, a procession of townsfolk making their way along the cobblestone streets to the beloved cathedral at the city's heights. Guided by old-country tradition, Vieste's inhabitants followed the beleaguered wife and mother in a spirit of compassion and community. They prayed together to the patron saint of Vieste, Santa Maria di Merino—the protector of sea travelers.

Antonietta would spend weeks looking for an airplane or an ocean liner with available space for an adult with children. Although there were many Atlantic Ocean liners, most were already taking on would-be passengers of the *Doria*. Four long weeks passed before Antonietta received the long-awaited phone call from the travel agent. "Signora Donofrio, we have found a cabin for you and your children on the *Cristoforo Colombo*. The accommodations will be spartan, I must tell you, because the ship is full. And you must be at the dock in Naples tomorrow morning."

The frantic Antonietta summoned her family to help her pack the bare essentials for the homebound journey. But how would she get to Naples and the dock?

"Don't worry, Antonietta," said her Uncle Marco. "I'll take all of you in a friend's truck. But pack quickly; we have a seven-hour road trip ahead of us."

Such a long wait for the opportunity to reunite with my family and such a short notice to make it a reality, thought Antonietta. In the rush to leave, she barely remembered her hurried good-byes to her mother and father. She would never see them again. Her focus was on getting home to her husband, whom she hoped and prayed was still alive.

Meanwhile, in Detroit, Antonietta's husband was beginning to recover. Germina spent her days at the hospital and her evenings at the home of the Rubino family, dear Italian friends who offered the traumatized young lady some solace and distraction from her anguish. Her brother Vincent, only sixteen years old, responsibly did his best to run his family's shoe-repair shop while his father recuperated. At last, Antonietta and her two other sons, Michael and Joseph, who had been separated from their loved ones by a vast and perilous ocean, were united once again. The family was convinced that prayers on both sides of the Atlantic had aided Giuseppe's recovery from his grave condition.

Germina's dutiful travel companion, Celeste, settled into her own routine of mother and homemaker, but not without lingering troubles from the tragedy she had endured. At night, she dreamed repeatedly of being hurt on the *Andrea Doria.* In a sweat, she would wake up, thinking, *Thank God I'm in my bed and not on the ship!* By November, the stress of the accident, plus the torn ligaments and pulled muscles from lowering her body by rope, resulted in a complete physical breakdown. Celeste was hospitalized, and her pain was relieved only by heavy doses of morphine.

Her nightmares persisted and worsened with time. Celeste, now a grandmother, still has nightmares of dying on a foggy night in July and not being able to raise her daughter, Diana. Perhaps the arthritis that has set into her right arm and leg will always perpetuate her painful and tumultuous dreams.

Germina's young nervous system did not escape unscathed from the harrowing experiences, either. She would suffer all her life from a chronic ulcer condition and a fear of sleeping in complete darkness—darkness too reminiscent of the black sea, which beckoned her to descend from the deck of the *Andrea Doria.*

Germina and the author now enjoy a very special friendship.

CHAPTER 5

When Her Watch Stopped

Second star to the right and
straight on till morning.
—J. M. Barrie, *Peter Pan*

NGELA GRILLO, A TWENTY-NINE-YEAR-OLD
MOTHER from Brooklyn, New York, had just finished the nightly ritual of putting her son, Anthony, to bed in their second-class cabin. As she cuddled
him in his red, white, and blue pajamas, she whispered affection-
ately, *"Buona notte, tesoro. Sogni d'oro.* Good night, my sweet one.
Sweet dreams."

Anthony, a playful three-year-old, knew that he only had "one
more sleep" before being reunited with his father in the morning.
As he had done for most of his short life, he fell asleep with his
cuddly Peter Pan doll in his arms, a comforting toy he had loved
since infancy.

Anthony's mother was also looking forward to morning, since
it would end her three-month absence from her husband, Carmelo, an Italian immigrant from Catania, Sicily. Angela had met him
on April 28, 1950, on the flagship of the Italian Line, the *Conte Biancamano,* on which he was serving as a young officer. When
Angela's brother-in-law, Frank, discovered that she was traveling
to Italy on the *Biancamano,* he had asked her to do him a favor.
"Angela, I have a friend on that ship, Carmelo Grillo. Would you
mind delivering this letter to him?"

The young woman, dressed in her beautiful travel suit and
matching hat, searched out the young officer and found a handsome, genteel man. It was love at first sight for both of them as
Angela looked into his eyes and handed him the letter. They decided to meet for strolls each evening, even though service men were
discouraged from socializing with passengers. When the
steamship's commander, Luigi Gulinelli, discovered the young

**Angela Grillo with her son
Anthony, in 1954 on Long Island.**

lovers' ritual of walking hand-in-hand each evening, he inquired, "Who is that young woman you are always with?"

Carmelo nervously made an excuse. "My cousin," he replied, seeing the incredulous look on the captain's face.

They continued their romantic rendezvous as discreetly as the situation on their "love boat" would permit. By the end of the voyage, the two were passionately in love. "Angela, I have a friend who's in love with you!" the young officer explained bashfully.

The baffled Angela could think of no one else who knew her on the ship, so she responded with "Who?"

"Me!" Carmelo gleefully replied.

Meanwhile, Commander Gulinelli continued to question Carmelo. But love prevailed over rules, and the young officer could no longer dodge the commander's suspicions. Carmelo finally confessed that he was in love with Angela and asked for permission to marry her on board the liner. The ship's rules would not allow this unless the officer renounced his future military commitment to the Italian Line. So Officer Grillo explained that he would be leaving the ship when it landed in Naples. The commander approved reluctantly. The young lovers were free to invite acquaintances on board to witness and celebrate their wedding, which took place without rings. The ship's chefs, however, gladly provided them with a wedding cake.

Upon arriving in his native Catania, the proud Carmelo introduced the new bride to his family. The blissful couple purchased two gold wedding bands, which they placed on each other's hand during a traditional Italian church ceremony on June 28, 1950, three months after their first meeting. Angela had to return to the United States while Carmelo finished his military duty. But they were reunited in January 1952, and one year later, their first child, Anthony, was born.

NOW, IN 1956, CARMELO AND ANGELA were living in Brooklyn. He was once again working for the Italian Line as the managing passenger officer for the *Andrea Doria*. The proud young father had decided to send Angela and Anthony to visit his family in Catania, so that his son could discover his paternal roots. On the morning of July 26, Carmelo planned to wake up at 5:00 a.m. for his family's arrival. Angela was returning one month earlier than originally planned, as she could no longer bear to stay away from her beloved husband.

She wanted to look especially pretty for the reunion. She placed several curlers in her shoulder-length brown hair, removed her beige tailored skirt and blouse, and folded them neatly on the chair. Then she removed her gold chain and her wedding ring and placed them on the small night table. She had never felt comfortable sleeping with her jewelry on. Before tucking herself in, she remembered to remove her Bulova watch, a present from Carmelo.

Angela gave the room a final inspection, making sure that her trunk and the large gift box carrying her son's new Italian toy—a car in the shape of an airplane—were ready for pickup in the morning. Angela had remembered her husband's instructions: "Don't place the trunk and the box in the corridor with all the others. Keep them in the cabin. My staff will load them into the car as soon as you arrive." That was a privilege of being an employee of the Italian Line, the company that owned many of the finest Italian passenger ships. Mrs. Carmelo Grillo was proud of her husband's privileges, which he had earned by proving himself worthy after only a few years in the Passenger Office.

It was now almost 11:00 p.m. Angela was tired and wanted a good night's sleep before the arrival. She pulled the blankets over

her body. But something told her to wear her three pieces of sentimental jewelry to bed after all. Was it because the chain was
adorned with a medal of Saint Anthony, a surprise gift from her
father-in-law? "Angela, I have something for you to wear to protect you on the trip," he'd said as she stepped onto the plank leading to the *Andrea Doria* in Naples. Or was it simply because she
was afraid to forget something in the morning's haste to dress herself and her son? In any case, she slipped on her precious possessions and turned off the light.

Angela said her prayers of gratitude before dozing off. *"O Signore, grazie per questa bella giornata sulla nave. Grazie per la nostra
famiglia unita, per la nostra salute e per la nostra prosperità. Benedici
tutti noi. Amen.* Dear Father in heaven, thank you for another beautiful day on our ship. Thank you for our good family, our health,
and our prosperity. Bless my dear ones." The thankful mother and
wife began what she expected would be a restful night's sleep.

Barely dreaming yet, Angela was abruptly awakened by a loud
noise. *Oh, those revelers,* she thought. *They are celebrating the last
night on board.* Then she heard strange noises in the corridor—running, crying, lamenting. She heard people calling out names.
Frightened, she opened her eyes, arose from her bed, and walked
in the dark to open the cabin door. Aghast at the sight of frantic
passengers pushing their way toward the back of the ship, she
slammed the door shut and began to shake her sleeping son.

"Anthony! You have to wake up! We have to leave the cabin!"
Although she tried not to alarm him with her pleas, she had to
shake the boy harder. "Anthony, wake up for your mommy now!"

"No, Mommy. I want to sleep some more," the innocent young
voice replied.

Angela slipped on her skirt and blouse, put on her shoes, and
dragged her son out of bed. She had no time to tell him to grab his
Peter Pan doll. In the dark, she felt a strange sensation, like that of
a rocking floor in a house of horrors. Then she heard a loud screech
and more rocking. In an instant, the heavy trunk and box slid
across the cabin floor, lodging themselves against the door. Angela
realized that the ship was listing, perhaps even sinking, and pas-

sengers were running for their lives. She used all her might to push the trunk and the heavy toy box away from the door, but to no avail. After struggling for twenty minutes, Angela realized that she and her son were trapped and no one could help them. She began to cry in despair. She heard more loud screeches and felt more rocking of the floor beneath her. With a stroke of luck, the cargo moved away from the door just enough to allow the mother and son to squeeze through the small opening and reach the hall.

"Return to your cabins and put on your life jackets," an officer implored the Second Class passengers. "Return to your stations with your life jackets on!"

The officer's voice repeated the plea firmly and loudly. Angela was close enough to her cabin to be able to find the entry and slip life jackets onto herself and Anthony before they ran into the corridor.

"Anthony, stay with your mommy. If you get away from me, I won't be able to find you in the dark!" the panicking mother begged.

Knowing that there were dangers from the stairwells, a swimming pool, and, of course, the stampeding crowd, Angela held Anthony tightly in her left arm. With her right arm, she tried to hang on to the railing. The floor was wet and slick. Suddenly, she fell on her right knee, sending a throbbing pain throughout her leg. There was no time to ask for help. Angela lifted herself up with Anthony clinging to her body and proceeded to the Boat Deck, two levels higher. There, she ran into her dining-room companions, Rigoletto and Anna Di Meo, an elderly couple who were to be very helpful to Angela and Anthony during this traumatic ordeal.

To everyone's surprise, the curtain of heavy fog that had filled the air and moistened all the surfaces throughout the day was abruptly and mysteriously withdrawn, allowing the passengers to witness the drama around them clearly. Angela gazed at the iridescent moon that was lighting the stage for a desperate scene— hundreds of passengers witnessing what seemed inevitable, the sinking of their beautiful liner.

"Guarda, le luci di una nave!" exclaimed an excited immigrant.

He was pointing to lights from another ship in the distance. The lights were an amazing sight to the *Andrea Doria* passengers, who were depending on the moon to see. Angela wondered if the twinkling reflections meant the possibility of rescue. *Are they here to rescue us? How can they possibly rescue us? We are sinking. They'll be afraid to get near us. How can we leave this ship and get onto the other one?* Angela felt despair and loneliness, especially without the support of her husband, who, as a former merchant marine officer, would certainly be of tremendous help now. *I wonder if he knows what's happening to us.*

Angela and Anthony continued to remain seated with their backs against the guardrail, praying with the other passengers for a miracle. Often, the fearful mother would touch the gold medal of Saint Anthony around her neck and pray that he would save her and her Anthony. A few more hours passed, but it seemed like an eternity to the pathetic souls whose lives were dangling above one of the deepest areas of the Atlantic Ocean. Angela continued to pray silently, as her voice would not emerge from her traumatized body. The passengers' moaning, sobbing, and praying continued. All the while, the wounded liner listed more and more. Each minute could be the last for the *Andrea Doria*'s nearly 1,700 people.

All of a sudden, a young man she did not recognize approached her, told her to stand, and urged her to prepare to throw Anthony overboard.

"Non posso! Non so nuotare!" she answered in a terrified voice. How could she throw her three-year-old into the ocean? She and her son couldn't swim!

"Signora, lo butti giù!" She heard a man's voice coming from several stories below. "We have a blanket to catch the boy. Throw him down!"

The bewildered mother picked up the boy, said, "Anthony, don't be afraid!" and proceeded to launch him into the hands of fate. She couldn't see the lifeboat below, but she heard her son's screams. Instinctively, she knew he was hurt. Without hesitation, the brave mother lunged over the guardrail to reach for a rope she saw dangling in the shadows. She swung her exhausted body down toward the merciful rescue vessel, only vaguely understanding the peril of her decision. She gulped in big breaths for strength and to keep herself from screaming. Fortunately, the lifeboat was still waiting as Angela dropped her limp body into it and then lost consciousness.

She awakened to people slapping her face.

"Thank God she's still alive! *Signora*, you are safe now. You are on the *Ile de France*."

As soon as she became conscious, the distressed mother started looking around and wailing, "Where is my son? I've lost my son!"

The people kneeling on the floor around Angela lifted her onto a deck chair and left to assist others whose needs were more urgent. Angela lay there crying. She felt helpless as the excruciating leg pain from her fall on the *Doria*'s deck prevented her from searching for her missing boy. She looked at her watch to bring some clarity to her confused state. The Bulova watch read 3:00, but she noticed that the hands were not moving. Before she could inquire about the time, a young man who recognized Angela as a friend of the Di Meos, the couple she had befriended on the *Doria*, asked, "*Signora*, why are you crying?"

"My son, my son, I've lost my son!" she lamented.

"What is he wearing, *Signora*?"

"He has on red, white, and blue striped pajamas."

"Well, don't worry. I know where he is. He is sitting with the Di Meos. Let me help you walk there."

The young man supported Angela's weight by holding her firmly under the arm. She limped along until she spotted the striped pajamas. Anthony was busily eating an orange until he saw his mother. He begged, "Mommy, throw me down in the blanket again. That was fun!"

Indeed, Anthony's resilience transformed his mother's grief into amazement, if not a little anger. She grabbed him and hugged him thankfully. Crew members and officials of the beautiful French liner were walking around to console their haggard, wounded, and unexpected passengers. A handsome official recognized Angela as the wife of a New York Italian Line employee. He offered his most gracious assistance to the distraught young woman. Unknown to Angela, the *Ile de France* was a survivor itself; it was the last of the French liners in operation during World War II. Over the next decade, it inherited the title "Saint Bernard of the Atlantic," for it would partake in ten rescue missions while transporting passengers from France to New York. Angela and Anthony became the beneficiaries of her benevolence.

CARMELO GRILLO'S OFFICE HAD CALLED HIM at around 1:00 a.m., shortly after the collision. "Come to the office immediately, Carmelo. There has been an accident with the *Andrea Doria.*"

Carmelo jumped out of bed, threw on some clothes, leaped into his car, and began speeding down the highway. A police officer pulled him over. "What is your hurry, young man?" inquired the officer.

"My wife and child are in a shipwreck. Turn on the radio, and listen about the *Andrea Doria.*"

The officer offered to escort him to the Italian Line offices. They traveled at breakneck speed down the highway. Arriving at about 2:00 a.m., Carmelo did what he was routinely expected to do for the arrival of the *Doria:* he printed a passenger list so that he could check in all of the passengers as they arrived at the Ambrose Lightship, the mouth of the New York port. Then it occurred to him that the *Doria* might not arrive in its usual manner. Carmelo began the laborious process of printing a passenger list for each employee and distributing them throughout the offices. This would facilitate the check-in of passengers who might arrive on different ships.

Finally, at about 2:00 in the afternoon, a colleague exclaimed, "Carmelo, what are you doing? Get on the Coast Guard boat, and go to the Ambrose Lightship! The *Ile de France* is arriving there soon, and your wife and son might be on it!" Roused from his worrying, Carmelo followed his advice. He arrived beside the grandiose French liner, praying to find his family there.

"Come aboard, Mr. Grillo. Your wife and son are by the swimming pool," he heard a voice yell down. A former colleague had recognized Carmelo. Thanks to the privileges of his job, he was able to board the *Ile de France* immediately.

Carmelo sought his wife and son amid the sad and fatigued faces, shrouded in gray woolen blankets. "Can you tell me the shortest way to the pool?" His urgency attracted the attention of his son.

"Mommy, Mommy, there's Daddy!" Anthony announced with glee.

"Anthony, are you dreaming?"

"Look, Mommy, there's Daddy!"

Angela turned her bewildered head and saw her husband, a frightful specter of the man she knew well. She was alarmed by what she saw. The twelve hours Carmelo had spent in anguish over the fear of losing his family had rendered him ashen and emaciated. In contrast, the apprehension of losing her life and her son's had made Angela's lovely body reddish and plump. Instead of hyperventilating as most people do in traumatic situations, Angela had resorted to gulping in air, with little exhalation. She appeared bloated and pounds heavier than normal. Carmelo hugged his wife and son as he cried. Angela felt safe for the moment but could not say anything, even when she tried to speak. The heavy load of gaseous trauma was locked inside her. She could barely pronounce his nickname: "Melo!"

Young Anthony, consoled by his father's appearance, hugged him tightly and implored, "Daddy, don't leave me anymore!"

THE NEWS OF THE SINKING *Andrea Doria* had traveled around the world. In Iran, Angela's sister Rita was preparing *spaghetti al sugo* for her husband, Frank, and guests. They were celebrating the Feast of Santa Anna, honoring the mother of the Blessed Virgin Mary. As Rita was carrying a large platter of spaghetti into the dining room, she happened to glance at the television. The dire scene of the *Andrea Doria* about to capsize froze her, sending the food platter onto the floor. Rita's screams drew everyone into the kitchen.

"What's the matter, Rita?" asked her husband.

"Look, the boat is going down. My sister and nephew are on that ship!"

Frank immediately sent a telegram to Angela's family inquiring about Angela and Anthony's predicament. The family wired back, "Angela and Anthony have arrived in New York safely."

THE GRILLO FAMILY LANDED IN NEW YORK early in the morning. They stepped onto land, but Angela was too dazed and sickly to feel relief. She barely noticed their arrival at home. When she did see her father, her mother, and her sister Elisa, she could not hug, cry, or speak. She pushed her way into the living room and sat on the gold satin couch.

Then the wretched young woman began to wail, exhaling the angst buried deep within. She plunged into grief with such mournful sounds that it alarmed her family. Carmelo called the doctor, who came to the house. After assessing Angela's condition, he simply suggested that they should let her cry until she could expunge her mind of the grief she felt. Carmelo sat by her side patiently, even though he was plagued with many questions and wanted answers about the horrific event. He asked his wife to watch the telecast of the collision with him, but Angela would have no part of it. She simply wanted to cry and try to lose her torturous memories.

Anthony's behavior showed no signs of unusual fears. His biggest regret was losing his Peter Pan doll. "I want my Peter Pan, Mommy!" he would cry when he thought of it. His doting father bought him another Peter Pan. Anthony pushed it away, exclaiming, "This is not my Peter Pan. I don't want him!" He would sit next to the washing machine, hoping that by some miracle, his doll would reappear as it had many times before. His daddy returned the new Peter Pan, since it only seemed to agitate the boy into begging for the original one.

Four years passed. Carmelo was still concerned over his wife's jittery behavior. It was evident that Angela was still burdened with the heavy trauma of her horrific experience. She would jump at every unfamiliar sound. Her nights were deprived of the therapy that humans derive from sweet dreams. Her *Andrea Doria* night-mares were variations on a theme of disaster aboard a sinking liner. At the suggestion of the Italian Line, she recounted her experience to a psychologist. Her private terror continued.

Carmelo knew something had to be done. "Angela, let's take a short trip on the sea. You need to get your fears out of your system. You can't continue living like this!"

At first, his wife was appalled at the idea, especially since she was expecting their third child. But she gave in. Carmelo used his maritime contacts to research what ship they could take that would pass another ship under a full moon. There would also have to be a greeting between the two ships that would remind Angela of her voyage home on the *Ile de France* and the whistle of good-bye as it abandoned the corpse of the *Andrea Doria*.

The night that would test Angela's strength arrived. With Carmelo holding one arm and a friend holding the other, she boarded the cruise ship. Angela felt paralyzed, as if her legs would not carry her. Evening approached, and the moon appeared. Angela anxiously listened and looked for signs of danger around her, like a hunted and captured animal. She waited in limbo for the acute pain in her chest to subside. When the ships' whistles blew in the night air, she felt as though a knife were piercing her heart. Carmelo reassured her, "You are very brave, Angela. I'm proud of you for doing this. You're going to be fine."

The afflicted passenger made it through the night and felt pride in doing so. She knew she could trust a passenger ship once again.

Her adoring husband, Melo, would spend months in search of a jewelry shop that would restore the movement of the Bulova watch. He finally resorted to visiting a Bulova factory, but his efforts were in vain. The watch refused to give up its 3:00 reading—always showing the hour when the desperate mother had hit her watch hard on the guardrail as she launched her trusting son overboard.

Angela, Carmelo, and their three children would take many trips to Italy again, with the Saint Anthony medal always gracing

Angela's neckline. Each time, she insisted on a cabin with a port-hole, through which she could see the foamy waves moving beside her. This reassured her that the ship was moving on the open sea, rather than being stranded amid the debris of disaster.

Angela's son Anthony became the founder of an *Andrea Doria* Web site[1] in 1996, and his passion for "keeping the memory alive," as he put it, was a part of him since childhood. For many survivors, the site has been the only way to connect with one another and share the experience. Moreover, it continues to inform the public of products and special events related to the *Andrea Doria*, and it also provides updates about the survivors. It has inspired short stories, articles, books, courses, and documentaries about the collision. Anthony Grillo, before his death in 2004, personally served as a liaison among survivors, divers, maritime experts, and the media for many years. He also helped organize reunions for survivors and their families. No one has contributed more time and energy toward keeping the *Andrea Doria* memory alive. Referring to his mission, Anthony exclaimed, "It has been a labor of love."

CHAPTER 6

Making Music and Memories

Music is the art which is most nigh to tears and memory.
—Oscar Wilde

ULIANNE MCLEAN, A CONCERT PIANIST from Wichita, Kansas, who had graduated from the Juilliard School of Music—and who was a survivor of the *Andrea Doria* tragedy—was settled into a successful professional music career in New York. Her mother, Elizabeth, had come to visit her gifted daughter and also planned to meet up with a longtime friend. As was customary during the 1950s, the ladies planned to meet under the majestic clock of Grand Central Station.

As Julianne and her mother were standing below New York's "Father Time," the tall, slender pianist suddenly felt a tight arm wrap around her waist. Her first instincts told her to protect herself and attempt to release the grasp. But she quickly recognized the face of Mr. McLean, who had been her friend and protector during the tragic *Andrea Doria* trip. Mr. McLean and his wife, not related to Julianne except by fate, had spent many evenings with the then-twenty-two-year-old musician, who had been traveling alone on the *Doria.* Julianne had just completed a year of intensive piano studies in Rome and performing on the concert stages of Europe. The McLeans had understood that the young lady felt lonesome, homesick, and fatigued after her year abroad.

"Hello, Julianne. How are you? I'm so happy to see you again. My wife and I have spoken of you often and wondered how you were saved from the *Doria*," the sixtyish-looking man said warmly.

"I have often wondered the same of you and your wife. It's so good to see you. I've always wanted to thank you."

"Thank me?" Mr. McLean asked.

"Yes, for retrieving our life jackets from our cabins. I attribute my survival in great part to you. Thank you!"

"We all needed one another that night, didn't we?" he replied. "Which ship were you rescued by?"

"I was taken to the *Ile de France*. What about you and Mrs. McLean?"

"We were rowed to the *Cape Ann*." As quickly as he had appeared, Mr. McLean excused himself for having to dash off to catch his train. The grand old clock towering above them seemed to say, "Moments in time are for remembering . . . even that tragic night off Nantucket Island."

Julianne and her mother resumed their conversation, relishing a renewed sense of well-being in their hearts. Her mother's friend arrived, and the three women went to lunch.

After the meal, Julianne went back to the historic Ansonia Hotel, where she lived. The hotel was a mecca for serious musicians, such as the late Arturo Toscanini, partly because of its solid and soundproof walls and floors. Dutifully, Julianne sat down at her beautiful grand piano to practice for her next performance. As she played Chopin's *Étude No. 21*, "The Butterfly," a piece that challenged her with its speed and lightness, her mind pulled her away to the encounter with Mr. McLean. She needed to practice, but at the same time, she wanted to savor the memories of her voyage on the ocean liner where they had met, where Captain Calamai had heard her practice and invited her to play for the First Class passengers.

Of course! I played Chopin études for the captain, his officers, and the passengers. Julianne had become very fond of Captain Calamai during her voyages on the *Doria*, describing him to everyone as "first class all the way, an elegant man in the Old World tradition." She had entrusted him with safely transporting her at least three times across the Atlantic, and he had delegated her informally as the ship's pianist. When she thought of him after the collision, she felt great sorrow for the way he had been treated by the media, the Swedish Line, and even some passengers. *I wonder if Captain Calamai is still alive? They chewed him up and spit him back out,* she remembered with displeasure. *He should have been commended for saving so many lives. Oh, I wish I still had the photo that was taken of me at the piano, with the captain and his officers. What a shame it went down with the ship. It was signed by all of them, too!*

The pianist's fingers were gliding across the keyboard, but her mind was drifting off to the last night aboard the pride of the Italian Line. *We were having a drink in the Cabin Class lounge on the port side. I was sipping on that pretty pink drink, a "house specialty," while the musical combo was onstage trying to get us to be festive on the last night on board. But there were only a handful of us there when we heard the huge crash.*

Portrait of Julianne McLean as she launches her musical career.

Julianne's hands were briefly immobilized on the keys as she remembered being thrown to one end of the room, with tables, chairs, and passengers piling up on top of one another. The musicians and their instruments had landed along the same wall, starting a cacophony of brass, strings, and percussion. The floor had tilted up drastically on the starboard side as it declined considerably on the opposite side. Then the floor had begun swaying, accompanied by ear-splitting sounds, as if metal were grating, scraping, clashing, and splitting wide open. Julianne's delicate interpretation of "The Butterfly" became ever more heavy as she recalled the discords of that terrible night.

The pile of people, covered with inanimate objects, had lain against the wall as if a sudden storm had blown them there. *Oh, those poor people.* They were moaning, with broken bones and bleeding heads. One by one, they picked themselves up slowly but wobbled and fell again as the vessel rocked back and forth. *We were so confused. Could it be a bad storm? Did we hit rocks? Did we crash with another ship?* Dire thoughts had run through their minds. In a mode of survival, the shaken passengers had battled their dilemma by moving upward on the inclined floor to the exit door. Although they had accomplished this, they would soon be challenged by the difficulty of making their way up the inclined stairs, competing for space at the railing. *Was it instinct that led us toward the Upper Deck, or was it the smoke and the stench of fuel oil that repulsed us and pushed us upward?* Julianne tried to remember.

"Let's hold on to each other going up the stairs!" Mr. McLean had implored his wife, Julianne, and some of the other passengers. They had formed a human chain stronger than any single link. *I held on tightly with one hand, unconsciously still clutching my pink, fruity drink in the other. It was shaking in my hand and spilling all over me. How did I hold on to it so long? Why didn't I put it down earlier?* She smirked at the sheet music as she remembered her foolishness. But at some point, she finally had put down her drink and kicked off her lovely black pumps. This was a painful memory, causing her G-flat note to turn into a G-sharp as she recalled the pain of her feet being trampled and cut by the sharp metal grating and the careless mob.

When they eventually reached the top deck, Mr. McLean had realized that their indispensable life jackets were still below in their cabins. "I'll go back down and get our life jackets. Wait here," he had instructed. The courageous man had battled the throng that was pushing its way up the stairwell.

As she continued to practice, the accomplished pianist realized that her rendition of "The Butterfly," intended to be *allegro vivace*, was moving much too slowly and heavily, unlike the airy and floating *Lepidopteron* it was supposed to emulate. *I have to concentrate now!* Julianne admonished herself. She continued to play. *Mr. McLean finally arrived with three life jackets. I put mine on inside out! I lost sight of the McLeans, and looking for them was futile. Lord, I could hardly stand because of that awful tilt! I sat on the slippery deck on my settee and slid down to the starboard side, finally crashing into all the suitcases.* Her "Butterfly" hit a sour note as she recalled smashing against the luggage that had been placed on deck for early disembarking the following morning; instead, it had become seating for the weary passengers, including a wailing woman from First Class. *Oh, that hysterical woman, wailing and screaming at the top of her lungs. She just made things worse for all of us—although she did stop eventually. I prayed for a miracle: "Dear Lord, please forgive me for what I've done and haven't done. Please help us."* Julianne remembered turning over her dilemma to the Almighty. Years earlier, she had become a Catholic convert, and she believed in miracles. After all, her life had been blessed with milestones. For one, she had been invited to play for the Vatican radio station and was the first American woman to perform live over those prestigious airwaves.

Julianne recalled sitting all alone observing the heroic efforts of the *Andrea Doria* crew. They made several treks down the steamy, slick stairwells to rescue passengers, especially the wounded. Each time they resurfaced, their faces and bodies were covered with grease and sweat. They sat people on the suitcases and tried to reassure them that the captain was attempting to reposition the list of the ship. Then there was that exceptional crewman who brought up a heavy elderly woman from below. The poor woman had broken bones, a welt on her face, and blood dripping from her head. He was apologizing to the woman for having to sling her over his shoulder. She just said, "Do whatever you have to do to save me."

As Julianne had continued to pray for a miracle, sitting on the ever more listing *Doria,* she had heard a loud plea for a heavy jack and seen two desperate men, the waiter Rovelli and Dr. Thure Peterson, whose wife was trapped under heavy wreckage below. She remembered observing the tall, handsome man wearing only a torn curtain around his waist. *Oh, how I prayed for his wife's rescue!*

By now, Julianne's practice session was suffering as her mind wandered off to the painful details of survival years ago. She closed the sheet music on her black grand piano and took a break so that she could reflect on long-ignored painful memories. She sat on a stuffed chair in her beautiful apartment near Times Square and indulged in the past. "Memories are to be made and remembered" had always been one of her steadfast beliefs, and now she was paying attention to it.

THE *ANDREA DORIA*'S FOGHORNS had blasted all day to warn other ships of its presence. The fog was so thick that people could hardly see what they were doing. Then, as if with a celestial swoop, the fog disappeared and revealed a full moon. Looking toward the heavens, Julianne saw a bright moon and sparkling stars. Soon after, looking over the railing, she witnessed another miracle—the twinkling lights of another ship, the *Ile de France*. Yes, the worn-out, lonely young woman realized, there was hope. She continued to pray even more confidently, knowing she would be saved: *Our Father who art in heaven. . . .* She wished other passengers had been more patient as she heard their cries from the water. Julianne saw some frantic people grabbing thick ropes and losing the skin on their hands as they descended into the shark-infested waters. They were crying out as they hit the salt water and bobbed on pieces of wood, hollering for nearby lifeboats to rescue them.

Julianne sat on the deck, trembling from the chill and from exhaustion. But she still had a long way to go to save herself. When she saw a lifeboat arriving from the *Ile de France* and heading toward the middle of the *Doria* where she patiently sat, she leaped up from the suitcase and headed for one of the dangling ropes. With her muscles vibrating like the tightly wound strings inside a piano that must respond when struck by a key, the young woman descended 20 feet from the First Class deck and into the *Ile*'s lifeboat. She felt completely spent, and her entire body quivered uncontrollably. As other passengers inched down, Julianne looked up and saw an unforgettable sight: the enormous funnel of the large vessel was hovering above their heads, like a menacing monster from a horror film. The incline had become so steep that it was forming a threatening load over them.

The desperate worshiper prayed: *Please, dear Lord. Let us escape. Help us get to the rescue ship. I don't want to die like this.* Her prayers were answered when the strong young sailors from the *Ile de France* began to row away from under the *Doria*, as if every second counted. They rowed like mad to reach the far side of the *Ile*, afraid that the whirlpool from the sinking *Doria* might take them all under. Still trembling violently, Julianne was faced with another emotional and physical challenge of endurance. Her lifeboat had stopped next to a rope ladder, which was leading straight up along the hull of the *Ile*. She knew that somehow she would have to make the climb to the small opening many stories above the sea. Fortunately, she received inspiration. The crewman of the *Doria* who had hauled the heavy-set injured woman over his shoulder from her cabin and then down the rope ladder was now engaged in the same maneuver. The courteous young man apologized once more for his unconventional comportment.

"Do whatever you need to do. Please help me," pleaded the helpless woman.

Julianne knew now that she could manage. Struggling to deal with a weakened body, she pulled herself up the steep, narrow ladder, step by step, with every ounce of strength remaining. *Dear God, please guide me to the top. I still have a lot of work to accomplish in your service.* The ladder seemed to stretch eighty stories high. Finally, she reached the bright opening at the top, where two French sailors greeted her. They helped her aboard the tall, majestic liner. One sailor immediately began removing her life jacket, which she had worn inside out. The other smiled and welcomed the trembling Julianne with a friendly *"Bonsoir."* The grateful young woman threw her arms around him and exclaimed, "It is a good evening. I'm so thankful to be here!"

She was safe. The gracious French hospitality on the *Ile de France* continued. The quivering Julianne was escorted to the ship's doctor, where her condition was assessed.

"Are you hurt?" asked the doctor in English with a French accent.

"No," replied Julianne, barefoot but still wearing her black button-down dress with its white collar.

"Did you go into the water?"

"No."

Julianne was not seeking pity but certainly appreciated the expressions of concern. Fortunately, she was unaware of the drama within the ship's hospital, which looked like a scene from the aftermath of a battle. Casualties of massive traumas were being wheeled out of emergency surgery. As their drugged bodies awakened, they began to wail, as much in pain as for their incomprehensible dilemma. Captain Raoul de Beaudéan walked from cot to cot, accompanied by a nurse who reported the condition of each wounded passenger. A Mexican bone specialist, who was an *Ile* passenger, worked alongside the ship's overwhelmed staff to set the bones and wrap them in plaster. In one corner lay a woman who drew compassion from all, including the sympathetic captain. She lay helplessly on a cot, in excruciating pain from a broken back and numerous fractures. With her body covered in purplish blue welts, she wailed—not so much for her condition but for the loss of her husband and two daughters.

A nurse sheltered Julianne from this horror by wrapping a blanket around her and directing her to the buffet table covered with comfort food: *brioches,* coffee, fruit, and sandwiches. Julianne helped herself to the aromatic coffee and a *brioche.* One of the *Ile*'s passengers brought her a pair of pink slippers, and Julianne appreciated her kindness. She walked instinctively to the outer deck, as she did not wish to be underneath anything again; the fear of being under a capsizing object remained fresh in her mind. Still wondering what had happened to cause such a calamity to the liner she so loved, she listened for news. No one was sure, and speculation prevailed. Meanwhile, Julianne was overcome with pity for a mother looking for her child, a man searching for his wife, and an uncle looking for his nieces and nephews. They paced the floor in a half-stupor, with barely enough strength to seek out their loved ones.

As day broke, Julianne watched the *Andrea Doria* sink farther beneath the waves, bringing her beautiful concert gowns to their final storage on the sea floor. Through her tears, she noticed tall, handsome Dr. Peterson standing alone and away from the crowd. As everyone wept, wailed, and lamented their losses, the mournful doctor watched the entombment of his beloved Martha in privacy. Julianne was quickly reminded of her good fortune to be alive. *Never mind my personal belongings! Dear God, this man tried to move heaven and earth to save his wife. Please take her to your kingdom.*

Suddenly, she saw a commotion on deck. Passengers from the *Ile* and the *Doria* huddled around a portable radio that was receiving news from New York: "The Italian liner *Andrea Doria* is sinking after being struck by the Swedish liner *Stockholm.* The number of casualties remains unknown, as survivors have been transported to several rescue ships. The *Stockholm* is seaworthy and is aiding in the rescue of the *Andrea Doria*'s passengers. Stay tuned for an update of what appears to be one of the most catastrophic collisions at sea, ever."

Exhausted, Julianne looked out at the ship with enormous sadness, wondering how the tragic accident could have happened on such a large ocean. *I thought radar was supposed to prevent such a thing! Didn't the* Stockholm *hear our foghorn blasting?* She believed it was miraculous that the *Doria* stayed afloat long enough for the rescue of so many. Nevertheless, the young woman had never imagined a sadder spectacle in her life. *Thank God so many of us are here on the* Ile. *I wonder how many poor souls didn't make it.*

The *Andrea Doria*'s alarm continued to echo on the Atlantic, with short blasts that reminded Julianne of a mortally wounded being crying for mercy. She had never considered the beautiful liner as just a thing; in her mind, it had taken on the role of a gracious hostess who welcomed the poor and the rich with the same luxurious hospitality. Julianne could barely tolerate the dissonant chords pulsating in a useless tempo. *Oh, dear God, let that ship be put out of its suffering,* she pleaded.

The lonely survivor then observed what seemed to be a light from the *Doria,* flashing with some purpose. Indeed, it was the *Andrea Doria,* using its Aldis lamp to respond to the *Ile de France*'s question "Do you still need us?"

"No, you may leave. Thank you," flashed back the *Doria* in Morse code. The two maritime masters, Captain Calamai and Captain de Beaudéan, bid adieu to each other as the *Ile de France* saluted the *Andrea Doria* with its flag and blew its horn three times in a solemn farewell. Some 700 pairs of survivors' eyes pressed themselves against the deck windows, straining through tears to grieve for the end of a reign of opulence.

Julianne felt comfort in knowing that she would be heading to her New York apartment at the Ansonia, which she shared with two roommates from Kansas City, Missouri. Misty-eyed and yet hopeful, she suddenly had an alarming thought: *If the sinking of the* Doria *is on the news, my mother might hear it and be frightened to death.* But she rationalized that it was too early in the morning for her mother to be awake. For several hours, Julianne drifted off into a secure slumber on one of the *Ile*'s deck chairs, hoping to free her mind from the haunting event.

Although she had no idea what to expect upon arriving in New York, Julianne would never have imagined such a media hubbub on the ship that was now her guardian. As the *Ile de France* approached the shoreline, Julianne observed a squadron of small boats encircling the *Ile* and instinctively knew that she did not want to take part in the media circus. *This is too much,* she thought, and fled from the microphones that were being forced in front of survivors' mouths. Journalists pleaded for interviews and placed cameras and microphones before Captain de Beaudéan. The smiling captain was flattered by questions posed only to heroes: "What made you decide to turn your ship in the fog to rescue the *Doria*? Weren't your men afraid of rowing so close to a sinking ship? How many passengers did you rescue? Did you save actress Ruth Roman?" The French master mariner chose to be dignified during these moments of glory; he chose not to respond. Since Julianne also chose to be silent, the public would not hear her stories of valor on the part of the crew. It was unfortunate that many passengers were portraying crew members as cowards and deserters, a picture she could have fiercely disputed. She did not feel strong enough physically or emotionally, however, to challenge the claims under such high-pressure circumstances. She made herself scarce until the ship finally docked.

As Julianne awaited instructions for disembarkment, she noticed arms waving furiously in the distance. She recognized her roommates, Ruth Riggs and Lewellyn Moss, who had heard of the horrific collision and wanted to bring Julianne home to the Ansonia. She was ecstatic. Finally, the ordeal seemed to be over, and comfort and familiarity were now a reality. She combed her fingers through her brown hair and ran off the gangplank to embrace Ruth and Lewellyn. "We heard about the accident on the radio. We decided we would meet every ship that arrived at the harbor until we finally found you. We're so glad to see you!" The three friends, musicians and roommates, engaged in an amazing account of misfortune and survival as they drove to their apartment.

"Have you heard from my mother?" inquired Julianne with apprehension.

"No. I hope she hasn't heard anything about the shipwreck."

Meanwhile, in Wichita, Julianne's mother had awakened much earlier than usual, having suffered a very restless night filled with nightmares about a shipwreck. She felt edgy and nervous. Not being able to explain this, especially since she should have expected to feel joyful at her daughter's arrival, she decided to go to the 6:00 a.m. mass at church. For companionship, she turned on the car radio. Almost immediately, it blared the breaking story of the tragedy on the Atlantic: "The collision of the *Andrea Doria* and the *Stockholm* is the worst maritime disaster since the sinking of the *Titanic*. There has been a considerable loss of life . . . "

Mrs. McLean began sobbing uncontrollably. Nevertheless, she kept driving, as she knew that her only solace at the moment would be inside the church. When she arrived, she sat in the back row. The kind priest noticed the distraught parishioner sobbing agitatedly, cupping her face in her hands. Although his mass was scheduled to begin, he took the time to walk to the back of his church in hopes of comforting the troubled woman. "What's wrong, Mrs. McLean? What can I do for you?"

The hysterical mother explained, "My daughter has been involved in a terrible accident on the Atlantic. She might have been killed!"

The priest said what he could to console her, then walked back to the altar and explained the disturbing event to his flock. He offered a special prayer for the mother and daughter. The entire congregation expressed compassionate support as the mother continued to sob.

When the three roommates finally arrived at their apartment, the exhausted and anxious Julianne ran immediately to the phone to call her mother. "Hi, Mom!" she said, trying to sound upbeat.

"Oh, thank God you're alive!" Mrs. McLean replied in a loud, trembling voice. "How are you? Are you hurt? Tell me everything."

"I'm fine. Everything is about as all right as it can be. I'm thrilled to be here with Ruth and Lewellyn. They're just loving me up, Mom! Don't worry!"

"Do you want me to come to New York, honey?"

"Oh, no. Let me come to you. It might take me a few days to get a flight, but I want to come home."

Within days, Mrs. McLean and some of Julianne's friends welcomed her home with more affection and attention than ever before. The young woman felt somewhat like a celebrity. Later, the *Wichita Eagle* came by for a long interview and photographs. Of course, they wanted Julianne to wear the black sleeveless button-down dress and pink slippers that she had been wearing when she landed in New York. Thus began her life-long relationship with the newspaper as the "in residence" survivor of the sinking of the *Andrea Doria.*

When Julianne returned to New York, her roommates decided to call the *Today Show,* hosted by Arlene Francis. The NBC studios sent a mile-long limousine to the Ansonia Hotel to pick up Julianne and deliver her to the set. When she arrived, she met with about fifty other survivors and crew members who had also been invited. To Julianne's amazement, Miss Francis zeroed in on her, perhaps because she was wearing her survival outfit, and concentrated on her story in great detail: "Where did you get the slippers? Did you fall in the water? Did you see the crew abandoning your ship? Which liner rescued you? Weren't you afraid since you were alone?" After the program aired, Julianne enjoyed recognition from old friends around the country whom she hadn't heard from for years. She was amazed at the power of television, at the time still in its infancy.

THE PIANIST OPENED HER HALF-CLOSED EYES. She realized that her mind, her hands, and even her soul felt uplifted. Was it from the therapeutic effect of confronting the past? Would the memories that fluttered inside her be freed from their mesh so that she could resume playing "The Butterfly" without distraction and obstacles? Julianne rose from her comfortable chair, exchanging it for the piano bench. Instinctively, her fingers flickered above the keyboard before descending on the ivories. Upon touching the first keys, she felt a sensation of airiness in her hands and in her heart. Indeed, Chopin's "Butterfly" was released. The smiling musician played, *appassionato*.

The rest of the practice session moved swiftly, without interruption—not even from thoughts of so many joyful events that had followed the *Andrea Doria* tragedy. She reflected on her courage in returning to Italy on an ocean liner just two years after the sinking. In the spring of 1958, she had resumed her studies and performances in Rome. There she had met a handsome young doctor named Carmelo Addario. By October, they had decided to marry, not just in any church but in Saint Peter's Basilica at the Vatican.

They were married during the wake for Pope Pius XII. The College of Cardinals had been meeting for weeks to pray for the deceased pope and to elect a new one. The church had been closed, except for that morning of October 18, when the basilica's smokestack had signaled a message in white smoke. The church was open! The Sistine Chapel Choir had sung the mass, as all the prospective popes sat in front of the main altar. It had been a setting as close to heaven as one could hope for, as the glorious voices reverberated within the frescoed walls.

As the "Butterfly" settled on its last four bars, Julianne reflected, *What great memories I have to share with my family and friends! I do hope I remember all of my interesting experiences and can retell them to my grandchildren one day.*

And now, whether performing Chopin's "Butterfly" in solo recital or Rachmaninoff's Piano Concerto No. 1 with great orchestras, Julianne continues to make memories on the stages of the world. And whether she travels by sea, by air, or by trains passing under the majestic clock in Grand Central Station, her memories— of tragedy and of joy—always accompany her.

IN COMMEMORATION of the forty-fifth anniversary of the *Andrea Doria* tragedy, Julianne McLean performed a work by Robert Schumann called *"Widmung"* ("Dedication") at the U.S. Merchant Marine Academy in Kings Point, New York. Survivors will certainly ask for an encore during the fifty-year commemoration.

CHAPTER 7

Sisters and Priests: Saving Spirits

We ourselves feel that what we are doing is just a drop in the ocean.
But the ocean would be less because of that missing drop.
—Mother Teresa

THE CABIN CLASS BALLROOM where Sister Angelita Myerscough was struggling to crawl up the slanted floor to reach her fellow sisters was a cacophony of frantic wailing, rolling instruments, and the shouting of Catholicism's last rites.

"I absolve you from your sins. . . ." Father Thomas Kelly crawled on all fours in his black suit, shoeless yet dignified, while delivering his spiritual message of absolution to those beseeching him for it. Hearing frantic cries from Italian passengers, the priest engaged his cultural awareness (which he had acquired while living in the hills overlooking the Vatican) by appealing to their faith in Saint Anne, whose feast fell on this day of July 26. *"Pregate Santa Anna affinchè siamo salvati,"* he repeated. "Pray to Saint Anne until we are saved." The young priest sensed a feeling of comfort on the apprehensive faces as they prayed to one of their favorite saints.

Sister Angelita, an American passenger returning from religious studies in Rome, watched in awe. *This is the priest who brought up so many life jackets to us,* she recalled. Father Kelly, who himself was returning from Rome after receiving a bachelor's degree in theology, had dedicated his studies to "the love of service to others," a motto he learned at a spiritual retreat. He and his cabin mate, Father Raymond Goedert, had already distributed dozens of life jackets after making several trips two stories below to retrieve them. Undeterred by the darkness, the smell of fuel oil, and the fear of being overcome by floodwater, Father Kelly had descended and ascended seesawing stairwells. Each time, the twenty-three-year-old priest loaded his body with a half-dozen life

Sister Angelita Myerscough.

jackets from abandoned cabins, then ran back up to the trembling packs of survivors, panting as he reached the muster station.

Sister Angelita was impressed by the inexhaustible strength of the young priest from Chicago. Her attempt to reach the higher side of the inclined room had failed brutally as she had rolled back down, crashing into a human pile of horrified passengers. Feeling overwhelmed, Sister Angelita approached Father Kelly and asked him to hear her confession. It was an awkward situation; they were trained to whisper their sins in dark silence, enclosed behind the curtains of a small booth inside a church. But this was an open ballroom, with people swarming and yelling from every direction. She hesitated. *How can I do this? Some people don't know about confession . . . well, they're going to learn now what it is*, the nun convinced herself as she began reciting the familiar ritual.

Father Kelly's missionary spirit had already lasted a couple of hours when a sense of fatigue set into his aching arms and legs—yet he told himself, *If I'm going to die, I might as well die for what I was trained for: serving others.* He had always known that he had something spiritual to share with his fellow man. He continued to hear confessions and offer absolutions.

In First Class, the deck of the perilously listing ship served as a temporary altar for the liner's chaplain, Monsignor Sebastian Natta. To reach out to the tormented souls around him who were seeking divine intervention, he leaned his body uncomfortably forward, following the slant of the ship, and calmly delivered parts of the holy mass—all while gripping the handrail behind him. As cries for last rites interrupted a hymn that was meant to console, the monsignor paused and raised his right arm to make the sign of the cross in forgiveness of the faithful ones. Chaplain Natta, known for his merciful efforts in other sea tragedies, had remembered to bring along the host from the ship's tabernacle, and he dispensed communion for several hours to the devout passengers before him.

All the while, Father Goedert was reciting a chain of prayers that encircled the piteous passengers on the port-side Promenade Deck. His words pierced through thick fog as he shouted across the deck and his audience strained to hear over the mournful, rhythmic blasts of the ship's foghorn. Time passed slowly, yet it could not stall death's deep and dark approach, as it slithered across decks and dark cavities, menacing the light of life. As the priest delivered Hail Marys in his T-shirt and trousers, he suddenly had a change of heart. The situation seemed bleak, as he was unaware of any rescue efforts in progress. While tightening his grip on the handrail that kept him upright, he began shouting the official words of general absolution, in both English and Italian, to everyone before him, regardless of their denomination: "I absolve you from your sins in the name of the Father and of the Son and of the Holy Spirit."

Feeling abandoned on the port side of the First Class deck were two other priests from Chicago, Father John Dolciamore and Father Richard Wojcik. They were returning from studies at the Gregorian University of Rome. Father Dolciamore had studied canon law with Father Goedert, while Father Wojcik had specialized in sacred music. A few hours earlier, the two cabin mates had been urged by another priest, Father Paul Lambert, to indulge in one more game of Scrabble instead of going to bed. This proved to be a lifesaving move. Immediately after the collision, when the priests went to their cabin to retrieve their passports, they faced a gruesome sight: Father Wojcik's bed had been severed in half by the *Stockholm*'s penetration of their corridor. The priests quickly placed their passports in their pockets and turned off the lights, without seeing the unconscious Dr. Thure Peterson lying under the bed.[1] After fleeing to their muster station, and before the ocean waters could rush into their corridor, the two priests immediately began calming passengers by praying with them. When their flock became too agitated for simple repetitions of the rosary, the men simply began shouting words of forgiveness. Putting their own distressed conditions aside, Fathers Wojcik and Dolciamore delivered the hope of eternal salvation to those who seemed destined to die cruelly.

"COME ON, SISTER! You've got to leave the ship now! Take off your shoes, and slide down toward me."

"I can't. I must go downstairs and tell the others that we're leaving the ship."

"There's no time. Let *us* take care of the others!"

Sister Angelita—once a tomboy, now a thirty-five-year-old nun—bunched her full-skirted habit into one hand and sat down on the slippery, slanted deck, sliding and landing against the crewman's legs. He urged her to hurl her body over the railing. With her heart pounding in her throat, she threw her black oxfords over her shoulders and dangled her purse on one arm as she prepared to take a leap of faith. But fear triumphed over courage as she remembered that she couldn't swim. Then, from the habitual reservoir of her mind, the sister spoke to God: *I surrender my life to you, dear Lord. Whatever your intentions are for me, I accept them.* It was then, while her life dangled in suspense, that she began to feel a great calm within her. Her destiny now lay in the hands of her savior. The petite nun pursued her descent into darkness on the swaying rope ladder, taking special care not to get tripped by her long skirt—one distant rung after the other, one fragile step at a time.

Sister Angelita reached the *Andrea Doria* lifeboat about 20 feet below her. Still bathed in a state of calmness, she admired the human spirit and bodily strength of the crewmen on the deck above her and in the lifeboat that sheltered her from the black sea.

How can they hang on to the rope ladder with the lifeboat riding the swell of each wave? At one point, she unintentionally let out a shriek as a wave drove the lifeboat in an upward sweep against the leaning liner, creating the sensation that the *Doria* was falling onto the smaller vessel. As the sister awaited the boarding of others, she prayed fervently, following the rosary beads between her fingers: "Hail Mary, full of grace, the Lord is with thee. Blessed art thou amongst women, and blessed is the fruit of thy womb, Jesus. Holy Mary, mother of God, pray for us sinners, now and at the hour of our death. Amen." This oration to the Blessed Mother—even with its ominous "hour of our death"—seemed to reassure Sister Angelita that she would reach safety.

Giovanna Zamparo, the sister's cabin mate, was now preparing to descend the Jacob's ladder, when a crew member noticed that the delicate-looking Italian beauty was not wearing shoes. "Take these, or you'll scrape your feet raw." He handed her a pair of worn black shoes. Giovanna descended safely and placed her chilled body next to Sister Angelita.

"Praise God that we're both safe, Giovanna. You saved my life! If you hadn't shaken me to wake up, I probably would still be groggy from the seasickness pill I took."

Giovanna, shoeless again after dropping the borrowed ones into the ocean, squeezed the sister's hand. "I'm glad I was awake. I was writing a letter to my parents, telling them about the magnificent trip we were having. Oh, I hope they don't hear about this until tomorrow when we're safe in New York."

Safe! The word planted itself in the women's minds as they watched the lifeboat fill up with weary souls. The two women from two different worlds—one in a humble black uniform, the other wearing an ivory-colored designer dress and matching purse—continued to pray silently in a spirit of mutual solace.

Suddenly, one of nature's miracles occurred: the fog that had shadowed their hopes of survival disappeared, unveiling a full moon and a bright spray of flickering stars. Sister Angelita marveled at the heavens. *Only a divine mind could do this for us. Thank you, dear Lord, for giving us light.* She made the sign of the cross, and another spontaneous prayer flowed from her soul: *Mary, Star of the Sea, I give you my thanks for this radiant miracle. Amen.*

The packed lifeboat, manned by sweaty crew members, inched its way toward another shining wonder, the French liner whose sole purpose was to assist hundreds of forlorn *Andrea Doria* passengers. Boarding the *Ile de France* would not happen so soon, however. As it reached each side port, the small vessel was directed to move on to the next. After circling the entire ship, the passengers finally climbed up a tall rope ladder and met their French hosts, who were prepared to feed, clothe, and medically assist them until their arrival on the shores of America.

Giovanna was pulled onto the French liner first. She felt comforted by the strangers who attended to her but was humbled by her pitiable condition—dirty, dead tired, and shoeless. Then, like a guardian angel, a young Frenchwoman in a beige trench coat approached Giovanna. Smiling meekly and without saying a word, the stranger discreetly opened her coat, where a pair of shoes was hidden. Both women understood that this gesture was meant to defend feminine pride and yet provide comfort. *"Grazie,"* Giovanna whispered to the compassionate foreigner, who quickly vanished into the chaotic crowd.

Sister Angelita was directed to the deck chairs, where rows and rows of traumatized survivors lay in either silent shock or overt despair. Some were all alone, while others had spouses and flocks of children with them. After sitting for a few moments, the sister felt her calling manifest itself. She moved about, first comforting a woman who complained of having lost her rosary. *"Suora, ho bisogno di pregare, ma ho perso il mio rosario."* Sister Angelita handed over her own beads in order to console the stranger in her urgent need for prayer.

The nun felt immense gratification as she realized that her studies of Italian at the University of Rome were bearing such helpful fruit. From the age of sixteen, when she had first taken her vows, she had proven herself intelligent and ambitious. Her order, the Adorers of the Precious Blood of Christ, had sent her and a team of sisters to Italy for two years. Upon their return, they were expected to bring to their convent in rural Ruma, Illinois, a better understanding of the language and heritage of those who had founded their order.

Now, as Sister Angelita made her way among the broken-spirited immigrants, she said prayers with them in Italian. Many of them kissed the crucifix around her neck as they prayed.

The sister noticed a man leaning precariously against the wall; he beckoned to her for help. "Sister, I'm feeling sick and weak. On the *Andrea Doria*, I was in the infirmary. Could you please help me get to a doctor?" With the help of a French crewman, the sister held the elderly man under his arms as they made their way to the *Ile*'s infirmary.

Throughout the morning, Sister Angelita was a tireless missionary of comfort. Mov-

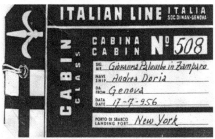

Giovanna Zamparo shared room 508 with Sister Angelita. (Courtesy of Giovanna Palumbo Zamparo)

ing from bed to bed, she held beckoning hands as she offered smiles and prayers to the distressed faces. Having given her rosary to the pitiful woman on deck, she dug into her shiny black purse to see what else she could offer. She pulled out a holy card with the image of Our Lady of Good Counsel—her favorite image of Mary since childhood. She placed it against her heart and felt its message: *Your Blessed Mother has been with you all along to give you strength.* As she passed the small card among the desolate Italian immigrants, each one kissed it and thanked the Blessed Mother for her role in saving their lives.

Pitying the exhausted nun, who, after all, was a survivor herself, the doctor in the infirmary suggested that Sister Angelita might want to attend mass. "Oh, yes, I think I could use a little respite," she responded humbly. As she wearily entered the chapel, she bumped her head against a statue of the French saint Thérèse. Rubbing her scalp, Sister Angelita asked Saint Thérèse in good humor, *Are you trying to knock me out, or are you happy to see me? Perhaps you're just thanking me for being here.* She genuflected along with dozens of other worshipers, feeling happy that she had not broken her fast with a sandwich earlier and could now receive communion.

Later, at breakfast in the dining room, Sister Angelita was delighted to see Sister Callistus Amsby and Sister Marie Raymond Baker, who had stayed across the hall from her cabin on the *Andrea Doria*. "Thank God we're all safe! Praise the Lord!"

"Have you seen Chaplain Natta?" Sister Angelita inquired.

They had not. The three women looked at one another anxiously and made the sign of the cross.

UNFORTUNATELY, THE NIGHT HAD NOT BEEN so spiritually rewarding for Father Kelly and Father Goedert. They had lowered themselves into a lifeboat powered by hand levers positioned in front of several passengers. The boat moved as the levers were pushed and pulled in unison.

"I'm sure glad to see you guys!" Father Goedert told the crewmen on their lifeboat. "What ship are you from?"

"The *Stockholm.*"

"That's great! By the way, do you know who hit us?"

"The *Stockholm,*" the crewman responded with an apologetic look.

The twenty-nine-year-old priest briefly considered jumping overboard—perhaps in anticipation of another calamitous event that was looming. The *Stockholm* seemed miles away, but the exhausted occupants of the lifeboat had to use every remaining thread of strength to reach it. It was a frightening and eerie journey in the pitch darkness of the night, since their small vessel had no light to guide them. Suddenly, they spotted the lighted mast of an enormous freighter heading straight on a collision course on their port side. *This must be the devil in disguise!* Father Goedert's thoughts brushed on the injustice of a second collision on this long night. *This isn't fair! We just got off a sinking ship—just to be sunk by another one?* He silently spoke to his maker: *Dear Father, I apologize to you for all my sins. Please forgive me. If you spare my life, I promise to be a better servant, to accomplish great deeds in your name. Hear my words, please!*

Several passengers hurriedly searched their pockets and purses for matches and lit some. The freighter continued on its course. They lit more matches; one person lit an entire pack. In return, the perspiring passengers saw a phosphorous light on the deck of the freighter. Then—as if a mass of prayers had been answered—lights flooded the panic-stricken survivors. Many made the sign of the cross as they realized they had been spotted. The Danish freighter stopped its engines, avoiding collision. Father Goedert felt clamminess and tenseness overcome his body. *This was worse than being on the sinking* Doria. *If we had been mowed down and drowned, no one would have known what had happened to us.*

With their muscles trembling and their emotions traumatized, Father Kelly and Father Goedert finally arrived at their rescue ship. But rest would have to be postponed. The two priests were asked by a Lutheran minister on board to attend to the *Stockholm's* crewmen in the sickbay. There they found several young men, mostly unconscious, some in need of blessings and some in need of last rites.

Finally, the two priests returned to the deck. They joined other curious gawkers who were inspecting the crumpled bow. They were awed by the miracle of having survived the monstrous assault inflicted by the ice beast's jaws. As Father Goedert leaned over the mangled mass of steel, he saw something horrible: the body of a woman who had dropped into the ocean. It was Jeanette Carlin, who had been catapulted from her cabin on the *Andrea*

Doria, had lain mortally wounded on the bow, and finally had fallen off along with tons of useless steel. Father Goedert simply made the sign of the cross.

Meantime, inside the salon of the liner, the Swedish hymn "No One Is As Safe As When in God's Hand" was being sung by *Stockholm* crewmen in an effort to soothe shocked survivors of the *Doria*.

ON THE *ILE DE FRANCE*, the three compassionate nuns continued their mission to offer support to the needy. An Italian couple approached Sister Angelita. "*Suora, non troviamo i nostri tre bambini,*" they said, describing their separation from their three children and not even knowing if they were safe. The sister offered words of comfort and recited the Lord's Prayer with them.

Later, two Italian crewmen shared their distress with the nun: "*Abbiamo provato a calare le lance del lato sinistro, ma era inutile!*" Sister Angelita understood their frustration, and perhaps their feelings of self-blame, as they relayed their futile attempts to lower the port-side lifeboats. "*Poi, le abbiamo abbandonate per aiutare gli altri che aspettavano sul lato di destra.*" The sister felt their grief at having abandoned those who had been waiting near the nonfunctioning lifeboats, choosing to assist others instead. "You did the best you could," she offered.

On a deck chair, a Jewish woman sat wearily alone. "I'm not Catholic, Sister. I wish I could pray with you," she implored.

"My dear lady, there is only one God. That's all that matters. Let us pray."

After circling the deck, Sister Angelita turned an unlit corner and noticed three frightened children in a huddle. She approached them and gently inquired about their parents. "*Non sappiamo dove sono,*" the frightened little pack answered, explaining that they had been separated from their parents. The sister took them by the hand and asked them to follow her across the large deck. There, the two anxious parents were ecstatically reunited with their offspring. *Thank you, Lord, for giving me this opportunity. These poor immigrants have lost everything they owned. The least I can do is help them find their families.*

Unfortunately, Sister Angelita could not reunite one elderly man and his wife, a sweet couple she had seen on the *Andrea Doria* voyage. The sister tried to speak to him in Italian, but he answered in a dialect she did not understand. He looked pathetic; she held his hand and prayed.

Sister Angelita's efforts were suddenly interrupted by a French crew member's announcement: *"Télégrammes, télégrammes."* Survivors were offered the chance to send telegrams to their loved ones. *I had better send word to my sisters in the convent,* she thought. Pulling out some change from the purse that still miraculously dangled from her arm, the sister paid the crew member and quickly wrote to her mother superior: "SAVED.[2] THANK GOD. SISTER ANGELITA."

What else do I have in here? It suddenly occurred to her that she had been able to keep other items inside her purse. She pulled out a gold-plated heart with a cross etched on its face; it was the symbol of her order, the Adorers of the Precious Blood of Christ. She rejoiced to think that not only had the Blessed Mary holy card been with her, but she also still had the precious symbol of her life's work. As she reached deeper into the bag, the thankful sister also found a small vial of holy water from Rome, which she immediately kissed. Ironically, she also found an Italian prayer, *"Preghiera dei naviganti,"* for passengers at sea.[3] Her passport, her boarding pass, and a list of Cabin Class passengers with photographs were there, too, as well as a postcard of the *Andrea Doria. Thank God I at least have a photograph of that beautiful ship.*

While the compassionate sister continued her rounds, Father Wojcik said an impromptu mass in the large Social Hall of the *Ile de France.* Before him, hundreds of survivors and *Ile* passengers worshiped their savior and gave thanks for being alive. It was 7:00 a.m.

AT LAST, THE FLOATING SANCTUARY called the *Ile de France* was nearing the harbor of New York, carrying its precious human cargo. Immigrants, movie stars, and crew members were all assembled without distinction on the decks of the French heroine.

They stared in awe as the shores were sighted. Sister Angelita realized that she had missed seeing the beloved Statue of Liberty, having spent most of her day in the infirmary. But it didn't matter now as she watched tears of hope streaming down the familiar faces of those she had met during the ordeal. *I wonder if anyone will be at the harbor to meet me.* Sister Annunciata and Sister Bernadine were scheduled to meet her at 9:00 a.m., the *Andrea Doria*'s normal arrival time.

It was now about 7:00 p.m. The passengers of the *Ile* were being escorted down the gangplank. Sister Angelita spotted the elderly man she had prayed with and realized he was still without his wife. The kind sister went over to the poor soul, whose crooked spine reflected a depletion of strength, and placed her arm under his. As they descended, she spied a blood-colored sash waving in the air. *Praise the Lord—it's the sash of my order! What a brilliant idea!* she thought. Her sisters were indeed there to welcome her home. Photographers also zeroed in on the blood-colored sash and took many shots of it. It would become a prize-winning photo worldwide, a symbol of God reuniting his flock in the most chaotic of times.

Sister Angelita led the elderly man onto shore, where a tall young fellow greeted him with an embrace and a joyous "Nonno!" His grandson had found him. Sister Angelita was happy but also worried for him. *Whatever happened to his wife?* She would always wonder.

The three nuns embraced warmly and exchanged brief pleasantries, not wanting to replay any wretched scenes from the previous night. A kind local woman approached Sister Angelita and offered to take her shopping at a fancy New York department store. "Do you need any clothes, anything at all, Sister?"

"Thank you very much, but Macy's won't have the kind of clothes I'm looking for," she replied, smiling.

The road to Sister Angelita's home in Illinois would first take a brief detour to another of the order's convents in Columbia, Pennsylvania. On the turnpike, Sister Bernadine and Sister Annunciata kept a watchful eye on their newly found survivor. Sister Angelita was amused. *They must think I'm going to suddenly scream or jump out of the car!* But no unusual behavior was noted; in fact, when the sister glanced at the turnpike map, she realized that they were near Valley Forge. To the amazement of the other sisters, Angelita remarked, "If we are near Valley Forge, I would like to stop and see it." Giving no thought to her lack of sleep, the inquisitive nun walked through the historic site, her strides swiftly kicking at her ample skirt.

Upon receiving the good news of survival, the mother superior, Sister Dorothy of Ruma, Illinois, informed her flock, "Sister Angelita must be feeling just fine. She asked to visit Valley Forge!" This brought joyful giggles to the relieved nuns.

Sister Angelita felt fortunate to be able to share the news of her survival with her order. But thoughts of Chaplain Natta continued to surface. *And what about the two sisters in Tourist Class whom I had intended to meet on the last day?* Her mind would not be at peace for a while.

IN CHICAGO TWO DAYS AFTER THE COLLISION, the *Andrea Doria*'s first survivor arrived. NBC's television crew had wasted no time, sending an official limousine to whisk Father Kelly off to the station's headquarters for a live interview. To the young priest's disappointment, the first questions were about the comportment of the *Doria*'s crew members.

"Did the crew abandon the ship?"

"I saw no evidence of that. To the contrary, I felt the crew members' presence throughout the ordeal. I heard garbled announcements on the loudspeaker throughout the night . . . a crew member escorted us from our cabins to our muster station . . . then another one came to the ballroom and tied a rope around furniture so that it wouldn't hit passengers. Three women crew members sang songs to comfort us while we awaited rescue . . . another one announced the arrival of lifeboats."

"Did you see a lot of Italian staff members on the *Stockholm?*"

"Yes. Perhaps it's because the *Stockholm* lifeboats were the first to arrive, and some of the service staff boarded them first. They returned to the stricken *Doria* several times to pick up more passengers."

Finally, after realizing that Father Kelly had no defamatory stories to share, the reporters' questions turned to the theme of benevolence.

"Were you able to help passengers abandon the sinking liner?"

"Yes. On the Cabin Class deck of the port side, the slant was tremendous; the curtains in the ballroom served as a plumb line to let me know how much the list was progressing. But fortunately, I was able to look out the windows and see lifeboats approaching. This was like a miracle, since our lifeboats were still dangling on their davits and couldn't be lowered. We had been waiting for three and a half hours. When we were told to abandon ship, we had to figure out how to get past the deck chairs that had slammed down against the inner walls and climb up to the ship's railing. So several of us men would take a woman or child by the arm and run upward until we grasped the railing. It was the only way to counteract the force of gravity. We continued to do this until everyone made their way down to the starboard side—you know, where the lifeboats were arriving."

"How did you manage to abandon the ship?"

"Well, I had to climb down a Jacob's ladder, but foolishly I tried to hang on to my shoes—which I had under one arm. I just didn't want to arrive in New York without shoes!"

The interviewer smiled at this story of pride and courage dangling in a precarious balance as the priest hung over the lifeboat, his feet often shifting above his head, obstructed further by the bulkiness of the life jacket.

"I dropped into the *Stockholm* lifeboat, happy to have my suit, my shoes, and my passport, which I remembered to take just before vacating my cabin."

The usually humble Father Kelly enjoyed being in the limelight. Besides, he thought, the interview would serve to document an important event. His confidence in speaking before a camera made him want to tell more—and there was much more he could have told the media, whose mission was to unveil the sensational.

Shortly after their arrival in Chicago, four priests who survived the collision are welcomed back by the cardinal. From left to right: Father John Dolciamore, Father Raymond Goedert, Samuel Cardinal Stritch, Father Thomas Kelly, and Father Richard Wojcik. (Courtesy of Father John Dolciamore)

"Father Goedert, my cabin mate, was in the same lifeboat. We got separated after arriving at our muster station, so I was really happy to see him safe. But then, just when we were beginning to feel safe, we were faced with another horrendous incident. The rescue ships were moving closer, and one of them, an old freighter, was heading straight at us in the dark."

Father Goedert had relayed the same horrifying story when he arrived in New York and met with Father Aloisious Wycislo, and later while driving to Chicago with his parents.

IN COLUMBIA, PENNSYLVANIA, Sister Angelita was finally feeling the toll of her long ordeal. She sat down at a large desk at the convent, and composed a heartfelt letter in Italian to the mother general of her order, Esther Graziosi:

July 29, 1956
Most reverend and dearest Mother General,

Many feelings emerge from my heart when I relive that terrible event on the night of July 25-26, on board the now lost Andrea Doria. *Without doubt, the Omnipotent, His infinite Goodness, and God's Providence were visible more than ever in all the circumstances that occurred during the disaster.*

I offer to you, Venerate Mother, to the other Mothers, and to my fellow sisters, my fervent thanks for the prayers and for the concern on my behalf. I would like to reveal to you and the others, the events that I lived through on that night.

Night of July 25:

Without any anxiety about the impenetrable fog, I decided to go to the chapel and pray, giving thanks for a marvelous trip. . . .

At about 10:30 p.m., I fell into a profound sleep. Then I groggily awakened to noises and shaking that I thought were insignificant; therefore I fell asleep again—until my kind cabin mate shook me awake. . . . Not wanting to leave behind my red sash, I placed it over my life jacket and ran toward the stairs that were already listing badly. With God's help, I stumbled up four levels, where there were about twenty people. . . . After about an hour, we found out that we had collided with a smaller ship. . . . Perhaps you are asking: Didn't you pray? Yes, dear Mother, I prayed and got others to pray—in Italian, English, Latin—saying brief prayers, the rosary, etc. A young American priest made it to our muster station (which was the Social Hall) and gave us general absolution. I accepted the will of God with more sincerity than ever before in my life. I prayed to our Madonna and our guardian angel; sadly, I must confess that I forgot all the other saints at that moment. . . .

The ship continued to incline sharply. I decided to go up on deck to investigate. Crawling on the floor (since it was impossible to stand), I made it to the stairwell, which was blocked by a small table. There was a man there having difficulty going up. I managed to move in front of him, pulling him by his arm and arriving up two flights of stairs—without letting him fall back down! . . .

> *It must have been about 1:30 a.m. when I reached the lifeboat.*
> *As I prayed, I saw an incredible sight. . . .*

Sister Angelita stopped writing for a moment and looked up toward the heavens, giving thanks once more for the illumination provided by the moon and the stars. She made the sign of the cross and thanked God for having safely guided men who descended with children in their arms and for having protected children who descended with ropes tied around their waists.

Now she was anxious to share how she had helped others on the *Ile de France*. Sister Angelita had long proven herself completely devoted to her order. But there was a time, during her teen years, when her mother superior had threatened to send her home for her rebellious behavior. She trusted her stellar behavior during the rescue would clear any earlier blemishes. She continued to write:

> *It was about 3:00 in the morning, the feast of Saint Anne. . . . I aided people crying, screaming, and fainting . . . the priest and the four of us nuns from the* Andrea Doria *attended mass and received the Sacrament . . . I tended to an Italian priest whose legs were broken and bloody. . . .*

Realizing that her story was getting long, she concluded:

> *This is my personal experience of this tragedy. . . . God saved my life, and for this I am eternally grateful. But if he had decreed otherwise, I would have also thanked Him. I learned during that night that truly "only God counts": "Te Deum laudamus, te Domine confitemur!"*
>
> *I ask for your maternal benediction as I offer you a prayer of thanks, and I confirm myself, your spiritual daughter.*
> *Affectionately,*
> *Sister Angelita Myerscough*

After several days of rest, Angelita was ready to return to the convent she called home. It had been two exciting years in Europe, traveling around the continent, studying at the University of Rome, and attending the beatification of Sister Maria de Mattias, the founder of her order.[4]

Sister Angelita received a warm welcome, with cheers and hugs and one very meaningful gesture. To her surprise, the sisters had prepared a special place setting adorned with the holy card of Our Lady of Good Counsel—the same one that had accompanied her during the ordeal. *She's following me throughout my return, too!* Within days, the order's celebrity received an invitation to speak about her harrowing adventure at a nearby hospital. The sisters there had a barrage of questions, which Sister Angelita answered with great care.

"Were there other sisters on the *Andrea Doria?*"

"Yes, there were six others, and I believe there were four priests, as well as Monsignor Natta, the *Andrea Doria* chaplain. Have you heard any news about him?"

There was good news: the chaplain was among the survivors. Sister Angelita wished she could have celebrated the last day of mass with him and made a proper good-bye.

"Did you have a chance to confess your sins before receiving final absolution?"

"Well, yes, but it was quite brief—and in front of everyone. I remember thinking, 'If people don't know what confession is, they'll know it now!'" The sisters in the audience giggled at the awkward situation. "A young priest named Father Kelly crawled from group to group giving the last rites; he stopped by me and gave me personal absolution."

"How did you manage to keep calm while you were waiting to be rescued?"

"We all supported one another. Even the bartender kept the panic down by telling amusing stories, joking, and explaining that the ship couldn't possibly sink. He went around and helped everyone in need. Other crewmen tied ropes across the room so that furniture would not slide and crash into us. A little boy, amused at all the commotion, said to his mother, 'Gee, won't we have something to tell the neighbors when we get home!'"

"Did some crew members abandon the ship before the passengers?"

"You must remember that the crew consisted of waiters, chefs, orchestra, and a host of other workers—not at all like a crew would be on a navy ship."

"But we read that crewmen were the first into the lifeboats!"

"Some lifeboats held seventy-five passengers or more, plus the crew. Someone with experience had to man the lifeboats, for you can't throw them into the ocean and expect them to stay there! Our crewmen worked efficiently and knew exactly what to do."

"It must have been difficult climbing a rope ladder into the *Ile de France.*"

"No, it seemed like the easiest thing I ever did!"

"What was it like on the *Ile de France?*"

"The French crew was very courteous; they passed out blankets, served coffee and sandwiches, and tended to the injured. It was as if they had been expecting us for several weeks!"

"What did you lose on the ship, Sister?"

"Well, certainly not as much as the immigrants who lost their life's belongings, but I'm sad to have lost my bachelor and master of arts certificates, about one hundred books, and the original recordings of the beatification of Sister Maria de Mattias." The nuns were saddened at the thought of losing the memories of a milestone in Catholic history. They didn't seem to mind that Sister Angelita had also lost gifts she was bringing back for them.

Finally, the curious assembly inquired about the habit. "Sister, were you wearing our order's habit during the night?"

"Oh, yes, except for the white collar, which was too large for the life vest. I even managed to put on my red sash. As I quickly dressed, it occurred to me, if I'm going to die, I want to be wearing the Precious Blood of Christ!" It was exactly what her audience wanted to hear.

Now Sister Angelita had a question for them. "Have you heard any news about the two sisters traveling in Tourist Class?" There was immediate silence followed by unsynchronized signs of the cross.

"They were not among the survivors, Sister. They are with our Lord."

Why didn't I go introduce myself, as I had wanted?

Finally, someone asked, "Do you plan to go back to Italy—and will you go by boat?"

There was no hesitation in the spirited sister's response. "The answer is affirmative on both counts."

In 1968, Sister Angelita made another trip to Italy; it would be the first of many. And indeed, she sometimes chose to travel by ship. Moreover, she insisted on traveling on an Italian liner, in support of the *Andrea Doria*'s crew. In the years after the sinking, she explained to many reporters, "I never felt that the *Doria* was to blame for the accident; Captain Calamai and his experienced officers were all on the bridge that night. On the *Stockholm*, the captain was not present; the young officer in command was inexperienced. Given those facts, I'm 99 percent certain that the *Doria* was not to blame." On her first return trip to Italy, the sister sailed on the *Rafaello*. This was a happy choice, for another passenger was Monsignor Natta, now chaplain of the *Rafaello*. Sister Angelita was ecstatic. "I'm delighted to see you, Father. I have always regretted not bidding you good-bye on the *Doria*."

"This meeting is truly by celestial intervention, Sister. This is my last trip as a chaplain, and then I'm retiring." *The Lord has been good to us*, Sister Angelita reflected later. *We have both been blessed with a life of service.*

The young girl who had spent her childhood in a rural town in Illinois was now a worldly woman who made many great trips across the sea. And whether she was living on a small farm or at the Vatican, Sister Angelita felt at home. In fact, she chose to make Rome her home from 1975 through 1987, where she continued to study theology at the University of Rome.[5] Her aim to master the Italian language became a reality. In fact, she now spends her days translating letters of Saint Maria de Mattias from Italian to English.

Now a senior consultant with her order, Sister Angelita looks back at her life with nothing but gratification for having served others through her religion. She explains, "I'm so grateful to the good Lord for all the good years of my life, my family, my pastor, my parish, and the sisters. I'm so grateful that God called me to this life."

She has kept in touch with the cabin mate who saved her from a somnolent death. Sister Angelita accompanied Giovanna to Rome, her second home. Giovanna never tires of retelling the story of the sympathetic Frenchwoman on the *Ile de France* who gave her a pair of shoes when she had none.

LIKE SISTER ANGELITA, THE PRIESTS from the *Andrea Doria* are still leading lives of religious benevolence. Father Goedert is the retired auxiliary bishop of Chicago, after having fulfilled his dream of practicing canon law and serving as pastor of Saint Barnabus Church. "My ministry has taught me that life is precious and fragile," he says. "The *Andrea Doria* tragedy reaffirmed to me that this life is not the end. But in looking back on that night, I really never felt totally hopeless while I was reciting the Hail Mary. Looking back at my life, I feel that I lived up to the promises I made to my maker as I was praying in front of that giant freighter."

Father Kelly is now a professor emeritus in sociology at Lake Superior College in Sault Sainte Marie, Michigan. He teaches a course in how various cultures respond when faced with trauma. He learned from his studies and from the *Doria* tragedy that people unite when facing a disaster situation—regardless of their culture. While he was in training as a counselor in marriage and human sexuality, he met a nun who would later become his wife. The two have spent a lifetime teaching sociology and religious studies together.

As if to test the depth of his faith, fate has dealt more life-threatening blows to Father Dolciamore. "I have been in two car accidents and a train accident where the car tried to beat a train and didn't make it! It's taken me a long time not to fear travel in general, including planes, trains, and ships. Nevertheless, I feel I've been very blessed and graced by the Lord. I could have been dead several times, but I have been spared. I think the Lord intended to have me accomplish some good. I've been able to do that in my priesthood, for which I'm very happy." The priest is still teaching canon law and remains judicial vicar of his parish in Venice, Florida.

Father Dolciamore's and Father Wojcik's careers have remained intertwined since that fateful night on the Atlantic. They are both members of the faculty of the Mundelein Seminary. Father Wojcik has dedicated a large portion of his life to re-creating from memory the sacred music he was carrying back from Rome in his suitcase. His most prized possession, *Liber Gradualis,* was a collection of original Gregorian chants, hymns, propers of the mass, ritual music, and performance rules he had painstakingly noted in the margins. Moreover, after Vatican II in the 1960s, he had to translate all of the works into English from the Latin versions. Father Wojcik sees the whole uncertain experience as like a game of chess played on the *Doria*: "Everything was designed for what we were going to be doing, but instead everything took another turn. You just pick up the pieces and go on. That night convinced me that one never knows what Providence has planned for us."

CHAPTER 8

The Rich and the Famous

Like the winds of the sea
Are the waves of time.
As we journey along through life,
'Tis the set of the soul
That determines the goal,
And not the calm or the strife.
—Ella Wheeler Wilcox

THE ALLURING *ANDREA DORIA* seduced travelers of all classes but offered an upgrade of prestige and pampering to those of comfortable means. These passengers wanted to relish the pleasures of the floating palace: silver plaques, wood mosaic, and stained-glass panels adorning the walls; statues created by skillful artists; china, silver, and gold gracing the tables; a fifty-car, air-conditioned garage;[1] and stunning staterooms in which to create cherished memories.

Some passengers whose reputations distinguished them from the crowd were:

Ruth Roman, a notable screen actress.
Mike Stoller, a young songwriter who would become an American legend.
Jerome Reinert, a young man from a prominent business family.
Madge Young, the fourteen-year-old daughter of a director of the American Bureau of Shipping, traveling with her prominent father, her mother, and her brother.
Linda Morgan, the fourteen-year-old daughter of popular ABC radio broadcaster Edward P. Morgan, and Madge Young's shipboard pal.

These *Andrea Doria* survivors have shared intimate first-person accounts, which follow here. Their stories, in their own words, reaffirm that the *Stockholm*'s bow spared no one in its indiscriminate destruction, regardless of stature and means.

Hollywood star Ruth Roman, reunited with her son, Dickie. (Associated Press)

RUTH ROMAN [2]

I WAS A PASSENGER ON THE *ANDREA DORIA*. Today, looking back on that terrible night off Nantucket, I know that in a way I profited from it. For I learned something which gave me a new feeling about my fellow man.

Of course I recall the frightening crunch of the *Stockholm* against our ship, the twisted steel, the shouts in the night, the fear born out of not knowing exactly what would happen to us. But even more vividly I remember the amazing strength and calm of the passengers and crew.

They taught me that within most human beings lies a great resource, normally untapped, but there, waiting, to be summoned up in moments of stress. Call it strength, courage—whatever it is, it pulls us through against the longest odds.

The last night out on the *Doria,* I was attending the "gala," an end-of-the-voyage party in the ballroom on an upper deck. Some of us were singing "Arrivederci Roma." Then it came—a crashing, crushing impact.

All of us knew that something horrible had happened. One thought ran from mind to mind: *The ship is in trouble.* Yet there was little hysteria. People set out, hurriedly but without panic, to do what they could for themselves or others.

I kicked off my pumps—on a listing ship, high heels are absolutely no help—and started running down, deck by deck, to the cabin where my Dickie and his nurse, Grace Els, were sleeping.

A sailor grabbed at me, fearing perhaps that I had panicked. Somehow I managed to get away. (I must have knocked him for a loop!) Then I ripped my sheath dress up the back, so I could move about more freely.

I got to Dickie and Miss Els—thin, gray-haired, a tower of strength. I brought them up to the listing Boat Deck and barricaded them with life preservers and blankets from our beds so they would not slip and roll down the deck. My calmness surprised me then—and now, in retrospect, it surprises me even more.

But I was not the only one who, consciously or not, was calling on his inner strength. I could not point to a single individual and cite him as a "hero." But I got a great feeling of confidence and reassurance from what I saw.

I remember a waiter who, in the midst of everything, heated milk and distributed it to mothers of small children.

I remember a ship's musician who went from passenger to passenger, ministering to the needs of each.

I remember our own Miss Els, who, on receiving a violent blow on the elbow, not only did not cry out, but didn't even mention it.

After I built the little blanket "trench" for her and Dickie, I lay down with them. I put my arms over my head and thought: *I may have to swim with Dickie; I'll need all my strength.* Then, restlessly sitting up, I spotted a deflated party balloon on the deck. I blew it up, gave it to Dickie and told him that we were going on a picnic.

Minutes later, a young sailor—I'll never forget him either—

calmly tied Dickie to his back and took him down a ladder to a waiting lifeboat. I followed, but apparently the lifeboat was full. It pulled away before I could get in.

As I stood there, Dickie held the balloon in one hand, waved to me with the other. "Picnic," he called. "Picnic!"

Later I learned that Dickie had been taken to the *Stockholm*, where total strangers took wonderful care of him—another act of kindness I'll always remember—until we were reunited the next day.

Finally, Miss Els and I were put aboard a lifeboat from the *Ile de France*. It was all over for us, and for the *Andrea Doria*—all except the realization of the wonderful inner quality which had turned tragedy into a lifelong lesson for me.

ACTRESS RUTH ROMAN HAD HER FIRST leading movie role in 1948's *Belle Starr's Daughter*. She also starred in *Lightning Strikes Twice* and Alfred Hitchcock's *Strangers on a Train*, both in 1951. Most ironically relevant to her *Andrea Doria* experience, however, was the film *Three Secrets* (1950), in which Roman, Eleanor Parker, and Patricia Neal portray distraught mothers who are waiting to learn whether their children have survived a plane crash. After a long and successful career on screen, stage, and television, Roman died in 1999 at age seventy-six.

MIKE STOLLER

I LOVED ITALY FROM THE MOMENT I arrived there. My first wife, Meryl, and I had spent three months of 1956 traveling through Europe, paid for with a royalty check I had received for the recording of "Black Denim Trousers and Motorcycle Boots." We were very excited about returning to the States on the *Andrea Doria*, our first time on an ocean liner. The travel agent who changed our initial reservations on a Greek ship said, "Take the *Doria*, you'll never forget it!"

The ship was beautiful and luxurious. I was twenty-three, and I was impressed with the elegant dining room and the uniformed

Elvis Presley was not aboard the *Andrea Doria*, but Mike Stoller (left) was. The King and Stoller are seen here with Stoller's songwriting partner, Jerry Leiber. (Courtesy of Mike Stoller)

waiting staff. I remember wondering what *farinaci* was. Of course, it referred to the pasta dishes, which were delicious.

There were always activities on board: dancing, card games, mechanical horse racing, Ping-Pong. I have the distinction of being the July 1956 Cabin Class Ping-Pong champion of the *Andrea Doria*. My award went down with the ship.

The night of the collision, Meryl persuaded me to join her and some young ladies who had promised to dance with some young, shy Italian fellows. I wanted to go to sleep so I could get up early and take movies of the Statue of Liberty and try to imagine what my grandparents had experienced when they arrived in New York some sixty years before. But I put on my slacks and corduroy jacket, and we went up to the ballroom. Meryl and the others seemed to be having fun, but I was bored. I ordered a glass of champagne and went to see if there was a poker game going on in the card room.

Suddenly, the ship struck something violently, and the deck

was sloped at a steep angle. I managed to keep my footing, but as I looked around, I saw something that looked like a giant letter opener ripping across the elliptical windows of the Promenade Deck, producing loud noises of glass and wood shattering and smashing. Since I had been reading *A Night to Remember* (the story of the *Titanic*) on board the ship, it briefly crossed my mind that we might have hit an iceberg, but this was July, and we were due to dock in New York the next morning.

The orchestra went abruptly silent, and there was mass confusion among the passengers. A teenage boy came running in and was yelling to us that he had seen another ship slam into ours. No one believed him. I kept hearing people murmuring the word "iceberg." We realized we needed to get life jackets.

The floor of the corridor leading to our cabin was filling up with oily water and debris. I saw some women sitting in this mess, praying with rosaries, while others were just screaming. I found our cabin door ajar. I quickly grabbed our life jackets and glanced at our new movie camera and the thirty rolls of film I'd taken in Europe but decided, *No way; I'm not carrying anything but the life jackets.*

I made my way up the leaning staircase with the jackets under my arm. When I reached the Promenade Deck, some people tried to take one away from me. I yelled, "It's not for me!" and continued up toward the Boat Deck. I had promised a friend of Meryl's that I'd get the life jacket from her cabin, but the trip there seemed too risky, and I told myself I could swim if I had to.

When I finally reached the Boat Deck, on the port side near the lifeboats, I found Meryl repeatedly calling out my name: "Mike, Mike, M-i-k-e!" She was gripping the railing; her face was ashen and expressionless, as if she were in a trance. I shook her by the shoulders and slapped her on the cheek. She calmed down. Finally, a crew member came by with extra life jackets and gave me one. We didn't have anywhere to go, so we just stood there holding on to the railing behind us while others leaned against the metal bulkhead opposite. Minutes were turning into hours; to keep our spirits up, we sang old popular songs.

Occasionally, we would look up at the lifeboats just dangling there, useless, because of the heavy list. Someone in our group tried to reassure us by saying, "Maybe they can pump the water out and right the ship." As if in response, a young fellow in our group who was an engineer sadly shook his head. I said to myself, *This is it.*

We remained on the Boat Deck, even though our muster station was on the Promenade Deck; at least we were near lifeboats (should they become operable) and on the outside of the ship. A few hours passed; the only thing we heard was one word over the loudspeaker: *"Calmi."* We knew it meant "Keep calm" but in a voice that made it sound more like "Help!" Then, when we had pretty much given up hope, we saw what looked like a ship sailing up the side of a mountain. It was surreal! We still didn't know it was the *Ile de France,* which had turned around to assist in rescuing us.

You see, after standing on a slant for hours and not seeing a horizon, our perspective was totally shot, and the *Ile* seemed as if *it* were on a slant. Then we saw people in lifeboats heading toward the *Ile* and realized that people were actually getting off the *Andrea Doria.* At first, our group was afraid to head toward the starboard side, thinking we might sink the ship if we all rushed over to the low side at once.

Finally, out of desperation and frustration, we decided to form a human chain and head for the starboard side. We placed children between adults and began our journey to the lower side. I remember a mother screaming repeatedly for her children, not realizing she was holding their hands. Eventually, we all crashed onto the starboard rail. A crew member tied a rope around Meryl's waist for security, but when she realized she would have to climb down a rope ladder herself, she froze. The lifeboat was waiting. One of the passengers inside yelled, "Leave them! Leave them!" I knew we had to hurry, so I told Meryl that I'd step on her fingers if she didn't move quickly enough.

Then things seemed to evolve from bad to worse. The lifeboat needed to hurry away, for fear that we'd be sucked down by the sinking of the ship. Urgently, the lifeboat crewman (who was actually an elevator operator on the ship) taught us how to operate the paddles by pushing back and forth on metal pipes, but the rudder was broken, and we couldn't steer. After swaying out of control for a while, we pulled away. I was so relieved to be out from under that leaning mass of twisted metal over our heads that I could have rowed all the way to New York! Some passengers, realizing we weren't headed for the *Ile de France*, and seeing that we were drifting off course, opted for mutiny. People began hollering, "That way, that way!" One man pulled out a gun and pointed it at the elevator operator, but he was quickly subdued by the others.

Somehow, without the ability to navigate, our lifeboat nearly collided with the prow of a freighter that was standing by. As we edged along the side of the *Cape Ann*, the water from its bilge pumps started pouring into our lifeboat and almost swamped it. A sailor on the freighter looked down incredulously and hollered, "What the f— are you people doing?" Meryl finally felt a sense of security. She said, "Gee, it's great to hear a real American voice!"

On board the *Cape Ann*, the crew treated us royally, preparing enormous plates of scrambled eggs and bacon and arranging to send telegrams for us. I sent a message in care of Atlantic Records to my partner, Jerry Leiber: "We're OK. We're on the *Cape Ann*. Coming in tonight. Please notify our families."

I felt as if I had been reborn. I finally managed to exhale all the air I had been holding in my lungs for three or four hours, and when I did, I burst into tears.

Meryl was angry about the lack of direction and information we'd received during our ordeal on the sinking ship. She decided to circulate a petition among 129 survivors. Ninety people signed it, although I'm not sure all the names were valid; some of the Italians, not understanding English, probably thought that they were adding their names to a survivor list. When we entered New York Harbor, a passenger named Arthur Fischer dangled the petition from a rope for the newsmen to grab. The grievances were published in newspapers everywhere.

In New York, my partner, Jerry, was waiting for us outside customs, along with Meryl's family. It was wonderful to see Jerry coming down the dock to greet us. He grabbed me and said, "Oh, man, you're OK! Hey, Mike, we've got a smash hit!"

"No kidding?" I said.

"I'm not kidding . . . 'Hound Dog.'"

"Big Mama Thornton?"[3]

"No, some white kid named Elvis Presley."

Our rhythm-and-blues song was now number one on the pop charts.

THE REUNION OF TWO YOUNG SONGWRITERS on a New York pier was the embarkation of an enduring career that would have an impact on America's musical culture for the next half-century. As one of the most successful songwriting-publishing-producing partnerships in the world, Jerry Leiber and Mike Stoller became influential creators in several musical genres: rhythm and blues, jazz, cabaret, and, of course, "good ole rock 'n' roll." Jerry writes the words; Mike writes the music. One commentator described them as "the power behind the throne of Elvis Presley." Recently, the songwriting team, whose show *Smokey Joe's Cafe* became the longest-running musical revue in Broadway history, has been working on new musicals.

Mike Stoller's survival of the *Andrea Doria* tragedy also bequeaths us melodies that have softened the harshness of our own daily struggles to remain afloat. Just as his inner strength guided him to stay alive in menacing times, his talent has imprinted our memories with melodies that transcend borders of time and geography. Americans have grown up with gems such as "Hound Dog," "Jailhouse Rock," "Yakety Yak," "Charlie Brown," "Poison Ivy," "Love Potion #9," "Kansas City," "Stand by Me," "Is That All There Is?" and hundreds of other popular hits.

When Stoller is asked to name his favorite song, his response is simply, "It's always the one I'm writing at the moment. But if I had to name my favorite recordings, I would say they are Big Mama Thornton's 'Hound Dog' and Peggy Lee's 'Is That All There Is?'"

Beyond the benchmark awards bestowed upon Leiber and

Stoller,[4] one of the most notable tributes to their enduring talent is the stellar delegation of artists who have recorded their music. These include the Coasters, the Drifters, Ben E. King, Elvis Presley, Peggy Lee, the Beatles, the Rolling Stones, the Beach Boys, Barbra Streisand, Jimi Hendrix, Johnny Mathis, Count Basie, Tom Jones, Edith Piaf, Aretha Franklin, Ray Charles, and many others.

Stoller modestly summarizes his amazing success: "Hey, I've been lucky."

When asked about long-term effects of the *Andrea Doria* collision, he replies, "I guess I've dealt with the *Andrea Doria* experience primarily by suppressing it. Today, Stoller tells us, "I'm writing music and enjoying my life. I've been happily married to Corky Hale Stoller, a jazz pianist and harpist, for thirty-five years, and I have three wonderful children: Amy, Peter, and Adam."

JEROME REINERT

WHEN I WAS A YOUNG BOY, my father would always tell me, "If you wake up in the morning and there is food on the breakfast table, you owe; how you repay society is your business. You can do it with money, expertise, or your talents, but you must pay your debt." In retrospect, it was my father's lesson that guided me through the *Andrea Doria* rescue.

After the crash, the First Class passengers like me quickly realized that we were not going to receive preferential treatment—as we had during the voyage. There were only two choices: to be immobilized by fear or to act on our own. Although feeling frightened, I was energized to do whatever I could to help. At first, I assisted people up the stairwells, cleared passages on the deck by throwing luggage overboard, and then went looking for my friends. Being twenty-one, I felt that my strength was inexhaustible and that I was nearly immortal. But as the incline of the ship increased and I watched all the lifeboats pull away, I realized that those of us who were on the Upper Deck had to devise our own plan, and fast.

As I watched the crew lowering people into lifeboats, I decided that the able-bodied among us could be helping them as well. I persuaded a couple of men my age to assist in lowering children and the wounded. My buddies then watched me as I dangled dangerous-

Jerome Reinert proudly displays the shirt he was wearing during the *Doria* rescue.

ly on a rope ladder, several feet away from the ship in its 30-to-40-degree list—all while holding a child in my arms. My feet were in front of me, my fanny was the center of gravity, and a swaying lifeboat was holding my ladder 30 feet below. It was exhausting!

We took turns going up and down the swinging ladder, carrying frantic children who were hollering and scratching at us. After delivering eleven children to the lifeboat, I helped my friend Gay Barton descend the ladder, one step at a time, because of her severely sprained ankle. My buddies and I spent a couple of hours doing these grueling descents and climbs. We had watched several lifeboats pull away with passengers when a crewman grabbed me and said, "That's enough. You're exhausted; you can't go up there anymore." I watched the last of our group descend; it was nearly 4:00 a.m. We were finally headed toward those neon lights, "ILE DE FRANCE," that had tempted us for hours. The *Ile* opened up a side hatch for us. When I saw the ladder leading to it, I thought, *This is a piece of cake in comparison to the* Doria *ladder! It's vertical, and it's actually lying against the hull!* Besides, I felt really hyper; I guess they call this euphoria.

As I stepped inside the hatch, a French crewman came toward me with a butcher knife. I was already feeling traumatized, so this frightened me. But at the same time as the crewman was cutting the straps from my life jacket, a kind-looking gentleman extended a glass toward me, offering me a drink. Being quite thirsty, I gulped it down—not realizing it was French cognac!

Then I was directed to the deck, where other survivors were being attended to by the French crew members and passengers. As I walked past some deck chairs, an Italian woman reached up and kissed my hand while her son smiled at me. I squeezed her hand and said, *"Grazie,"* thanking her for her kindness. At the same time, a distinguished-looking Frenchman was standing nearby. Noticing the recognition I had just received, he approached me.

"I am Monsieur Guy de Berc. Why did the woman kiss your hand?" he inquired.

"I don't know, but I might have lowered her son into a lifeboat."

M. de Berc seemed quite impressed by my explanation and invited me to his cabin. I had seen beautiful cabins on the *Doria,* but I had never seen anything so luxurious as this. The quarters were quite large, and the walls were lined in mahogany paneling displaying maritime art. The Frenchman offered me an opportunity to clean up and refresh myself before explaining that he was the general manager of the French Line for the United States, Canada, and Mexico. Fortunately, I was not shy, or this could have been quite intimidating.

M. de Berc was very hospitable and very curious about who I was. It became obvious that he wanted to hear a firsthand account of the collision and rescue on the *Andrea Doria*—after all, his company had contributed a lot of resources to this event. I talked with composure, never breaking down or giving in to my fatigue and injuries.

"After my engineering studies at Rensselaer Polytechnic Institute,[5] I traveled to England, France, and Italy for five weeks—a graduation gift from my mother. In Rome, I met a young lady from South America who had just graduated from a finishing school in Switzerland; she was lovely, and I wanted to continue seeing her."

M. de Berc looked at me with interest, probably wondering why I was telling him this detail, so I continued.

"When she told me that in two days she would be boarding the *Andrea Doria* in Naples, I canceled my flight on TWA and booked a ticket on the *Doria*—for the same trip as the lady."

"Ah, so you had a romance on that fateful voyage?"

"Well, sir, not exactly. Mackie and I met for dinner the first night on board. Later, as we were dancing, I sensed four eyes glaring intensely at me—it was Mackie's father and her female chaperone. I decided to end this fifteen-hour romance and make other acquaintances."

I continued describing my voyage to this inquisitive stranger. "The night of the crash, I was with my new friends: Gay and Andrea from New Orleans, Isa from New York, and a Canadian gentleman. The popular actress Ruth Roman was celebrating with us. We were all exchanging contact information—the way one does after summer camp—when all of a sudden, the ship began to rock. I noticed that the drapes were swaying away from the windows. It was obvious we had hit something, but we didn't know what."

M. de Berc excused himself for interrupting me, explaining that he wanted to make a phone call: "Forgive my oversight, Mr. Reinert. It's 5:30 a.m., and you must be starving. Besides, there is someone on this ship who should hear your story."

In the dining room, I was introduced to our breakfast companion, William Geisen—the same gentleman who had welcomed me on board with a glass of cognac. "Thank you for joining us, Mr. Reinert. What can I get for you?" he asked.

With the bold attitude of a recent college graduate, I responded, "I'll have a Scotch."

"The bar isn't open yet. Why don't we talk over some breakfast?"

I still felt quite hyper and, curiously, not even tired. M. de Berc explained that our companion, Mr. Geisen, was the general manager of the Maritime Association of the Port of New York. At this point, I realized that I had better retell my experience with all my ducks in a row, so I continued my personal account as if I were the expert.

"Immediately, there was chaos. We heard an announcement telling us to get our life jackets and report to the lifeboats. I headed downstairs for the corridor to my cabin, but when I got there, the entire corridor was gone; it was as if a bulldozer had razed a building and it lay in a long pile in front of me."

My hosts' eyes stared at me in amazement.

"When we all went out on the deck, we were faced with mounds of suitcases; it was hard to move. Besides, the swimming pool had spilled over, and the deck was covered with water. We made our way by throwing suitcases overboard to get to the lifeboats. Later, the lifeboats were lowered, but they filled up quickly; we waited a couple of hours until we devised a plan to evacuate more people."

At this point, I explained to the two powerful men just exactly how I had participated in rescuing children and friends. They looked very impressed.

"How was the crew involved in rescuing?" Mr. Geisen inquired.

"The officers and sailors gave directions and helped evacuate passengers. But some of the other employees got into the lifeboats with the passengers." I quickly added, "I don't blame them, however. They weren't trained for rescuing people, so they saved their own lives the best they could."

My account seemed acceptable to these maritime managers.

"I owe my life to the *Ile de France*," I continued. "The *Stockholm* lifeboat had to take us to the *Ile* because their ship was full. Thank you!"

At this point, M. de Berc explained to me, a twenty-one-year-old kid, the risks taken by the *Ile* in coming to our rescue.

"It was a complicated decision," he said. "The maritime law of the 1880s assigns value to the ship based on the value of the freight. We were already exceeding the insurance limit. Captain de Beaudéan and I discussed this matter, plus the added expenses of postponing arrival in France—not to mention the danger of navigating in a fog rescue. But we agreed that the value of people's lives already in peril was more important, and the potential loss of lives on the *Andrea Doria* seemed enormous!"

Feeling privy to important facts, and thankful for this overwhelming kindness from the French, I went back on deck and dozed off. Later in the morning, I was awakened by a ruckus. I looked over the railing and saw tugboats full of press personnel; they were climbing on board. To my astonishment, I also saw among them Harry Maze, my brother's father-in-law. Being an assistant district attorney of Brooklyn, he had used his connections to come on board to try to find me. I had been stoic until now, but when Harry hugged me, I fell apart; I couldn't stop crying. Once again, M. de Berc offered his cabin. While I cried like a baby, the Frenchman related my whole story to Harry.

Our arrival in New York Harbor was very emotional for me. As I passed the Statue of Liberty, I thought about my father's arrival in America. He was a Romanian Jew who had immigrated in 1906. I paid tribute to his memory by imagining the courage he had to leave everything behind; unfortunately, my father passed away when I was only fourteen.

Harry and I breezed through customs as he flashed his legal badge to officials. As there were no cell phones and the cab ride to my sister's apartment in Manhattan would take only minutes, we didn't stop to call the family.

When I walked into the apartment, my family seemed to be having a wake for me, thinking I had died in the collision. My sister's face looked as if she were seeing a ghost. She walked toward me very slowly, but then she hugged me really hard and wouldn't let go. My poor mother looked as if she were in shock over everything, including my return.

Other than walking around in a daze with a fractured finger and sprained ribs for a few weeks, I have since lived every day to the fullest. The *Andrea Doria* experience taught me an important lesson: Live for today, because tomorrow is an uncertainty. Since knocking so closely on death's door, I'm much more willing to take risks. Everything seems easier after that experience, even trading a great deal of money every day on the New York Stock Exchange! I'm in my seventies now, but I ski and travel around the world for business and pleasure.

My life has been blessed with luck as well as hard knocks, but I believe that life changes as you are living it, so I go with the flow. One thing I will never give up is the lesson my father taught me: "Pay back your debt to society." That's what I did on the *Doria* for others, and that's what the Frenchmen on the *Ile* did for me. Since that night, I have never stopped paying back.

JEROME REINERT REMAINED IN CONTACT with William Geisen and Guy de Berc until their deaths. Mackie later sent a letter to Jerome that included five dollars. It was money Jerome had given her to call her family from the *Ile de France*. She was repaying him for his kindness.

Reinert was president, chairman, and CEO of Reinert and Company in New York City. Since 1960, he has held a seat on the New York Stock Exchange. He has also been a consultant in the securities industry and director of two other companies: Securities and Investment Planning of Chatham, New Jersey, and S.I.L. of Pozzilli, Italy.

His philanthropy, paying back his debt, reaches far and wide. Among many humanitarian causes he has supported are the Rensselaer Polytechnic Institute (national fund-raising chairman, President's Advisory Council, and life patron donor of an endowment that finances the scholarships of two graduate school students), the National Kidney Foundation of New York City (president, trustee, and recipient of the Humanitarian of the Year award), the Wellness Community of Southeast Florida (cofounder of this cancer support group), and the Boca Raton Museum of Art (Board of Trustees member, donor of oil paintings, exhibitor of Winslow Homer).

Reinert is also very proud of his teaching appointments at various institutions throughout his career, including St. John's University, Rensselaer Polytechnic Institute, New York University, New York Institute of Technology, Florida Atlantic University, Georgia Technical University, Marymount Manhattan College, Hunter College, and the University of Denver.

MADGE YOUNG

Recollections from a teenager's diary[6]
and a father's journal[7] alternate here.

MY PARENTS, MY BROTHER, AND I had been touring Italy and were now in Naples, from where we were to sail home to the United States for a vacation. We had been living in Europe for three and a half years: six months in London and, before that, three years in Antwerp.

> *My wife, Virginia, and my two children, Madge, 14, and David, 11 . . . were due for home leave in that year and had been planning our travel arrangements for some months. The era of great transatlantic passenger ships was still at its height and thus we could make a choice as to which of these magnificent floating palaces we would use for the ocean voyage. Although we had lived in Europe for several years,[8] we had never had the opportunity to visit Italy, so we decided to make a slight detour and spend a week in that beautiful country . . . then sail on one of the luxurious liners owned and operated by the Italian Line. . . .*
>
> *This fine ship was . . . 697 feet long, had a beam of 90 feet, and boasted 11 decks, with a gross tonnage of 29,100. . . . Built . . . in 1952 by the Ansaldo Shipyard at Sestri, Italy, she was modern in every respect, complying with all the requirements of the 1948 Convention for Safety of Life at Sea.*

Wednesday, July 18, 1956, we boarded the *Andrea Doria* at 4:00 p.m. bound for New York. I met many people on board, among them Peter Thieriot, Dorothy Bollinger, and Linda Morgan. They became my shipboard buddies, since we were all teenagers. The

**In October 1956, the Young family returned
to Europe on the S.S.** *America.*

days went by quickly. We swam in the pool and had lunch up on deck. In the evenings, after dinner, we went up to the ballroom, where we played either bingo or the mechanical horse races. After that came dancing.

We were due in New York on Thursday, July 26, at 6:00 a.m.

[On the last day of the voyage] Virginia and the children went to our cabins to start packing. . . . I stayed on deck for the better part of the afternoon, watching the fog, listening to the rhythmic bellow of the Doria's *foghorn, and straining my ears in an effort to pick up a similar sound from other ships in the vicinity. The fog was vertically stratified, meaning that our course alternated between areas of dense fog and patches of clear air, so that we were playing an in-again, out-again game. In my opinion, this is a far more dangerous type of fog than one of a homogeneous nature.*

At 10:30 Wednesday evening, we left the ballroom after the horse races and went down to our cabins. For the first time, we did not stay up for the dancing. David, my brother, who was eleven years old, was already asleep.

At approximately 11:20 p.m., I was standing in the bathroom brushing my teeth. Daddy was just getting into bed. Mummy was washing Daddy's nylon shirt. All of a sudden, there was a terrible crash. I fell into the bathtub. The crash felt like two hard bumps. There was also a horrible jarring noise with it.

I grabbed the part of my pajamas that was lacking, and rushed into the stateroom. David was still sleeping peacefully. Daddy had his life jacket, and Mummy had grabbed a coat because she had on a rather revealing nightgown.

I wasn't scared at all. I just thought they had stopped the engines suddenly. Before the crash came, I had been wondering whether we had slowed down for the terrible fog that we had been coming through all afternoon. I was bewildered and wondered why Daddy told me to get my life jacket. I thought, *What a big do Daddy is making out of this whole thing.* But I thought it would be fun to wear the life jackets with pajamas. Daddy was trying to rouse David.

"David, wake up," said Daddy.

"Why, what's the matter?" mumbled David.

"Grab your life jacket," was the reply.

David did as he was told but asked, "What's the matter? Is the ship sinking or something? This is a funny time to have a drill."

The four of us rushed out into the hall, which was full of smoke. Daddy thought there had been a boiler explosion or a fire, so we ran. The ship was already listing 20 degrees. Women in slips and nightgowns all opened their doors and asked what the matter was. Nobody was panicky. An officer passed us and said, "Be calm, be calm."

During the lifeboat drill, we had been told to go to our muster station in an emergency. Ours was in the main lounge, so we headed in that direction. Nobody talked or screamed or pushed. Everything was done orderly and in silence.

The main lounge was on the Promenade Deck. We were on the Upper Deck, one deck below. When we arrived on the Promenade

Deck, people were pouring out of the main lounge and the ball-room onto the glass-enclosed deck, so we followed them. After we had been sitting (or standing, whichever was easier, because the list had increased considerably) for half an hour, and David was just a little bit upset, having been quieted down with the idea that he might be going the rest of the way to New York on a destroyer or a helicopter, we began to see women and children from Tourist Class coming up from below—covered in oil. We assumed that the oil tanks had burst.

Meanwhile, I thought it was all great fun, and many of us started singing "It's a Long, Long Way to Tipperary." (It should have been "It's a Long, Long Way to New York.") People tore down curtains to use as blankets for the children whose clothes were all a sopping wet, oily mess.

Finally, up at the other end of the deck, I caught sight of Dorothy and wanted to go say hi to her, but Mummy said I had to stay with her.

> *Orders were being given from the bridge over the ship's intercom in Italian, and there was some criticism among the passengers that these should have been in English. I do not speak Italian, but I understand a few words and I knew that the orders were being given to the crew. . . . The instructions concerned launching of the lifeboats and other operations necessary for the rescue efforts.*

All of a sudden, the pea-soup fog began to lift. We could see a few other ships standing by. By this time, most of the lights on the ship had gone out, except for the emergency lights in the hallways. The windows of what had been the glass-enclosed Promenade had either been removed or broken.

Daddy suddenly saw moving out from behind the stern of the *Doria* some tremendous letters all lit up spelling out "ILE DE FRANCE." What a beautiful sight! This was at about 1:30 a.m. All this time, orders had been coming over the public address system in Italian, directed at the crew.

At about 2:00 a.m., word went around that women and children were to get into the lifeboats. We kissed Daddy good-bye, which felt funny. I didn't think there was any danger of anything happening. Good thing, too! All this time, I had been wondering whether this would be in the newspapers or not.

I was very much relieved after I had kissed my family and start-ed them on their slide across the deck, and could feel confident that they were now safely in a lifeboat. My children could not quite understand why I wanted to kiss them good-bye.

I discovered I had a handful of hair curlers that I had been holding since the confusion of getting out of the cabin. I gave them to Mummy, who put them in her purse, which she had grabbed at the last minute. She also put in her slippers, which she had had to remove, so as to be able to keep a foothold on the deck.

The ship was now listing heavily to starboard, and we were on the port or high side. The rope ladders went down to the lifeboats from the Boat Deck on the starboard side, so we had to slide down the slanting decks on polished floors because it was impossible to stand up. Then up the stairs to the Boat Deck, where, one by one, people were climbing over the side and down 50 feet into lifeboats. Our turn came. David went first, then Mummy and myself. At the top of the ladder, just before we climbed down, there was a pile of shoes on the deck that people had to take off because it was easier to go down barefoot.

The lifeboat was already full (about one hundred people), but as we looked up, people kept coming over the side. The ship was listing so badly by now that it felt as though it would roll over on top of us at any minute. Sitting next to me in the lifeboat was a woman about sixty-five years old, whose head was bleeding through a bandage, and her life jacket was soaked in blood. She had slipped on the polished floors, and her head had gone through a glass door. She looked so weak that I don't know how she had climbed down the rope ladder.

Meanwhile, people were still coming over the side of the *Doria*. Some people in the lifeboat started yelling, *"Basta! Basta!* Enough!

Enough!" Still people kept coming. Eventually, we started to row away while a woman was still on the ladder, leaving her hanging in midair. When she screamed, we went back and took her on. Two more people came down, and then we rowed away. It was then that we saw the big gash in the *Doria*'s hull. Only one thing could have done that: collision with another ship! But where *was* the other ship?

> *After all the women and children had been helped to slide down the deck, the men took their turn. When I got to the starboard side, I took up a position at the top of the rope ladder and helped other people to get down. There were quite a few elderly people who needed such help, but there were some not in that category who seemed to have a fear of the ladder, even though at that time the drop from the Promenade Deck to the lifeboat was not much more than 10 feet. One man, a cleric, was so frightened that he had gripped the deck rail with both hands and froze in that position, blocking the exit. It took two of us to break his grip and get him onto the ladder.[9]*

Fortunately, it was a warm and calm night. In about half an hour, we reached the *Ile de France*. The French liner looked deserted except for a couple of men up above who spoke nothing but French. Somebody in our boat asked for a volunteer who spoke French. I volunteered along with another man, and we asked where we were supposed to come aboard. Finally, someone opened a port about 20 feet above our heads. A rope ladder was lowered.

Everybody insisted that the injured lady sitting next to me go first, but she said that she was too weak to climb the ladder. They then lowered a sort of harness that she put on, and they pulled her up. Two or three more people went, then came my turn. They told me to take off my life jacket, because it would be in the way while I climbed up. I would have liked to keep mine for a souvenir. By the time I got to the top of the ladder and inside, there was no one in sight. I walked down a long hallway. It sure felt better to be walking on level decks again. After a few more people had arrived, a group of us got into an elevator and went up to the Promenade Deck. We were all given blankets and cushions to put on the deck chairs. We lay down and watched as more of our fellow passengers wandered in. We soon learned that we had crashed with the *Stockholm.*

Within a short time, most of the deck chairs were full. Shortly afterward, I saw Dorothy come down the deck. She said that her mother was in the hospital on the *Ile de France.* She told me that at the time of the crash, she was lying in bed while her mother was standing up. Her mother was knocked over, and something fell on top of her. They were in cabin number 50—right near the point of collision. Cabins 46 to 56 were the damaged ones. Dorothy held the wall of the cabin up while her mother crawled out from under the debris at the far end of the cabin. When they went to open the door, they found it was jammed, but they were able to kick out the vent at the bottom and crawl through.

Dorothy and I talked about what each of us had done in the past two hours. Then we got up and walked up and down the deck, stopping to say hello and ask how various people were. All along, we hoped to run into our shipboard buddy Linda. We saw Peter, who at the time of the crash had been in a different part of the ship from his parents. He was worried about them because he had not seen them yet. We all told him that his parents were probably on another ship, but actually nothing was ever heard of them again.

At about 5:00 a.m., dawn came. We had drifted now and were within about 500 yards of the *Doria.* We could see everything quite clearly: the three swimming pools, the slide on our swimming pool, and the sun deck where we had spent many sunny days. We usually had a buffet lunch up there in our bathing suits. It all looked deserted and miniature. We could see the water pouring over the deck from the swimming pools. They were being emptied the hard way. It made you feel sorry for the *Doria.*

A few minutes later, Daddy came walking down the deck toward us. Mummy ran to him; she had been worried about him ever since we left him. I just said, "Hi, Daddy!" as he walked up. Mummy couldn't understand why I hadn't been the least bit worried about him. Well, I didn't know there was any danger. Mummy asked him for any news about people we had befriended on the *Doria*. Daddy tried to keep David and me from hearing his response. But I heard the awful news anyway: Linda Morgan and her sister, Joan, had died in the crash! I figured it had to be a mistake, so I refused to believe what he said.

The *Ile de France* lifeboats were being pulled up, and the crew stepped out onto the Promenade Deck right in front of us. At 7:00 a.m., we left the scene and headed for New York. Daddy told us that he was very nearly the last passenger off the *Doria*. He had been checking the ship's list ever since it began. He said that from the time we got off to the time he got off, it didn't list much more.

He thought they would probably tow the *Doria* into New York. Thanks to the generosity of the *Ile de France* passengers, we all managed to acquire at least some outer clothing. Daddy got a khaki shirt and a pair of black trousers from one of the French waiters, and then he went below to have a shower. There he met an *Ile de France* passenger who had just gotten up—it was 11:00 a.m. This man didn't know a thing about what had been going on the previous night. When Daddy explained, he insisted that he take his bedroom slippers, as Daddy could not find any shoes to fit.

Meanwhile, I had been having a nap in my deck chair. The girl who had been jokingly saying that the *Doria* was going to sink was in her chair next to mine. As I awoke, she greeted me with "She sank! See, I told you she would."

I wouldn't believe it and went around questioning several people. It was confirmed that the *Doria* was now probably making its way slowly to the bottom of the Atlantic's gigantic bed. Even now, I still can't imagine our belongings down there slowly rotting and becoming part of the shifting sands.

At about 3:30 in the afternoon, we passed Ambrose Lightship and entered New York Harbor shortly afterward. Never was it such a beautiful sight. As we steamed in—as the first rescue ship to reach shore—every ship, from tugs to liners, greeted us. They all gave us three blasts, which we returned. The noise was deafening. We were really being welcomed. It was a wonderful feeling, especially since I had not been back to the States for three and a half years.

We stopped at quarantine where the customs and immigration officials came aboard, along with hundreds of newspaper reporters. We assembled in the lounge, where we were handed a notice that read, "Due to the unusual circumstances of your arrival, we are dispensing with all formal immigration proceedings. However, we ask you for your name and address." Next, we went to a desk where a man asked us a few questions and said, "Have you anything to declare?"

Mummy proudly displayed her bundle of three pairs of pajamas (she was using mine as underwear), and he duly put a chalk mark on it.

Finally, we docked and were allowed to disembark. The pushing and shoving were much worse than getting off the *Doria* itself. As we came down the stairs off the pier, the TV cameras were on us, and I really felt like a VIP.

At that point, my worldly possessions were one wristwatch, one locket, one pair of pajamas, and a handful of curlers. David at least had his dental braces. I was brushing my teeth at the time of the crash, so I had the braces out and left them along with some spares we'd had made especially for the trip.

We went by car to the hotel—and were we a sight as we walked into the lobby in bedroom slippers and borrowed clothes! Friends and relatives were there with clothes for us.

The next day, I went to the hospital to visit Linda, who for twenty-four hours had been presumed dead. The *Stockholm*'s bow had scooped her out of her bed, and she had been found unconscious in the wreckage. She said she remembered nothing until a seaman found her. She also said they found her autograph book on the deck of the *Stockholm*. Linda kept saying sadly, "When they find my dad and my sister . . ." Mummy and I didn't tell her what we had heard on the *Ile de France*.

The *Andrea Doria* was a beautiful ship, and I still can't believe it is lying at the bottom of the Atlantic, but I guess I'll have to accept it as a fact. The *Andrea Doria* is no more.

> *The* Andrea Doria *was a fine ship; she met all the standards for strength and seaworthiness of the ABS, as well as all the safety requirements of the 1948 International Safety of Life at Sea Convention, referred to as SOLAS.*
>
> *Many people have asked us if this experience did stop us from ever traveling by sea again and our answer has always been a categorical "no."* . . .
>
> *In fact, upon termination of our home leave in 1956, we returned to Europe by ship.*

MADGE YOUNG DESCRIBES HER LIFE and that of her family as "a very average life since 1956." While her parents remained in London until 1968, Madge returned to the United States for prep school at Concord Academy in Massachusetts. She graduated from Tufts University in 1965. After dedicating herself to a career in programming and systems engineering, she changed her focus to motherhood. She and her husband, Nick, have four children. Her brother, David, graduated from Purdue University. Upon his retirement from corporate finance, he and his wife, Rosemary, went into farming.

Robert Young, Madge's father, became vice president of the American Bureau of Shipping and in 1979 was named its chairman. He passed away in 1996. Virginia Young, at the age of ninety-three, is still living in New Hampshire.

LINDA MORGAN

I WAS FOURTEEN YEARS OLD when my parents decided to enroll me in an American boarding school. I had been living in Europe most of my life, most recently in Spain. My stepfather (from when I was age two) was working as a *New York Times* correspondent in Madrid. When he was granted a leave, my mother, my seven-year-old sister, Joan, and I boarded the *Andrea Doria* in Gibraltar and headed for the United States. I was really excited. I had only been to America once, to visit my father, Edward P. Morgan, a broadcaster for ABC Radio.[10]

The trip on the *Andrea Doria* was fun. It was like a small town: it had movies, a nursery, a

The autograph book, which was found lying on Linda Morgan's mattress on the bow of the *Stockholm,* is a reminder of her miracle.

newspaper store, a pool, and a beauty shop. Joan and I made friends with other children. One of my friends was Madge Young, with whom I had a lot in common; she was an American living in England and was also fourteen years old. Since we lived in Europe, we could speak to each other in different languages. So we palled around often, especially at the pool.

The last night of the trip, my family and I were invited to dine at the captain's table. I was really excited about meeting Captain Calamai and was planning on getting his signature for my Campfire Girls autograph book.[11] When we arrived at the dining room, the maitre d' explained that the captain would be spending the evening on the bridge because of the fog. We were disappointed and even surprised that he didn't send a subordinate.[12] During dinner, my stepdad—who never stopped being a correspondent— made a remark that was unsettling to my sister and me. He quipped, "Wouldn't it be fantastic if the *Andrea Doria* crashed in the fog? Just think of the exclusive we'd have for the *Times!*"

Realizing that we didn't share in his humor, Dad quickly asked us whether we wanted to go to bed early or go to the game room. We decided to stay up. Dad was really lucky that night: he won money at bingo and betting on the mechanical horse races. When he figured his luck was probably running out, we decided to return to our cabin for a good night's sleep. Joan and I were in room 52, adjoining my parents' cabin, number 54. I slipped on my yellow silk pajamas with Chinese writing on them. I tucked myself into my bed next to the porthole, and Joan tucked herself into hers, along the opposite wall. Mom and Dad came in and wished us good night, then admonished, "No talking. We have to get up early, so you must get a good night's sleep." My autograph book lay on the nightstand beside me, so I flipped through it briefly—I was still hoping to get Captain Calamai's signature in the morning.

I don't know how long I had been sleeping when I heard a really loud noise. The next thing I remember is waking up outside, under stars, with ocean all around me.[13] I was really confused! Had the roof of my cabin disappeared? I looked around me and saw that I was on my mattress, which was stripped of sheets and covers. My left arm was just dangling beside me—and I couldn't move it! I began crying out for my mother in Spanish, my mother tongue. *"Mamá, Mamá!"* All I heard were the sounds of a woman moaning and sobbing,[14] then silence. *"Mamá, dónde estás?"* I cried again.

Then, mysteriously, a sailor approached me speaking Spanish. He tried to console me, but he seemed rather bewildered himself. "My name is Barnabé Polanco García.[15] You are hurt. I will take you to the infirmary."

As he pulled me toward the door leading into the ship, a man asked me my name.

"Linda Morgan," I told him.

He looked at his passenger list and replied, "You're not on the list."

"Look under Linda Cianfarra, my stepfather's name."

Looking perplexed, he asked me, "Where did you come from?"

"Madrid."

It was written on his face that something was really wrong. His expression and the fact that he spoke with a different accent from what I was used to made me cry. Still trying to understand, I asked, "Isn't this the *Andrea Doria?"*

"No, this is the *Stockholm."*

Now I was completely bewildered. When I got to the infirmary, there was more chaos. Swedish sailors were coming in with oil, blood, and gray paint all over them.[16] Meanwhile, the doctors gave me some morphine, anticipating that I might have internal injuries.[17] Emotionally and physically, I was shutting down because of the shock and the morphine, only waking up in short episodes. When I did wake up, I asked the doctors to notify my parents that I was on the *Stockholm* and that I was OK. I told them this several times, always assuming that my family was fine. Since everyone was speaking in Swedish, I couldn't grasp what all the commotion was about. Fortunately, Mr. García, the sailor who had found me, came to visit me and brought me my autograph book.[18] It was comforting to speak in my native language.

When we arrived in New York, I was put on a gurney and transferred into an ambulance. The press was all around us asking questions. There was discussion among the authorities about where to take the injured, so that we would not all arrive at the same hospital. The ambulance sound was frightening, and I was scared of all that was happening—still not comprehending anything.

At the hospital, I was comforted by my nurse's announcement: "Your father is coming to see you." I assumed they meant my step-father, Camille. When my father walked into the room, I was disappointed. I didn't know him well, and I wanted to see the family who had tucked me into bed a few days earlier. But I hid my disappointment. My father told me he had met me at the pier when the *Stockholm* arrived, but being semiconscious at the time, I did not recall seeing him.

My father acted happy to see me, but my piteous state must have scared him a lot: one arm was in traction, and both legs and one arm were in a cast. My father explained that there had been an accident at sea and that several vessels had gone to the rescue. He told me that my mother had arrived on the *Ile de France* and was recovering in another hospital. He paused and then added that my dad and sister were probably on one of the other vessels.

I was in a private room with a private nurse whom I liked very much; nevertheless, I had no true privacy for about four days. There was pandemonium all around me as the press was in and out of my room constantly for interviews and photographs. My father, being a broadcaster, believed the media should have easy access to my story and me. I admit that I enjoyed the attention I was getting while I was awake, but the nights were disturbing. I would wake up from nightmares feeling frightened and disoriented. One day, I was surprised by a special visit from my friend Madge and her mother. I thought to myself, *Lucky for them—they didn't get hurt at all!* I asked them to sign my autograph book.

I spent more than two months in the hospital. It was then that I found out how courageous my father had been through this ordeal. First, he told me that I had been reported as missing in all the newspapers around the world, since no one had placed my name on the survivors list when I was found on the *Stockholm*. He explained to me how he had boarded the *Ile de France* in New York Harbor and found my mom in the sick bay. "She looked so awful that I hardly recognized her," he sadly told me. Then, reassuringly, he added, "But don't worry, she's doing very well now." My father even told me that a few minutes before his nightly broadcast, a journalist called and asked for my picture. When my father asked why, the journalist answered, "You know she's dead!"

In spite of this shock, my father got on the air and gave an ad-lib, live radio newscast to the whole United States. This is a part of what he said:

> Good evening. Here is the shape of the news. Tonight it is the shape of disaster. There are other headlines . . . but the main story—the story around the world tonight—is the story of the sinking of the Italian liner, the *Andrea Doria*. . . .
>
> This reporter has just returned from a trip down to New York Harbor to board the liner *Ile de France*, and has

come back after interviewing a number of the first survivors to reach New York City. . . . You get aboard and then
the story comes—told in little fragments. . . .

There was Camille Cianfarra, the Madrid correspondent of the *New York Times*, his wife, his stepchild, and
another child. Where were they? one asked.

One was told that Mrs. Cianfarra was badly hurt and
was in sick bay of the *Ile de France*. One finds her. She is
badly hurt but she is not on the critical list. She has multi-
ple fractures and cuts. She asks about her husband. It is
reported, but it is not confirmed, that Camille Cianfarra of
the *New York Times* is among the dead. The children may be
aboard another ship. It is not proved. It is not certain. . . .

She and her husband were in the stateroom—perhaps—which suffered the direct hit of the prow, the bow of
the *Stockholm*. She was trapped. Her husband was trapped
in another part of the room. She tried to call to him. She
tried to get to him and could not. And he did not answer.
She thought that the door to the children's stateroom was
open. She did not know. She was not sure. She did not hear
their cries. . . .

Slowly, little by little, torturously for the persons who
don't know—happily for the persons who do—the whole
pieces of the disaster will be fitted together. It is a horrible
thing—but an inspiring thing—to see the way people react
under duress. . . .

This is Edward P. Morgan, saying good night from New
York.[19]

This broadcast was printed in all the newspapers that covered
the tragedy. It amazed everyone that he could report this story
while thinking that I might be dead. He never revealed that he was
talking about his own family.

At some point, which I don't remember because of the pain
medication, I found out that my sister was dead. I felt awful! I
wished I had told her that I loved her. But instead, I recalled the

fights we had had, and I felt remorseful. Not long after that dreadful news, I found out that my stepdad had died also. It was almost too much for me to comprehend—I was very close to my stepdad, who had raised me since the age of two.

Finally, I received a phone call from my mother, who was also still hospitalized. We both cried, sharing in self-pity and grief for having lost half of our family. The entire event seemed surreal, no doubt because of the medication but also because of the concussion I had suffered in the collision. Nothing had any time frame— and I wished I could wake up from this nightmare that was only too real!

By the time I got out of the hospital in September, I knew why I had been dubbed the "Miracle Girl." The photograph of me shortly after being discovered by Mr. García was in all the media. I hated being reminded of how I had lain on top of that giant heap of twisted steel—and had been spared being dropped into the ocean within moments! Sometimes I tried to imagine how I might have been catapulted from my bed to that awful place. *Why are people fascinated by such a gruesome event?* I just wanted my former life back, with privacy and family intimacy.

Upon leaving the hospital, my father took me to my mother's apartment. Again, I was shocked. Her hand was still in a cast, and she had evidence of a deep cut across her face. I found out that her back had been injured and one leg fractured. We cried a lot. To make us feel better, my father bought tickets to *My Fair Lady* on Broadway. I was in a wheelchair, with one leg and my arm still in a cast. By then, I wasn't surprised by all the attention I was getting.

A few weeks later, both casts came off, and my father brought me to my new school. I was really anxious to fit in, especially since I was arriving one month after school had started, so I was furious when he insisted on arriving in a black Cadillac limousine. It was my first time in an American school, but fortunately I had gone to English-speaking schools in Europe. Everything was different from what I was used to in European schools, where girls didn't go out alone and we had never heard rock and roll (I loved Tchaikovsky). Because of the recent tragedy in my life and getting adjusted to a whole new life in America, my first semester was really hard.

But life went on as normally as possible. I tried not to dwell on the *Andrea Doria* tragedy and wanted everyone to forget my title of "Miracle Girl." Unfortunately, on the anniversary date, reporters came around for updates. I tried to avoid them and refused to read anything about the collision. One day, as I was reading the newspaper, I happened on a reprint of one of my father's broadcasts, the one from Friday, July 27, 1956:

> Good evening. This is the shape of the news. Tonight it is still the twisted lines of tragedy interspliced with the thread of happiness and even maybe miracle spiraling from the collision at sea between the Italian liner *Andrea Doria* and the Swedish liner *Stockholm*. . . .
>
> The known death toll is 10, although a late report indicates three more injured have died. That leaves, unofficially, 36 persons missing. . . .[20] The daughter of this reporter, Linda Morgan, accounted for one of the incidents of the tragedy which some would classify as a miracle. Sleeping in a stateroom on the starboard side of the *Andrea Doria* which bore the full brunt of the *Stockholm*'s crash, she was officially reported as killed. Instead, she was catapulted apparently onto the bow of the *Stockholm*, where a crewman found her alive in the wreckage. She was among the litter cases brought to New York today, not in critical condition. . . .
>
> Within the space of 24 hours this reporter has been pushed down the elevator shaft to the subbasement of despair and raised again to the heights of incredible joy, washed, one suspects, with slightly extravagant rivulets of some heavenly champagne.
>
> Last night, as far as the world at large was concerned, a girl, age 14 . . . nationality American, named Linda Morgan, was dead. She happens to be this reporter's daughter. She had been killed, by the incontrovertible evidence of an eyewitness. . . .[21] But Linda is NOT dead.

There is something sacred, I feel, about the mystery of life which, in the alchemy of the unknown, enables people as they face the supposed tragedy of death, their own or that of another. It makes other things seem so petty and unimportant. . . .

A wonderful human being from Philadelphia named C. Jared Ingersoll once told me in recounting how he kept right on going after the death of his wife and then his son. "I try to live fully," he said, "so that when my luck changes there will be little room for regret or recrimination over time lost or misspent." This reporter hopes tonight he has learned that lesson well enough to teach it with tenderness to a girl young enough to grow with it into a full blossom that will give joy to others for her very living. Perhaps, perhaps, she has learned it already herself.

This is Edward Morgan, saying good night from New York.[22]

Reading my father's words was very touching and important to me. My father and I had become closer already, but his words helped me remember how brave he had been to take care of my mother and me during our physical pain and our emotional turmoil. I also realized that he loved me as a father.

LINDA MORGAN'S LIFE CONFIRMS that she has fully lived her father's wishes. The young girl has blossomed into an accomplished woman. Besides being a wife and mother, Morgan has flourished in the art world. Her résumé displays her roles as museum curator, librarian, lecturer, and publisher. Moreover, she has transcended the painful "miracle" of the *Andrea Doria*. She recently spent two years living on and sailing a yacht with her husband, Phil. "My only stipulation was that we could see land at all times," she says gleefully.

CHAPTER 9

History's Greatest Sea Rescue

All the world's a stage, and all the men and women merely players:
they have their exits and their entrances; and one man in his time
plays many parts, his acts being seven ages.
—William Shakespeare

I: THE ACTION AND THE PLAYERS

THE FINAL ACT IN THE DRAMA of the *Andrea Doria* can be told no more vividly than through the protagonists' script. Thanks to the measures taken by the directors of the rescue and by those who indirectly assumed leadership, I am here to tell the story.

The curtain rises on the night of July 25, 1956, at 11:22 p.m. EDT, unveiling a setting 180 miles east of New York and 45 miles southwest of Nantucket Island. Two ocean liners, shrouded in fog, can faintly see the glow of each other's light from a distance of a mere two miles. As yet, they remain unidentified to each other—in spite of the fact that ten minutes earlier, they had interlocked as the Swedish ship impaled the Italian liner.

On this seemingly calm summer stage on the Atlantic, the action seems to be lulled, but that is deceiving. The *Andrea Doria* is still moving forward, propelled by the recent crash, and is headed for a second collision with the stationary *Stockholm*. The Swedish commander orders all full speed astern and a hard starboard turn, but the ship ignores his direction. Its 700-foot-long anchor chains, which had unraveled during the collision—dropping nineteen-year-old kitchen boy Evert Svensson to the sea floor—are impeding all movement.

When the *Andrea Doria* finally stops its forward motion, it is sitting one mile from its accomplice. The condition of the *Stockholm* is seemingly stable, but its steel-reinforced bow is mangled and compressed inward. On the other hand, the *Andrea Doria* is leaning heavily to starboard, its hull exposing a gigantic hole.

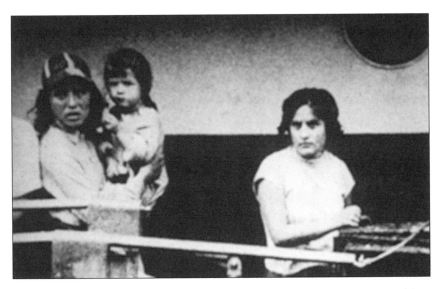

Liliana Dooner and her daughter Maria are on board the rescue ship
Cape Ann. **Liliana plunged into the ocean to save both Maria and**
Cecilia DiPaola (right), who had slipped off the rescue ropes.
(David A. Bright Collection, courtesy of Liliana Dooner)

Unwillingly, 1,134 passengers and 572 crew members on the
Andrea Doria are staging a drama of survival on oil-slicked decks
and corridors, aggravated by a 20-degree slant. Immediate action
is imperative.

Captain Piero Calamai seeks an assessment of damages from
his staff. The report is grim: three watertight compartments[1] have
been damaged, the bow area directly under the bridge wing is
ripped open up to the Passenger Deck (see the diagram, pages 228-
229), and there is flooding from every direction. Two adjacent compartments are also rapidly flooding. This dire information compels
the captain to begin directing a concise script in technical language, setting in motion the most dramatic and effective sea rescue
operation of our time. The U.S. Coast Guard monitoring station on
Long Island picks up the astounding announcement:[2]

11:22 p.m. S.S. *Andrea Doria*: SOS—SOS—DE-ICEH. [This is
the *Andrea Doria*.]

11:23 p.m. M.V. *Stockholm*: CQ—CQ— [Attention all stations.] Collided with another ship—Message follows.

These first SOS messages are being sent simultaneously from the *Andrea Doria* and the *Stockholm*. Morse code messages and alarm signals are received on ships along the Atlantic shoreline. Within 40 minutes, coast guardsmen on eleven cutters launch their roles as emissaries of survival.

Racing to the main scene of the calamity are the following vessels:

Campbell, a cutter, once a hunter of German U-boats in World War II.

Yakutat, a 311-foot watch-standing vessel.

Eagle, a sailing ship.

Hornbeam, a buoy tender with about thirty men on board.

Evergreen, a cutter assigned to seek out icebergs.

Owasco, a 255-foot cutter.

Legare, a small 125-foot cutter.

Cape Ann, a 400-foot freighter of the United Fruit Company.

Private William H. Thomas, a troop transport vessel.

Edward H. Allen, a training ship for the Navy.

Heyliger, also a Navy training ship.

Robert E. Hopkins, a 425-foot tanker.

U.S.N.S. *Jonah E. Kelly*.

Tamaroa, a Coast Guard cutter.

Coast Guard planes and helicopters are on standby in New York, laid up by the impeding fog.

The Coast Guard tells Captain Calamai that the nearest (and the smallest) rescue vessel is the *Cape Ann*; it is 30 minutes away. He will have to wait three hours for the largest rescue vessel, the *Ile de France*, to arrive.

The main focus now turns to the *Ile de France*, 29 minutes after the collision, when the luxury passenger liner receives a radio message from the *Stockholm*. Captain Raoul de Beaudéan reads the message handed to him by his chief radio operator: "Just collided with another ship—*Andrea Doria*."

The French liner is 44 miles from the disaster scene. It is headed for France with 1,767 persons on board. The fifty-three-year-old nobleman diverts his preoccupation over dense fog swallowing even his funnels from view to consider a rescue mission. Captain de Beaudéan discusses the implications of such an action with his boss, Guy de Berc, who happens to be a passenger: the unknown necessity of the rescue, added costs resulting from a delayed arrival time, insurance issues of overloading the vessel, the danger of intermingling in the blindness of fog with other ships, and concern for alarming his passengers. At 11:44 p.m., Captain de Beaudéan radios a response that will initiate a rescue plot of epic proportions: "Am going to assist—will arrive 05-45 GMT [1:45 a.m. Eastern time]. . . . Are you sinking—what assistance do you need? Captain."

The *Andrea Doria* responds: "Master *Ile de France*, need immediate assistance."

Wanting more information, the captain asks the *Doria* for clarification: Do they need a tug? Lifeboats? An escort? The response is silence. He radios the freighter *Cape Ann:* "What can I do to help—several boats ready."

The *Cape Ann* responds: "*Doria* says she immediately needs lifeboats for about 1,000 passengers and 500 crew."

Captain de Beaudéan immediately orders his crew: "Prepare to launch 11 lifeboats."

The firm command is given in spite of the gloomy setting reported by the Nantucket Lightship: "Weather foggy—visibility 15 yards."

MORE THAN ONE HOUR HAS PASSED, and the *Andrea Doria's* list is rapidly increasing. The danger of sinking appears imminent.

Second Deck Officer Junior Guido Badano places a call for help to the engine-room watch personnel: "You must stabilize the ship by any means possible."

The second watch personnel, with "fog crew" reinforcement, are on duty. They are in charge of operating a power station furnished with boilers, generators, diesel dynamos, turbo dynamos, air-conditioning, and compressors. The area extending nearly the length of the ship is flooding as water pours in not only from the starboard hull but also from above. The men are working furiously to stabilize the ship and keep the power functioning. As the diesel engine situation becomes critical (because of flooding), one engine after another is stopped as another is turned on. The boiler room and the main engine room begin flooding. The bilge pumps are turned on to suction the water. Violent short-circuiting begins to incapacitate the pumps one by one.

By 12:30 a.m., the main electric power station is abandoned, and the electric load is transferred to the auxiliary unit. This will feed the emergency cables while the two turbodiesel generators are feeding the machinery still working. The list is at 27 degrees and increasing rapidly. Because of the incline and the greasiness, walking becomes nearly impossible; grab lines are hooked from wall to wall to facilitate movement. By 1:00 a.m., the list is 30 degrees, and the machinery on the starboard side is partly submerged in water. The men continue working, but under greatly reduced lighting.

On the *Stockholm*, the situation is intense, but sinking is not an imminent threat. Since the reinforced steel plating of its bow had sliced through the *Doria*'s steel hull like a carving knife in butter, many passengers remain fast asleep. But one passenger, who is standing on the outer deck, is feeling the swipe of death's hand as she hears strains of "Arrivederci Roma" resounding from the pitch blackness of night. Another passenger is hoping that her anxiety is just an illusion from her traumatized past: having survived the *Titanic* as a young girl, she is now fretfully making her first ocean voyage since that tragedy.[3] Others gather in public meeting places, donning their life jackets.[4]

Captain Harry Gunnar Nordenson makes his way to the bridge to find Third Officer Ernst Carstens-Johannsen bewildered and shaking. Demanding information, he learns that there's been a collision with another ship. He immediately orders the shutting of the watertight doors, which Carstens has already done.

"Who is she?" Nordenson brusquely inquires, watching the wounded stranger disappear into the fog's anonymity.

"I don't know," Carstens responds, still perplexed and traumatized.

Captain Nordenson orders the start of the ballast pumps to address the leaning of the *Stockholm* by 3.5 feet, 4 degrees to starboard. Shortly thereafter, Chief Officer Gustav Herbert Kallback reports more troubling news: the first bulkhead is smashed, twelve cabins are crushed, and at least five crewmen are gravely injured.[5] Seawater is up to 11 feet in the cargo hold, being smashed from the violent impact. If the water rises to one more deck, it could potentially sink the ship.

Captain Harry Gunnar Nordenson and Third Officer Ernst Carstens-Johannsen of the *Stockholm*. (Associated Press)

Nordenson inquires about the ability of the second bulkhead to withstand the force of gushing seawater, which has now risen to 14 feet. Officer Kallback gives him reassuring news, at which point the captain asks the radio operator to inquire about the identity of the other ship.

Meanwhile, radio communication from the *Doria* to other vessels continues. The results are productive. The first rescue ship, *Cape Ann*, is located three miles from the *Andrea Doria* and the *Stockholm*: "Three miles from you now—have two lifeboats—no motorboats."

Although help is on the way, the rescuers wonder if they will arrive on time. One hour and 18 minutes after it is struck, the *Andrea Doria* makes an urgent appeal to its adversary, the *Stockholm*: "You are one mile from us. Please, if possible come immediately to pick up our passengers."

Captain Nordenson of the *Stockholm* radios the *Doria*: "Here badly damaged—whole bow crushed. No. 1 hold filled with water. Have to stay in our present position. If you can lower your boats, we can pick you up. You have to row to us."

One minute later, at 12:21 a.m., the *Andrea Doria* replies: "We are too bending. Impossible to put lifeboats at sea. You have to row to us. Please send lifeboats immediately."

An hour later, at 1:39 a.m., the tension of the drama lessens as the *Stockholm* replies: "Now launching lifeboats—headed for you."[6]

The *Andrea Doria* crew is struggling to lower its lifeboats since the incline is greater than ever predicted: 27 degrees.[7] Crewmen tug on the davits of the port-side lifeboats that are designed to release the rescue vessels at the muster stations, but it's to no avail. Other crewmen are trying to gather passengers for boarding from the Promenade Deck on the starboard side. The list makes this impossible as the lifeboats are hanging away from the ship—too far for passengers to enter them. Captain Calamai realizes that the starboard lifeboats must be launched without passengers. He orders his staff to move the passengers, huddled at their muster stations, to the lower decks (which are closer to the sea) and near the stern. His experience as a naval commander during World War II guides him to evacuate the ship in the fashion of disembarking troops: using rope ladders, Jacob's ladders, cables and hoses, and emergency scramble nets (like the ones used to cover the swimming pools). The heavy list and wet decks (from emptied swimming-pool water) are impeding this procedure.

Finally, the first two crafts begin rowing furiously away from the inclined liner. It is apparent from the color of the life vests, gray for the crew and staff and orange for passengers, that the lifeboats contain both. Survivors looking out at the sea are concerned about seeing so many gray vests in the rescue vessels and fear they are being abandoned.[8] The official announcement to report to muster stations, wearing life vests and staying calm, is concealed by screams and short-circuits in the wiring.

The setting is one of panic and chaos. As the corridors and then the decks of the *Andrea Doria* overflow with people, the human side of this drama unfolds. Some survivors will leave a legacy of remarkable inner strength, while others will resort to cowardice and selfish self-preservation.

ON THE STERN IN TOURIST CLASS, Liliana Dooner, unconcerned with her appearance (covered by only a purple half-slip pulled over her upper torso), is desperate to leave the listing ship with her two-year-old daughter, Maria. But there are no lifeboats in sight. Mustering all her courage, Liliana seeks help in tying ropes under the arms of her daughter. She proceeds to dangle the child over the railing in hopes of luring a lifeboat. Maria raises her arms and yells, "Mommy, Mommy!" Her tiny arms slip through the rope, and she falls into the ocean. As bystanders try to restrain her, Liliana jumps into the black ocean after her daughter. As she surfaces, her body swipes another—it's Maria! As they swim to the lifeboat, Liliana sees thirteen-year-old Cecilia DiPaola, dangling from a rope. She begs her to let go and land nearby. The mother then drags the two girls to the lifeboat, swimming under the inclined hull of the *Doria*.

Dangling precariously above them, Livia Benvenuti, a grandmother, is lowering herself to the lifeboat. But the lifeboat rows away, leaving her to hang along the side of the ship for nearly two hours. She fears that her arms will give out from pain and fatigue; she continues to pray as she watches a woman on a rope nearby fall into the water and disappear. A lifeboat arrives, and Livia finally lets herself drop to safety.

In First Class, thirteen-year-old Peter Thieriot is desperately searching for his parents. Running down the slanted stairs of the Promenade Deck, then the Upper Deck, and finally the Foyer Deck, he stops suddenly when he sees a man, wearing only boxer shorts, sloshing through oily water and debris. Peter continues to move toward the ballroom, where he witnesses another perplexing sight: Italian crewmen are inflating an emergency raft; they proceed to heave it into the ocean and then jump into the water after it. The young man cannot reach his parents' cabin. Unaware that the cabin has been destroyed and his parents have disappeared into the ocean, he returns to the Promenade Deck, where a priest asks him to help lead a rosary vigil.

The spotlights flashing across the moonlit waves sight a desperate couple struggling to float in the oily water. Journalist David Hollyer manages to pull himself into a *Stockholm* lifeboat, but his wife, Louise, keeps slipping back into the ocean; she is covered with oil and can't grip the rope. Finally, a Swedish sailor pulls her over the side of the lifeboat. He offers her an orange from his pocket. The young couple, who had earlier vowed to go down holding hands should the ship sink, are safe and together—eating an orange.

Moonlight and stars light the treacherous passage of Francesco De Girolamo and his family crossing the Tourist Class deck. The two parents and five children between the ages of three and eighteen are doing everything possible not to get separated. As they approach the starboard railing, crewmen begin lowering the mother and daughter. As the men of the family begin their descent on a rope, the lifeboat with mother and daughter departs. Francesco is holding three-year-old Gino, while a crewman is lowering Mario. Antonio and Nicola, ages seventeen and fourteen, are bravely descending on their own. They all reach the lifeboat and hold on to one another, agonizing over the whereabouts of the mother and daughter.

On a high deck near the bow, Elizabeth Hanson, struggling with her decision to throw her three children into the ocean, finally launches twelve-year-old Andy. Then she drops seven-year-old

Ardith, who flounders in the water until someone dives in to fetch her. Meanwhile, ten-year-old Donnie is protesting, refusing to jump. The six-months-pregnant mother musters all her strength to heave Donnie over the rail for his descent. Then she climbs over the railing, pulls her knees toward her chest to protect her belly, and drops into the water. As the Hansons sit numbly in the lifeboat, they witness a catastrophe. Tullio and Filomena Di Sandro, still on deck, are desperate to save their four-year-old daughter, Norma. Tullio spots a *Stockholm* lifeboat bobbing below. He grabs little Norma and yells down, "Catch the child!" But before waiting for a blanket to be extended for protection, the father launches her outward to avoid the side of the *Doria*. Mrs. Hanson covers her children's eyes, but their sensitive ears detect the loud thud of Norma's little body hitting the lifeboat gunnel.

BY ABOUT 2:00 A.M., Captain Calamai looks toward the stern from the starboard wing and sees that the shadowed figures, looking like toy soldiers descending the nets, are thinning out. The bloodcurdling screams are also subsiding. The master now directs his attention to another rescue, that of his ship:

> 2:30 a.m. *Andrea Doria*: We need tugboats immediately for assistance.

The radio transmissions accompanying the rescue operation are unrelenting. Finally, more than four hours since the initial SOS announcement, the uplifting climax to this tense plot of survival is being announced:

> 3:38 a.m. *Cape Ann*: Have about 120 survivors on board— more coming.
> 3:40 a.m. *Thomas*: Have about 50 survivors on board—more coming.
> 3:50 a.m. *Stockholm*: Urgent—nearest Coast Guard Station. Have three serious casualties aboard—need immediate attention—please send helicopter to our position—40-34N—69-46W.

4:25 a.m. *Stockholm*: Have approximately 425 survivors aboard.

4:57 a.m. *Ile de France* to *Stockholm*: All passengers rescued—proceeding New York full speed—*Thomas* standing by *Andrea Doria*. No more help needed.

5:04 a.m. *Cape Ann*: Have approximately 175 survivors aboard. . . . Proceeding to New York.

5:34 a.m. *Stockholm*: Please—any word of helicopter?

5:45 a.m. *Manaqui* to *Thomas*: Request release from scene.

5:45 a.m. *Thomas* to *Manaqui*: Release granted.

6:06 a.m. *Thomas*: CQ—CQ—plenty ships now—no further assistance needed.[9]

The radio chatter sending waves over the Atlantic Ocean is temporarily silent. The New York Coast Guard confirms it: "No more radio contact with *Andrea Doria*—believe off the air."

For now, it is presumed that the flooding of the emergency power area has dowsed all essential circuitry. Nevertheless, the rescue mission must proceed for all those saved and anxious to leave the scene. Only the *Doria* master and forty-five members of his crew remain aboard the dying liner, in spite of its 45-degree starboard list.

The long-awaited helicopters arrive at the *Stockholm* to pick up the gravely injured.

It is now nine hours and 45 minutes after the collision. The cutter *Hornbeam* transmits one of the last radio messages: "Picked up 45 crew members and master from *Andrea Doria*."

The *Thomas* adds its tally of survivors to the roster: "Have 156 survivors on board."

Then, as if the director of a bittersweet drama anxiously prompts the denouement of the key player, the calamitous ending is announced: "*Andrea Doria* sank in 225 feet of water—position 40-29.4N, 69-50.5W. . . . Area cleared."

The rescue operation concludes with excellent sea visibility: "Wind 3 mph, sea slight swell, moderate visibility—3 miles." Before the curtain closes on the last scene, spectators from all the

Above: Coast Guard sea rescue of an *Andrea Doria* crewman near Nantucket in 1955. The same procedure was used to rush little Norma Di Sandro to a Boston hospital. Below: Crew members of the U.S.N.S. *Jonah E. Kelley* witness the rescue efforts by the *Ile de France* (foreground) and the cargo ship *Cape Ann* (far background). (Courtesy of Nautical Research Group)

Above: The morning light reveals a desperate rescue: makeshift ropes and nets hang from the abandoned *Andrea Doria*. (David A. Bright Collection) Below: Captain Raoul de Beaudéan (center) of the *Ile de France* savors an overly optimistic report of the rescue along with two crew members. (Associated Press)

rescue vessels feel themselves summoned to the railings, as if enticed to become part of the grand finale. They bid a silent farewell to a beautiful liner and Italy's symbol of postwar maritime pride. Free-flowing tears make ripples on the smooth waters.

THE CULMINATION OF THIS CLASSIC-STYLE DRAMA takes place in New York, where, one by one, the rescue ships arrive.[10] The audience, consisting of families, friends, and the press, offer a heroes' welcome: tears of joy, handkerchiefs waving, and tight embraces. All are thankful that the rescue vessels were in the vicinity of the collision and that the *Doria* stayed afloat long enough for every survivor to escape.[11] Each rescue vessel proudly discloses its roster of survivors.

> *Ile de France:* 730
> *Stockholm:* 545
> *Cape Ann:* 168
> *William H. Thomas:* 156
> *Hornbeam:* 45 (mostly crew and Captain Calamai)
> Total: 1,644 survivors

II: THE CRITICS' REVIEWS

THOSE WHO STUDIED THE COMPLEX RESCUE give us their insights. Those who played a role in the drama share their lasting impressions.

The Professionals

FRANCESCO SCOTTO, RETIRED NAVAL ARCHITECT on the technical staff for the Italian Line, embarked on a full investigation of the *Andrea Doria-Stockholm* collision and rescue. His collaboration with ex-officials, deck and engine-room officers, and a maritime attorney became known as the Working Group.[12] Their work culminated in an impartial technical research document called *Collisione Andrea Doria-Stockholm—The Round Table.*[13] In response to the media, the public, and some passengers' accusations that the *Doria* crew was mostly ineffective, Scotto writes:

Above: Friends and relatives of *Andrea Doria* survivors wait anxiously at the *Ile de France* pier in New York. Below: The damaged *Stockholm* passes the Statue of Liberty as it carries 545 *Andrea Doria* survivors into New York Harbor. (David A. Bright Collection)

Calamai gave orders to the starboard squad to launch the eight starboard boats and organize the disembarkation of the passengers at the stern, slowly moving the passengers aft from the various muster points.

This operation was entrusted to the remainder of the crew who were not engaged in other activities. While the Deck seamen were busy with the lifeboats, while Engine Room staff battled against the water . . . the passengers remained in the hands of our Cabin and Catering Service crew who, in effect, accounted for most of the 572 crew.

Staff Captain Magagnini and Captain Calamai, convinced that the embarkation of the passengers into the lifeboats would take a long time and be more difficult than normal, gave the order to strengthen each boat's crew with approximately five people, mainly from the unused crews of the port lifeboats. The number of seamen who . . . found their way into the lifeboats was higher than that originally provided for, though not always with the desire to escape, but also voluntarily or to reach an objective of numbers.

In addition, some passengers, seeing dozens of crew members get into the lifeboats, thought they were being abandoned and decided to take to the boats themselves. Moreover, some young "kitchen hands". . . threw themselves into the sea to be picked up by the lifeboats.

The officer in charge of lifeboats in the sea ordered that they gather at the stern to regroup (where the disembarkation was taking place). He found that the boats already contained a high proportion of crew members and a certain number of passengers. So, using sound logic, he decided to "lighten" the boats, making full use of the waiting time, while the passengers descended very slowly into the boats. Thus, he sent two full boatloads of seamen (with gray life jackets), a few passengers (with orange life jackets) to the *Stockholm.* . . . As such, when the boats came alongside the *Stockholm* and the Swedish crew opened the side ports to take the survivors on board, they saw many people in gray life jackets and only a few in orange life jackets. Unfortunately, they began talking about betrayal of the renowned sea tradition of "women and children first" into the lifeboats. In fact, this was not true. . . .

Medical Service Personnel . . . led by Dr. Bruno Tortori-Donati worked with the elderly, the disabled, those in the ship's hospital, those who took sick that night, plus passengers trapped among the wreckage of their cabins crushed by the bow of the *Stockholm*. . . . The stewards and stewardesses and all the other Hotel Service staff . . . accompanied all the passengers to the lifeboats, sometimes physically transporting them. . . . Monsignor Natta (the chaplain) . . . crawled from group to group administering the Eucharist and Last Rites.

Over and beyond all the controversy regarding the subject, we can confirm that most of the Italian crew behaved in a first class manner during the rescue.

Third Officer Eugenio Giannini recalls how he played a critical role in the rescue of passengers:

When Second Officer Guido Badano, in charge of the port-side lifeboats, informed the captain that these were incapacitated, I received my instructions from Calamai: "Giannini, go get the passengers on the port side and bring them to the lifeboats on the starboard side. Go by way of the stern."

Since I was in charge of the Cabin Class muster station, I went to round up those passengers who were gathered on the Promenade Deck. I had to convince them, explaining in Italian and English, that there were truly lifeboats on the starboard side. We formed a line by holding hands while maintaining our balance. It was extremely difficult to move. Then I heard voices from the deck above us, and shouted for them to come down and join us.

When we all reached the starboard side of the stern, I had a brilliant idea that I got from watching World War II movies: I explained to other crew members that we needed to remove the net covering the swimming pool and hang it over the side of the ship; this is how marines were lowered into boats. When we realized some older and injured passengers couldn't manage the nets, we procured fire hoses to tie around their waists so we could lower them. We rounded up life preservers and ropes; perhaps 100 passengers per hour were descending using these combined tactics. All the staff members were helping, even the ship's baby-sitter.

I know that some passengers felt abandoned at their muster stations. To this I respond: have them examine their conscience. They are alive because we were able to rescue every passenger that was not killed on impact. We did everything possible to rescue our people. And I still believe the captain was wise in not giving an "abandon ship." Panic was minimal considering we didn't have enough lifeboats. Besides, look what happened during the *Titanic*—there was pandemonium.

It was daybreak when the remaining staff made their way to the bridge to board the last lifeboat. The captain offered Dr. Peterson assistance in removing the body of his wife, but Peterson refused, saying: "It's too dangerous. My wife is gone. I don't want anyone else to die."

Looking back, I don't consider what the staff did as heroic—we simply did our duty. I also don't believe the reports of cowardice; they were distorted. Besides, one can't expect every staff member out of 532 to all display optimal courage.[14]

Second Officer Guido Badano was in a position to explain and critique the organization carried out during the rescue:

Chief Engineer Giovanni Cordera on the S.S. *Rafaello* in 1970. (Courtesy of Giovanni Cordera)

The evacuation (into lifeboats) continued slowly and with difficulty . . . children, the elderly and invalid were being carried in the arms of crew members . . . there was much fear but little panic. From the starboard bridge wing one could see directly the disembarkation on the lifeboat deck managed by First Officer Kirn and Third Officer Donato, while on the stern Staff Officer Magagnini and Third Officer Giannini were directing the operation. Second Officer Franchini was sent to direct lifeboat operations to the ocean. . . .

The captain continued to give orders calmly and precisely: put the rafts into the sea, throw out life rings, find and set up nets to descend passengers onto lifeboats, require . . . almost too strictly the order of children, women, elderly, etc., orders that in some cases . . . divided families who arrived to New York on different ships. . . .

Our lifeboats . . . made at least 16 trips . . . carrying nearly 70 percent of the people that were on board. . . .

Here is the response that was never shared with the public and that explains the actions of our crew during the rescue, which resulted . . . in a success, if one considers that all passengers on board were saved and those lost were all located in cabins destroyed . . . by the crash. . . . The captain continued to give various orders from the bridge . . . one was to go around the ship by lifeboat to pick up any possible survivors in the water.

At about 4:00 a.m., Officers Kirn, Magagnini, Giannini, Donato, etc., reunited on the bridge. Magagnini assured the captain that all the passengers had disembarked. . . .

The engine room had already been evacuated (at 2 a.m.). . . . Only the emergency power was still working. Four hours after the collision, the ship's evacuation was nearly complete. . . .

At 4:30 a.m. (five and a half hours after the collision) moving on board was nearly impossible because of the incline (about 40 degrees).

Staff Captain Magagnini advised the captain that everyone remaining should board a lifeboat . . . the captain refused to abandon his ship. The incline was making it impossible to even remain sitting on the deck. Finally, the captain conceded.[15]

Second Engineer Giovanni Cordera sheds light on the performance of the engine-room personnel—called "invisible" by some:

The entire platform was crowded with day crew and those who were off duty. . . . Orders were given by Chief Engineers Chiappori and Pazzaglia. Some received the task of pumping dry the bilges in the diesel-dynamo space where flooding was in course . . . then the SOS emergency pump . . . was set in motion. This was met with difficulty as the heavy list did not allow the pump to work and the engine was consequently unable to take the load; it was necessary to abundantly feed the emergency engine carter, taking pails of oil from the engine room, carrying them . . . along the service passageway, leaning one's back against the bulkhead. In this way the engine started and worked until the end.

All these operations were carried out in precarious conditions due to high heat (114 degrees) . . . and the vessel's list. . . . Meanwhile new, vast leakages occurred. . . . The SOS pump kept working and the watertight doors pump also. . . . When nothing more could be done both due to lack of electric energy and . . . due to the list, it was decided to abandon these spaces and to transfer some of us to . . . the Boat Deck near the bridge wing. Only then did these personnel . . . go up on deck to embark on the last lifeboat when only a few were still on board the vessel.[16]

The Passengers

PASSENGERS ON BOTH THE *ANDREA DORIA* and the *Ile de France* became eyewitnesses to this heroic rescue on the Atlantic Ocean. Most of their impressions were positive;[17] some were less than favorable.

A First Class passenger on the *Doria*, Robert T. Young, a marine engineer and naval architect with the American Bureau of Shipping,[18] wrote in *USA Today*:

> Captain Calamai has been criticized for not sounding the general alarm. Whether to do so or not was a difficult decision for him to make. I personally believe he made the right one, because, had he sounded it, an uncontrollable panic could have ensued.
>
> Accusations have been leveled at some members of the crew for abandoning the ship and leaving the passengers to their fate. Although I was not an eyewitness to this, I must accept the evidence of those who were. I did, however, see quite a few crew members giving their life jackets to passengers who had been unable to get their own. It must be kept in mind that passengers' life jackets were colored a bright orange, whereas those of the crew were a dark gray. Also, it must be realized that it took eight

crewmen and a helmsman to man one lifeboat. . . . A lifeboat loaded with people wearing gray life jackets did not necessarily mean that they were all crew members. In the area where my family and I were located, the crew members remained at their post and carried out their duties as far as it was possible to do so.[19]

Psychologists Paul Friedman and Louis Linn, who interviewed survivors while traveling on the *Ile de France*, concur with Young:

The facts are that the crew of the *Andrea Doria*, with the expected exception, acted with generosity and even heroism. . . .

The most frequently voiced charges were: that no announcement had been made about the nature and gravity of the accident, and that no concerted rescue effort was made. These have been answered by the fact that the first impact of the collision caused a power failure on the *Andrea Doria*, putting the public address system out of commission. Moreover, the ship rapidly developed a severe list which, coupled with oil slicks on the decks, made it imperative for each person to save himself from sliding into the sea. . . . As a matter of fact, Italian crew members did make their way about on the sharply inclined decks, urging passengers to remain calm, and there was indeed very little panic.[20]

Third Class *Doria* passenger Luciano Grillo cites examples of incompetence:

Our lifeboat's engine wouldn't start and the crew didn't know what to do. With my experience as a boat machinist I told them how to create a spark. Then they couldn't find the handle for the motor. I blame the maritime industry for not checking the condition of the lifeboats regularly. When we finally boarded the *Stockholm*, I saw our bartenders there. I heard some Swedes say, "You cowards, go back and pick up your survivors."

Cabin Class passenger Meryl Stoller felt abandoned by the *Doria* crew:

No one knew we were waiting to be rescued.[21] During the hours we were waiting for help, we didn't hear any directions, so we just kept waiting. We didn't see any crewmen either. . . . There were no life jackets left inside the benches and no sand to spread on the slippery deck. . . . Why weren't there enough operable lifeboats on one side of the ship to carry all of us?. . . I thought for sure we were going to die when we discovered that our lifeboat had no working rudder. We just floated aimlessly.

Chris Guitaut, a passenger on the *Ile de France,* offers:

We saw a few cases of hysteria; mostly women who had been separated from their children and were afraid they had not been saved. . . . Another woman suddenly started to sing from *Aida* so loudly you could hear her from one end of the deck to the other. A doctor promptly gave her a sedative and took her to the infirmary.

It was now 4:00 a.m. and most of the passengers of the *Ile de France* were up and trying to give some assistance. Everyone was marvelous. An appeal for shoes and clothing was soon sent out, and almost every passenger donated some of his clothing or shoes to the survivors, and took up a collection as well.

First Class *Andrea Doria* passenger Elizabeth Quinn gives her impressions in a letter written on September 6, 1956:

Captain Calamai refrained from broadcasting a warning for fear of panic. Perhaps he was wise. . . . "Abandon Ship" is an awesome and solemn thing to hear.

I'm writing this largely in praise of the unflinching courage displayed in that life-saving drama of the *Andrea Doria.* [The crew] all seemed to be yelling at once at the top of their voices instructions to one another and with complete understanding.

When the final chapter is written, I'm sure it will be recorded that July 25 and 26 will mark the finest, most heroic life-saving epic of peacetime history.

WORDS, AS IN THE QUOTES ABOVE, empower us to grasp the human elements of this event, but numbers concisely give us the bottom line. The mathematical data of this monumental rescue, especially when compared with other maritime rescues, are notable:

The *Andrea Doria-Stockholm* collision resulted in the loss of 46 *Doria* passengers: 43 during the impact and 3 more soon thereafter (from a total of 1,706), Survival rate: 97.3 percent.

The *Titanic*, built to withstand any accident, sustained damage from hitting an iceberg, resulting in 1,522 deaths out of 2,033. Survival rate: 25 percent.

The *Empress of Ireland*, known as the "Canadian *Titanic*," sank fourteen minutes after being rammed by a Norwegian coal carrier in 1914. Out of nearly 2,000 passengers, only 465 survived. Survival rate: 23 percent.

The *Lusitania*, considered the largest and fastest ship in the world in its era (1915), lost 1,201. Survival rate: 39 percent.

The *Vestris* was shipwrecked in 1928 with 325 people on board. Survival rate: 62 percent.

The *Admiral Nakimov* sank in seven minutes on the Black Sea in 1987. Survival rate: 68 percent.[22]

Fortunately, there has been no other collision between two passenger or cruise liners since the *Andrea Doria-Stockholm* disaster. Moreover, stricter safety measures and advanced technology now provide for safer rescue operations. The improvements made for locating a collision site and abandoning a ship are as follows:

The Global Maritime Distress and Safety System (GMDSS) and the Emergency Position Indicating Rapid Beacons (EPIRBS) assist in locating a shipwreck quickly.

Every liner has enough lifeboats on either side of the vessel to accommodate all passengers and crew.

If passengers cannot reach the lifeboats, inflatable escape slides provide for a swift descent into the life crafts already in the water.

Lifeboats are motor propelled and have enough fuel for 24 hours, traveling at a speed of 6 knots.

All crew personnel are better trained for emergency action situations.

Passenger safety, especially with the advent of the immense popularity of cruise ships, is continuously being studied. The Marine Safety Commission emphasizes regulations to prevent casualties at sea. Nevertheless, should an accident occur, it is recommended that ships provide a safe haven for passengers as the ship proceeds to port. This is based on the time-honored principle that a ship is its own best lifeboat.

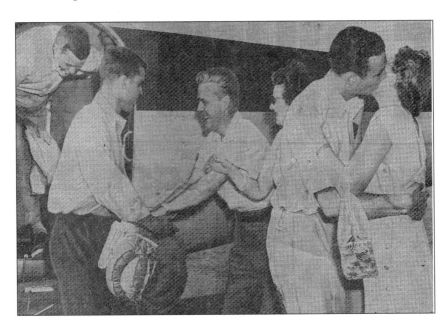

Three Grosse Pointe, Michigan, teens are met by their parents at Detroit's City Airport: Lawrence Fitzpatrick (stepping out of the airplane), Peter McKee (center), and Robert MacDonald, embracing his mother. The three *Doria* survivors were unhurt.

An *Andrea Doria* Photo Gallery

First Class passengers relax in the enclosed Promenade Deck's Winter
Garden area, showing Gambone wall panels outside the ballroom.
(David A. Bright Collection)

Overleaf: The First Class menu.
Menus were printed in Italian and English.

Tv. " ANDREA DORIA „
Capt. PIERO CALAMAI

Pranzo di Gala

Coppa d'Arancio al Maraschino   Succo di pomodoro o di vongole

Caviale Beluga Malossol   Tostini Melba
Prosciutto affumicato di Vestfalia   Burro   Sardine di Nantes all'olio
Perle Svizzere   Giuliana di pollo al Pimento rosso
Olive assortite . Funghetti all'olio   Salame di Milano

Consumato freddo Madrilena
Consumato chiaro in tazza   Crema di vegetali
Vermicellini in brodo   Vellutina di Pollo Orleans

Langostina fredda in Bellavista, salsa maionese
Filetti di Sogliole alla Bella Mugnaia

Ventivola alla Parigina

PUNCH ALLA ROMANA

Lombata di bue arrosto Hôtellière
Cavoli nani   Patate fritte alla Francese.   Pomodori gratinati

Cavolfiore alla Polacca

Cappone del Padovano allo spiedo
Insalata Florida, Club dressing

TAVOLA FREDDA

Cosciotto d'agnello alla menta   Zampone di Modena
Tacchino arrosto ai Mirtilli   Galantina di pollo ai tartufi
Lingua affumicata   Pasticcio di cacciagione
Terrina d'anitra Rouenese   Prosciutto di Boemia al rafano
Maialetto all'Alsaziana   Costata di bue Orticoltore

Torta Mille foglie al lattemiele
Soufflé Arlecchino   Coppa ghiacciata Aurora
Cassata Siciliana   Desiderio di Re
Cestini di frivolezze

Frutta fresca e secca

Moka

GRAN SPUMANTE ITALIANO

Gala Dinner

Orange cup with Maraschino   Tomato or clams juice

Beluga Malossol Caviar   Melba toast
Westphalian smoked ham   Butter   Sardines of Nantes in oil
Switzerland cheese pearls   Julienne of chicken with Pimento
Assorted olives   Mushrooms in oil   Milan salami

Cold consommé Madrilene
Clear consommé in cup   Cream vegetable soup
Consommé Vermicellini   Chicken cream soup, Orleans

Cold shrimps, Russian salad, mayonnaise sauce
Fillets of Sole à la Belle Meunière

Vol - au - vent à la Parisienne

ROMAN PUNCH

Roasted sirloin of beef, Hôtellière
Buttered Bruxelles sprouts   French fried potatoes   Gratinated tomatoes

Cauliflowers à la Polonaise

Padua capon on the skewer
Florida salad, Club dressing

COLD BUFFET

Roast lamb, mint sauce   Zampone of Modena
Roast turkey, Cranberry sauce   Chicken galantine
Smoked ox-tongue   Roebuck patty
Tureen of duckling Rouennaise   Prague ham with horseradish
Suckling-pig Alsacienne   Prime ribs of beef Gardener

Feuillantines tart with cream
Harlequin soufflé   Ice cream cup Aurora
Sicilian cassata   Desir du Roy
Frivolities pastry baskets

Fresh and assorted dried fruit

Moka

ITALIAN SPARKLING WINE

Above: The elegant First (Prima) Class dining room with a beautiful
wood mosaic on the back wall, incorporating pieces from every kind of
Italian wood. Below: The most elegant cabin on the *Andrea Doria* was
the First Class premium luxury cabin. The Zodiac Room was designed
by Piero Fornasetti, depicting a mythological theme in blue and white.
A painting of the Madonna and Child surrounded by a wreath of flow-
ers is displayed in a modern white frame that looked like a 1950s television set. (David A. Bright Collection)

PART TWO

Stories of the Ship

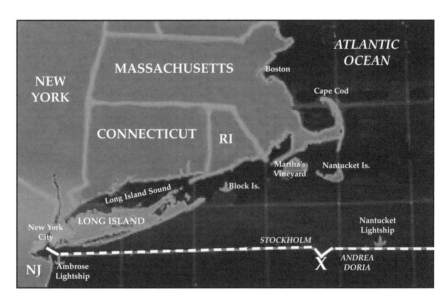

Where it happened.

CHAPTER 10
Anatomy of a Collision

In more than 90 percent of the groundings and 75 percent of the collisions . . . human error is present.
—Captain Robert Meurn

H AVING EXPERIENCED the *Andrea Doria-Stockholm* collision firsthand has had an impact on me beyond the trauma that my family and I endured. One result of this impact has been an insatiable curiosity to find a scientific explanation for what really happened on that foggy night near Nantucket. To embark on this mission, I first read several books on the subject written by journalists. It seemed they had reconstructed the collision mostly from media coverage, personal accounts, or information provided by the Italian and Swedish American Lines. Although they maintained that their accounts were factual, their conclusions seemed biased and bent on casting the Italians in a negative light—without providing hard evidence and without naming their sources. In my pursuit of real, hard facts, I consulted maritime scientists, seafaring people who could give me data based on experience, logic, and evidence that went beyond issues of pride, legalities, and sensationalism. I wanted an updated version of the accident, explained with the use of modern technology, unavailable a few decades ago.

This chapter presents conclusions derived from taking the content of the pretrial depositions and re-creating each scenario with today's technology. The reader will learn the other side of the *Andrea Doria* "mystery," a side that has been surprisingly ignored. Because the conclusions will be reported in the voices of the nautical experts, it is hoped that the "mystery" will finally be called the "explanation."

THE STORY OF THE *Andrea Doria-Stockholm* collision begins some twelve hours before the fatal tragedy, when, at 11:30 on the morning of July 25, 1956, Captain Harry Gunnar Nordenson, commanding officer of the motorship *Stockholm,* moved his liner away from its Swedish American berth in New York and headed east for the open sea. He ordered the use of a lane 20 miles north of the one assigned to his vessel, which placed the *Stockholm* in the path of westbound traffic. Nordenson had used this route dozens of times before in order to save two hours of steaming time.[1] The *Stockholm* was traveling at 18 knots[2] (full speed) as it headed for Gothenburg, Sweden. In normal anticipation of ice that drifted in Scandinavian seas, it was equipped with a steel-reinforced bow able to slice its way through any such encounters.

At the same time, from a pier a half-mile downstream, Captain Raoul de Beaudéan commanded his luxury liner, the *Ile de France,* to leave its berth. The French vessel moved ahead of the Swedish motorship as they worked their way past the Ambrose Lightship and headed for the Nantucket Lightship, 200 miles to the east.[3] By 3:00 p.m., the French liner, traveling at 22.5 knots, had pulled far ahead of the Swedish liner and was rapidly disappearing from view. Its destination was Le Havre, France. Given their distance apart, Captain de Beaudéan could not have fathomed that his journey would be entwined with that of the *Stockholm* before day's end.

During the same afternoon and inbound to New York, the Italian luxury liner *Andrea Doria* was on its eighth day of a nine-day journey, which had commenced in Genova, Italy.[4] On the morning of July 26, Captain Piero Calamai was due to arrive at Pier 84 in New York, as he had done fifty times previously. In accordance with the North Atlantic Treaty, the *Doria* was in a prescribed lane in its approach to New York Harbor.[5] What happened en route to these ships' destinations can be explained only in terms of a combination of bad decisions and poor luck. A collision takes place, on the average, every 86 million nautical miles logged on ocean travel—making such an occurrence highly unlikely. It is fascinating to decipher the unfortunate circumstances that led up to the calamity that took place at 11:11 p.m. on July 25, 1956. In pretrial depositions before the Federal Court of New York, the accounts given by the two ships' officers are in direct opposition to each other. First, here is the *Andrea Doria* version.

On bridge duty on the *Andrea Doria* were Captain Piero Calamai, Second Officer Curzio Franchini, Third Officer Eugenio Giannini,[6] a wheelsman, and a lookout. Another lookout was stationed
on the bow. Midway through the day of July 25, the senior watch
officer of the Italian liner notified his commanding officer that fog
was closing in rapidly around the ship. Captain Calamai went to
the bridge and immediately ordered the ship's engines to be
placed under "standby" conditions,[7] thus reducing its speed from
23.00 to 21.85 knots. In compliance with navigation law, the automatic timer was set to sound the fog whistle every two minutes.[8]
At 10:10 p.m., the ship's radar indicated that the *Andrea Doria* was
passing the Nantucket Lightship three-quarters of a mile to the
south. The course was set for a compass heading of 269 degrees,
the normal heading for the 200-mile run to the Nantucket Lightship. Because of dense fog, the *Doria* officers could not visually see
the Nantucket Lightship as they passed it, but they had it positioned on their radar. As they passed one mile to the south of the
lightship, the officers heard its distinctive coded foghorn signals.
Captain Calamai and Second Officer Franchini, the senior officer of
the deck, monitored the radar screen. Third Officer Giannini, the
junior watch officer, moved back and forth from the outer bridge
wing to monitor the radar as well.

At 10:45 p.m., twenty-six minutes before the collision, a single
target appeared on the *Andrea Doria*'s radar screen. It was the
Stockholm. The target was at a distance of 17 miles, bearing 4
degrees over the *Andrea Doria*'s right (starboard) bow. As the *Stockholm* approached, the angle of bearing continued to increase slowly. The radar plotting of the target indicated a continual increase of
the bearing angle and that the ships were on parallel courses,
headed in opposite directions.[9] At this time, Captain Calamai
determined that there would be a starboard-to-starboard (right-to-
right) meeting situation, at a distance of about three-quarters of a
mile. Third Officer Giannini described the bridge situation at a
conference of the Round Table.[10] His statements concur with those
of the other officers on the bridge:

> The target observed is a ship proceeding at the speed of 18 knots,

on a course presumably parallel and opposite to our own; it ought to pass at about one mile abeam of our starboard. Franchini continuously follows the echo of the ship under observation, and the latest situations are reported to the Master, who, every so often, personally verifies the situation. There is concentration on the *Doria*'s bridge, without tension. At 11:05 p.m., so as not to reduce the distance of the passing abeam,[11] now imminent, Master Calamai orders to steer 4 degrees to port, at 265 degrees. At the time of this turn, the *Stockholm* was at about 3.5 miles distant.

It's now 11:08 p.m. (three minutes before the collision). Due to fog, there is no visual sighting (of the target). But I'm surprised at not hearing a foghorn yet. I ask my Master, "Why don't we hear her? Why doesn't she whistle?"

At 11:09 p.m. (two minutes before the collision), the *Andrea Doria* plots the echo at little more than one mile away, approximately 30 degrees to starboard.

Now the course of the other ship seems such as to reduce passage abeam to 0.9 mile, but 1668 meters is still a considerable and reassuring distance. Now we can sight the glow of the approaching vessel, and a few seconds later, we are able to clearly view the two white range lights, the lower one well to the right of the upper one.[12] Master Calamai has also sighted them. I am watching the vessel, and in my binoculars, with astonishment, I see that she is rapidly hauling to starboard!

"She's bearing down on us," I shout. "She's coming right at us!" But the Master had already appraised the situation: too late to swing to starboard. Collision was by now inevitable.

We try to escape: "Hard to port," I hear the Master command. We signal our turn with the ship's whistles. Franchini asks, "Captain, what about the engines?"

"No. Let them be! We need all the speed we've got now!" the Master replies.

The *Stockholm* is, by now, coming full at us, right into us, without a signal. The *Andrea Doria* is beginning to respond to the helm, but it's too late![13] Little more than a minute had passed, yet it seemed an eternity. The *Stockholm* rammed us right under the bridge, crushing more than 20 meters of the reinforced bow into our hull. She slid along the full length of our starboard side.

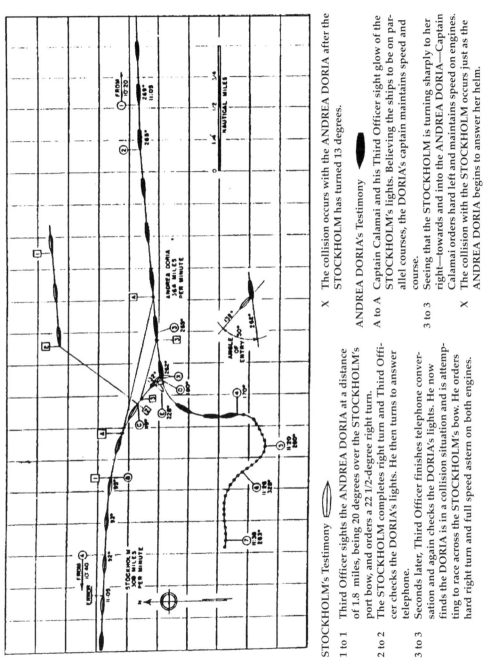

STOCKHOLM's Testimony

1 to 1   Third Officer sights the ANDREA DORIA at a distance of 1.8 miles, being 20 degrees over the STOCKHOLM's port bow, and orders a 22 1/2-degree right turn.

2 to 2   The STOCKHOLM completes right turn and Third Officer checks the DORIA's lights. He then turns to answer telephone.

3 to 3   Seconds later, Third Officer finishes telephone conversation and again checks the DORIA's lights. He now finds the DORIA is in a collision situation and is attempting to race across the STOCKHOLM's bow. He orders hard right turn and full speed astern on both engines.

X   The collision occurs with the ANDREA DORIA after the STOCKHOLM has turned 13 degrees.

ANDREA DORIA's Testimony

A to A   Captain Calamai and his Third Officer sight glow of the STOCKHOLM's lights. Believing the ships to be on parallel courses, the DORIA's captain maintains speed and course.

3 to 3   Seeing that the STOCKHOLM is turning sharply to her right—towards and into the ANDREA DORIA—Captain Calamai orders hard left and maintains speed on engines.

X   The collision with the STOCKHOLM occurs just as the ANDREA DORIA begins to answer her helm.

Figure 1. (Courtesy of John Carrothers)

The Italian liner was penetrated directly under the starboard bridge where Captain Calamai and Officer Giannini were standing.

We turn now to the *Stockholm* version of events, paraphrased here from Third Officer Ernst Carstens-Johannsen's testimony under oath at the official inquiry in New York.

At 8:30 p.m., Third Officer Carstens[14] relieved Second Officer Lars Enestrom from his watch. The course was 90 degrees, but there was uncertainty about the vessel's position, as the currents were setting the vessel off course. Enestrom estimated his vessel to be 1.5 miles farther north than expected. Captain Nordenson appeared on the bridge at about 9:00 p.m. and summoned Carstens to the chart room to determine their position. Using radio direction fix (RDF), the officer took two bearings.[15] At 9:20, the captain entered the chart room, looked at the chart, and asked Carstens to order helmsman Peder Larsen to steer at 87 degrees. (His orders indicated that he wished to pass nearer the Nantucket Lightship than usual.) "Keep it north at not less than one mile and not more than two," he ordered. He also requested a passage distance of no less than one mile. At 9:45, Captain Nordenson returned to his quarters, telling Carstens to call him when Nantucket came into view. Third Officer Carstens, helmsman Larsen, and lookout Ingemar Bjorkman, who was in the crow's nest above the bridge, manned the bridge at this point.[16] At 10:48 p.m., after taking another RDF, Carstens became concerned about his ship being increasingly (three miles) to the north of its preestablished course. He noted the time in the ship's logbook and ordered a slight change in course to the right (south) to compensate for the drift caused by the currents, which he assumed were the cause. The course recorder graph indicated that there had been a change in course from 92 to 95 degrees.

Shortly after this, Carstens observed a weak echo of a target on his radar screen, noting it at 12 miles' distance. He assessed that the radar target was bearing slightly over the *Stockholm*'s port (left) bow. Five minutes later, Carstens continued to note that the target was to port by 2 degrees at a distance of 10 miles, but he was not sure of his bearings. Therefore, he began a series of radar plots at regular intervals. Every radar plot confirmed for him that it would be a port-to-port meeting situation. Carstens stated that four minutes before the collision, the *Andrea Doria* eventually exposed itself right at the point where his radar plotting told him it would appear, at a distance of six miles. Carstens also testified that at 11:08 p.m., three minutes before impact, the bridge lookout shouted, "Lights to port!" He stated that at two miles' distance, he sighted the *Andrea Doria*'s port-side red light. Although he still anticipated a safe port-to-port passage with his target, the officer ordered a 22.5-degree turn to starboard, as a further precautionary measure.

Carstens testified that he was astonished by two things: the speed of the approaching vessel and the fact that he was not able to see the vessel's lights with the naked eye. He nevertheless continued to maintain that it was a clear night and that visibility was not an issue. Although the Nantucket Lightship was emitting a fog alert, Carstens still did not suspect that fog was disguising the other vessel (in which case, he might have called the captain, who had asked to be notified of fog conditions).

The bridge telephone rang, requiring Carstens to cross the entire bridge and turn his back on the bow. It was the crow's nest lookout warning him of lights 20 degrees to port. At 11:10 p.m., Carstens turned toward the bow and suddenly noticed, to his horror, that the two ships had totally changed relative positions. The *Andrea Doria* was now showing its green, or starboard-side, light. From the port-side bridge wing, Carstens witnessed a greatly illuminated ship crossing the *Stockholm*'s bow. Realizing that conditions were "in extremis," he ordered a hard right turn and rang up an "all-out emergency full-speed astern, hard a-starboard"—just before the *Stockholm* ran headlong into the *Andrea Doria*'s starboard side.

THE *STOCKHOLM,* BEING THE SMALLEST LINER at sea, rammed one of the largest on the Atlantic at full speed, piercing just under the *Andrea Doria*'s bridge wing. The force may be compared to that of 200 missiles calibrated at full speed, hitting without explosion, in one blow.[17] The nine-meter-deep puncture was incurred swiftly, within approximately seven seconds. Initially, the *Doria* continued its forward movement for about 2.6 nautical miles, in spite of the *Stockholm* being planted within its hull. Soon, the speeding *Stockholm*'s advance was abruptly halted—but not stilled, as the energy of motion from the *Doria* transmitted itself to the *Stockholm*. Consequently, the *Doria* dragged and swung the *Stockholm*'s ice-breaking bow 90 degrees to the right. Because Carstens had ordered, just before the collision, "stop engines" and "full astern," a partial retreat of about six meters (and lasting only seven seconds) turned the *Stockholm*'s bow into a 75-foot jackhammer gone mad. This jagged steel mass ripped open the *Doria*'s hull with the force of a giant can opener, as it smashed portholes and side ports, widening the breach ruinously. Witnesses watched in disbelief as the tearing, breaking, and chafing produced a spectacle of fireworks.[18] Incredibly, this devastation of unimaginable proportions took only ten minutes of time.

The destruction was so great that the wide breach of a once immaculate liner resulted in the penetration of three of the *Doria*'s watertight doors,[19] compromising the ship's seaworthiness immediately. The inflicted vessel quickly began taking on 500 tons of ocean water, which filled the nearly empty fuel tanks. This sudden and unexpected heavy ballasting produced an immediate 20-degree list.[20] Moreover, this slant to the starboard side, along with a rocking motion, created a scooping effect that flooded seawater onto Deck A, then Decks B and C, and finally the engine room. Some passenger compartments were crushed and vanished into the sea. Inside the ship, people were overcome by heat, acrid smoke, and the smell of fuel oil. These events resulted in more damage than any ship was ever built to sustain. The *Andrea Doria*'s descent to the ocean floor was imminent. (See figures on pages 228-231.)

The *Stockholm*, although greatly damaged, would retain its seaworthiness, as most of the damage was sustained within its armored bow. Chunks of steel were lost inside the *Doria* or simply dropped into the ocean, resulting in a 22-meter destruction of its fore body.[21] The *Stockholm* would remain floating nearby, gazing upon its victim from a distance of one or two miles.

A FEW WEEKS AFTER THE ACCIDENT, the Swedish American Line, representing the *Stockholm*, filed suit in New York Federal Court. It claimed that the *Andrea Doria* was responsible for the accident. Soon after, the Italian Line, which represented the *Andrea Doria,* filed a lawsuit in the same court, stating that the *Stockholm* was the perpetrator of the collision. In spite of what would be testified under oath, no one could dispute the human toll that had resulted from the crash. On the *Andrea Doria*, forty-three lives were lost almost instantly within the collapsed structures. Other people were simply released from their beds to find eternal rest in the black sea. Five crewmen on the *Stockholm* were immediately crushed on the bow they had been guarding only seconds earlier. Hundreds of injuries, especially on the *Andrea Doria*, were later reported. Two more fatalities occurred after evacuation from the sinking Italian liner: a little girl who died from a fractured skull and a passenger who suffered a heart attack upon arriving on the rescue ship *Stockholm.*

Countless depositions were taken in anticipation of a trial; the two captains, their crew, and passengers shared their personal accounts. Combining these with the two opposing versions of events on record (that of the *Stockholm* and that of the *Andrea Doria),* more questions arose than were answered. Maritime experts, journalists, the public, and baffled passengers continued to ask:

- How was it that Third Officer Carstens insisted the night was clear, when most other sources—the Nantucket meteorological station, passengers on both liners, the crew of the *Andrea Doria*, the *Ile de France,* and other rescue ships—reported dense fog in the area?[22]
- Why weren't there navigational rules preventing ships from taking sea-lanes that placed them in the paths of other vessels?

- Why did Carstens maintain that his radar placed the *Andrea Doria* on the port side of the *Stockholm*, while Calamai ascertained that his radar positioned the *Stockholm* on the starboard side?
- When visual sighting was finally made, why did Officer Carstens testify that he saw the *Doria* on his port side, while Captain Calamai reported the *Stockholm* on his starboard side?
- Why did Officer Carstens order a hard-to-starboard turn as he sighted the *Andrea Doria* crossing ahead and to starboard of the *Stockholm?* And why did he not indicate his turn with the prescribed whistle?
- Why didn't the *Stockholm* reverse its engines when the danger of collision should have been deemed imminent?
- Why was Captain Nordenson of the *Stockholm* in his quarters in a region known by seafarers as "the Times Square of the Atlantic" (and an area often obscured by fog)?
- Why did the bridge watch of the *Stockholm* consist of only three young seamen, whose average age was twenty-two and who had limited experience?
- If Captain Calamai had ordered a hard-to-starboard turn just as he sighted the *Stockholm,* would the collision have occurred?
- If Captain Calamai had plotted the course of the *Stockholm* at regular intervals, would he have avoided its path?[23]
- Were both vessels traveling at an excessive speed in foggy conditions?
- Were the captains under pressure from their companies to maintain schedules?
- Would a more moderate speed have avoided the collision?[24]
- What is considered a safe passing distance on the open sea in fog conditions?
- Should the two liners have created more distance between them?[25]

WHILE EXPERTS AND THE PUBLIC ALIKE pondered these questions, depositions continued for three months. During this time, damage claims for loss of baggage and criminal lawsuits for loss of life began pouring into the insurance offices of Lloyd's of

London (which, coincidentally, was the insurer for both the Italian Line and the Swedish American Line). Additionally, court costs and attorney fees were amounting to millions of dollars. It was evident that this could easily become the costliest maritime settlement in history. This was especially true since both claimants continued to give opposite accounts of the accident, and assigning blame correctly would be a lengthy process. Less than four months after depositions had commenced, the attorneys for both companies announced that because of difficulty in obtaining evidence,[26] a settlement would be in everyone's best interest. The agreement was to be businesslike, with no culpability assigned to either party, declaring that time would allow truth to become clear. As for the reimbursement for death, injury, and loss of personal belongings, it would be $6 million, which was the assessed value of the two ships.[27]

Needless to say, this infuriated the claimants who had carefully itemized all their losses and had requested $85 million. It was obvious that Lloyd's of London would be the winner—saving $79 million. Without a trial, which would have determined culpability, it appeared that truth would be a casualty of this agreement.

Because of the swift out-of-court settlement between the two lines, many witnesses had not been heard; most of them happened to be Italian officers.[28] These men were enraged and protested that the Italian version would never be heard. Third Officer Giannini was one of the crew members silenced by the ruling. In 1988, he revealed the resentment he had felt for many years because there had not been a trial "that could have clarified many things." "I saw what happened: who was right, who was wrong. I know who told the truth," he said at the Round Table discussions in Genova. "We who lived this tragedy are here to tell the truth—truth which was known by many others and which could have been told . . . ours are voices that nobody heard."

THE EXPEDIENT RESOLUTION reached in New York did not pacify people of principles. What appeared to be a final declaration of appeasement simply initiated a further quest for the truth.

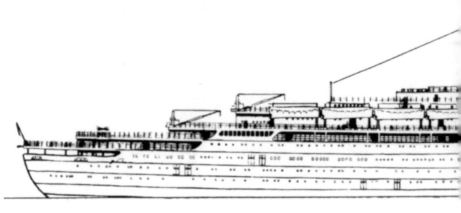

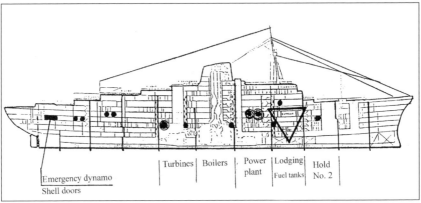

| | | Turbines | Boilers | | Power plant | Lodging | Hold |
| | | | | | | Fuel tanks | No. 2 |

Emergency dynamo
Shell doors

Top: Profile diagram of the *Andrea Doria*. Above: The triangle represents the areas penetrated by the *Stockholm*'s bow. Facing page: The bow pierced the starboard passenger areas and fuel tanks. This resulted in the flooding of cargo hold No. 2 and the power plant generator. Upon striking the *Doria*, the bow of the *Stockholm* compacted 75 feet within itself (including its massive serrated structure) by penetrating about 30 feet into the interior of the *Doria*. The forward movement of the *Doria* dragged the *Stockholm* with it. While the *Stockholm* stayed

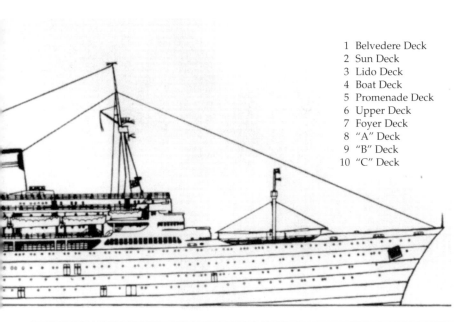

1 Belvedere Deck
2 Sun Deck
3 Lido Deck
4 Boat Deck
5 Promenade Deck
6 Upper Deck
7 Foyer Deck
8 "A" Deck
9 "B" Deck
10 "C" Deck

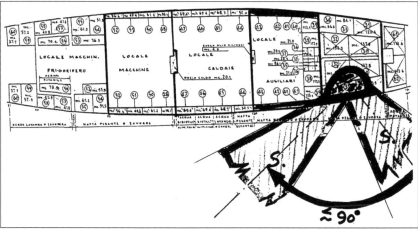

implanted in the *Doria*, it rotated nearly 90 degrees, cutting the *Doria*'s hull like a lathe. The *Stockholm*'s penetration and pullout caused extensive flooding by rupturing vertical and horizontal walls and pipelines. During these seconds of extensive friction, witnesses reported seeing a display of fireworks. (Courtesy of Francesco Scotto and the Round Table)

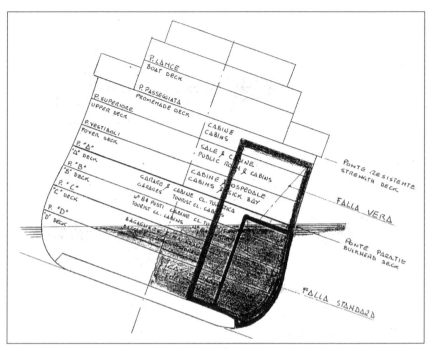

A cross-section of the various decks shows that the penetration affected the deep fuel tanks, the baggage and storage compartments, and all
three classes: Tourist, Cabin, and First. The rectangle represents the
decks penetrated by the *Stockholm*—the highest being the Upper
Deck, containing First Class cabins. (Courtesy of Francesco Scotto and
the Round Table)

Five decades later, we have volumes of conclusions from master
mariners, nautical engineers, and scientists. These experts from
both sides of the Atlantic, whether working independently or col-
laboratively, whether of American, Italian, or Swedish ancestry,
have given us their results. Astonishingly, they have reached the
same conclusion: if both vessels had altered their courses to starboard sooner, there would not have been an accident. So, given the
circumstances, the *Stockholm*'s actions just before the crash were
the main cause of the collision. These findings have been published in scholarly journals, addressed at maritime conferences,

and reported by the *New York Times* and others. All of the living experts consulted for this book are willing to place their opinions on record. Therefore, here, unlike in most earlier publications, their identities will be revealed. With named expert sources, quotes from their findings, and excerpts from testimony at the pretrial hearings in New York between August 1956 and January 1957, the reader will finally learn the other side of the debate.

Captain Robert Meurn, professor emeritus at the U.S. Merchant Marine Academy, provides his version of the collision:

A monumental factor in the *Stockholm's* overall defense hinges on the answer to the vital question, "At what time did Carstens alter the ship's course to compensate for the drift indicated by his alleged 11:00 p.m. fix?" The *Stockholm's* course recorder graph shows a 3-

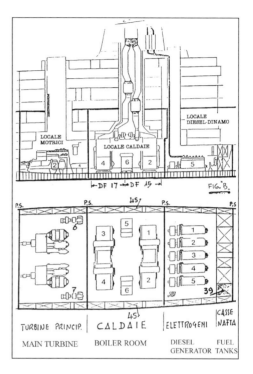

A layout of the power plant where the emergency generator was maintaining circuits and where two turbo generators were feeding the machinery still running. It also shows the deep fuel tanks on the starboard side; No. 39 was being used at the time of the collision. Flooding occurred in all three chambers of the power plant: the generator room, the boiler room, and the main turbine room. (Courtesy of Francesco Scotto and the Round Table)

degree change in course (92 to 95 degrees) was made at 11:05 p.m., plus or minus a few seconds. But under oath, Carstens testified that he picked up the *Andrea Doria* by radar at a distance of

12 miles, just as he ordered a slight change in course following his 11:00 p.m. RDF fix. In cross-examination, the Italian Line attorneys were quick to point out to Carstens that his testimony was "impossible and untrue." Logically, they proved to him that at 11:05 p.m., when he ordered the slight change in course to compensate for the drift he had indicated, the *Andrea Doria* was only 4, and not 12, miles away from the *Stockholm*.

The following excerpt from the pretrial testimony[29] gives credence to the likely error in navigation made by Carstens. The examiner is Eugene Underwood, attorney for the Italian Line.

Q: At your speed of about 18 knots, how far would the *Stockholm* have advanced in nine minutes?
A: Let us see now . . . 2.7 miles.
Q: If the *Doria* was 10 miles away nine minutes before the collision, and if the *Stockholm* advanced 2.7 miles in the same time, then the *Doria* had to cover 7.3 miles, did she not?
A: Yes, but what I understand from this question, you mean 2300 [11:00 p.m.] as a fixed time, but I have said it was about 2300.
Q: If the *Doria* covered 7.3 miles in those nine minutes, what would her rate of speed have been, could you figure that out?
A: 7.3 miles?
Q: Yes. That is the difference between your advance and the 10 miles that you observed.
A: It would be something over 40 nautical miles.
Q: I get it as 47 knots.
A: Yes.

This was precisely what Underwood wanted to obtain: an incongruous response from Carstens to indicate that the third officer had indeed erred, either in calculations or in his notation of the time. The *Andrea Doria*'s maximum speed was only 26.67 knots.[30] Faced with this irrefutable fact, Carstens modified his story somewhat. He stated that he did not change course at 11:05 p.m. and that the indication of change on his course recorder graph was only a yaw in the ship's steering. In fact, he testified under oath that the steering of the helmsman was erratic and unreliable: "He is more interested in the surrounding things than the compass." This gave Underwood the opportunity to demonstrate, by producing the course recorder of the *Stockholm* as evidence, the significance of the wavering helm:

> Q: Inasmuch as your ship was yawing 3 or 4 or 5 degrees and the bearing was a very fine bearing, it was of the utmost importance to be certain about your observations, was it not?
> A: Yes.
> Q: But you did not look at the compass, you asked the helmsman what the heading was, is that right?
> A: If I had left the radar, he may have gone away from 91, so I had to rely upon the helmsman in a case like this.
> Q: With your ship equipped as it was, that is, having no repeater,[31] you had no alternative but to rely on the wheelsman, did you?
> A: Yes.
> Q: And if the helmsman is in error by 1 degree, that may throw off your bearing by as much as 50 percent, may it not?
> A: Yes.

As the third officer found himself in a bind, he claimed that the Sperry course recorder expert, who had identified the change in course at 11:05 p.m., was wrong. In spite of the self-contradictions and resulting uncertainties, the attorneys never readdressed these issues; thus, the contradictions were never officially established.

Meurn continues to explain John Carrothers's theory:

> The third officer's denial of the 11:05 p.m. change in course placed him in an unsound position. Now it was necessary to revert to the last previous slight change in course at 10:40 p.m. (obviously made as the result of drift found in his 10:30 p.m. RDF fix) as the time he picked up the *Andrea Doria* by radar at a distance of 12 miles. After informing his readers of this in *Collision Course*,[32] Alvin Moscow justified the discrepancy by arriving at his own conclusion: that the "about 11:00 p.m." RDF fix was actu-

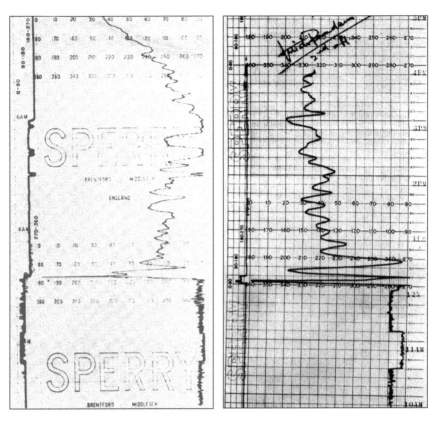

Left: The *Stockholm* course recorder graph clearly shows the lack of concentration of the ship's helmsman in approaching the collision point. The two starboard turns appear opposite on a course recorder graph. By working backward from the collision point, it is clear that the *Stockholm*'s third officer was mistaken about when he said he first visually detected the *Andrea Doria*. The difference in times on the two graphs was a result of the time setting of the course recorder by the ship's officers: 0311 for the *Stockholm* and 1211 for the *Andrea Doria* (the local time was 2311). This made no difference in interpreting the approach of each vessel. Right: The *Andrea Doria*'s graph shows the collision approach to have been recorded in the 270 degree—360 quadrant column. This quadrant shows that the *Doria* had been steering a course of 279 degrees for about 43 minutes before the collision. The tremendous impact caused the course recorder to jump up and down, clearly showing the collision point.

ally taken at 10:48. Neither of these contentions is acceptable. If true, Mr. Moscow is affirming that Carstens altered his course at 10:40, as a result of the drift found at 10:48! (At 10:40, the ships were 20.66 miles apart, not 12 miles.)[33] How could Carstens alter course at 10:40 to compensate for drift he did not know existed until eight minutes later at 10:48?

Carrothers addresses Moscow's contention that Carstens's testimony "correlated closely" with the *Stockholm*'s course recorder graph:

> Moscow writes that the third officer waited for three minutes, until the distance between the ships had been reduced to 10 miles, before starting to plot the oncoming *Andrea Doria* by radar. This is technically impossible! In order to correlate the *Andrea Doria*'s action with the abovementioned, while recognizing that the *Stockholm* was running at a speed of 18.5 knots, it would have been necessary for the *Andrea Doria* to have increased her speed to 194.72 knots in order to reduce the distance between the ships in three minutes. The *Andrea Doria* would then have resumed her normal speed of 21.85 knots when the third officer allegedly started his plotting procedure. This is unacceptable and untrue. For the aforesaid sequence to be correct, and to place the *Andrea Doria* at the collision point, it would have required the *Doria* to then make an "S-turn" in front of the *Stockholm*, at a speed in excess of 2,500 miles per hour, in one minute's time![34]

Andrea Doria historian, educator, and diver David Bright agrees with Meurn's conclusions that Carstens misread his radar: "The exact decisions Carstens made regarding the coordinates, at the time he said he made them, according to his own testimony, point to him believing that the *Andrea Doria* was farther out. Everything aligns perfectly. This clearly relates to his mistake in reading radar."

Marine engineer and writer of nautical journals John Carrothers, described by colleagues as a man of integrity and brusque honesty, originally inspired Meurn and Bright to consider the theory of a "radar-assisted collision."[35] Meurn says:

I am of Swedish decent. I was aboard the *Stockholm* seeing my family off to visit other family in Sweden. My grandfather was a professor at the Swedish Merchant Marine Academy. I was taught that my people (Swedes) are always logical and clear-headed. But after discussing the collision with my colleague John Carrothers, I began to do my own research. It was then that I realized that I had allowed social prejudices to taint my views.

Undaunted by the two contradictory versions deposed at the pretrial hearings in New York, Carrothers put his technical savvy to work, on his own time. In 1972, his findings were published in the U.S. Naval Institute magazine, *Proceedings.* He explained how the court should have investigated the accident, based on established procedure, and demonstrated, with graphs, what must have happened for the accident to occur. One of his figures shows the approach of the two vessels, and another illustrates how the third officer probably misused his radar by assuming that he was using the 15-mile range scale when in reality the range scale was 5 miles. Carrothers summarized this error as follows:

> At the official inquiry, Carstens testified that he had changed the range on his radar equipment from the 5-mile to the 15-mile to the 50-mile ranges from time to time during the course of his watch. In those days ranges were determined by range rings, which assumed a different range for each vessel. The scale was not illuminated and there was no variable range indicator. In this case the cause was most likely the failure to use available equipment correctly. When one considers that the range in radar equipment is changed with the turn of a dial, as one would change channels on a television set, it is understandable how easy it would be, in the pitch black of a darkened wheelhouse, to commit such an error. This is not an infrequent kind of error; however, in the majority of cases, it is detected before any damage is done.

In 1997, James Shirley, senior president of the legal firm that represented the Swedish American Line for the New York hearings, agreed that Carrothers's theory of a "radar-assisted collision"

**Computer Assisted Operational Research Facility (CAORF)
simulation of the collision. (David A. Bright Collection)**

was plausible. In a letter to Captain Hugh M. Stephens, president
of the Council of American Master Mariners, he referred to a visit
to the U.S. Merchant Marine Academy:

> I enjoyed . . . particularly the CAORF [Computer Assisted Oper-
> ational Research Facility] radar and visual simulation. . . . I find
> the suggestion of Carstens-Johanssen's error as to the range at
> which his radar was operating very believable. It is an error I
> have seen all too often (perhaps even made myself) with radars
> much better equipped to prevent such mistakes.

Carrothers, for his part, declared that his theory would be the
one "that finally places the corpse of the story to rest":

> Fortunately, there exist two vital documents upon which is
> inscribed the full story of how the ships arrived at the collision.

These documents are the Sperry gyrocompass course recorder graphs that had been officially presented by both defendants and recorded by the Court as evidence. . . . Had this inquiry been conducted under the jurisdiction of the Coast Guard, or Navy, the first order of business undoubtedly would have been to produce a plot or diagram illustrating that which was scribed on the graphs. As each witness testified, his testimony then would have been compared with the graphs' evidence. In this manner the correct answers would have been apparent. But this was not done, since neither the U.S. Coast Guard nor the Navy investigated the collision which involved two foreign ships in international waters and was therefore not under their jurisdiction. Let us, then, reproduce a plot of our own.

Figure 1 [reproduced earlier in this chapter on page 221] was produced from the course recorder graphs. The plot is to scale and has been worked back minute by minute from 11:11 p.m. to 11:05 p.m. where the actual collision sequences began.

Figure 2 [facing page] is an enlarged illustration of the testimony of the *Stockholm*'s Third Officer as lifted from Figure 1. The "S"-turn illustrated in Figure 2 is the fastest, most direct route for the *Andrea Doria* to get from point 2, where the Third Officer placed her one minute before the collision, to point 3, where he put her seconds later at the end of his telephone conversation. . . . The *Andrea Doria* would have been required to increase her speed to better than 2,500 miles per hour to maneuver herself from point 2 into the collision situation at point 3.

Neither the Swedish American Line, the owners of the *Stockholm*, nor its attorney, the late Charles S. Haight, agreed with the interpretation of the *Andrea Doria*'s graph as outlined in Figure 1. In his book about this disaster, *Collision Course*, Alvin Moscow informs us that they contend the *Andrea Doria* executed a long three-minute turn of 110 degrees to port going from compass heading of 275 degrees to a heading of 165 degrees. He continues by crediting Haight with the statement that the accident must have happened at the end of this long port turn.

Figure 3 is an illustration of this contention made by Haight. The *Andrea Doria*'s reduced speed of 21.85 knots is indicated in the one-minute (X-4 Min.) period prior to X-3 Min. [For this to be true] she would have been required to double her speed to reach this collision position. Furthermore, in no way can the condition of the *Stockholm*'s bow after the collision be reconciled to the roll-type collision illustrated here.

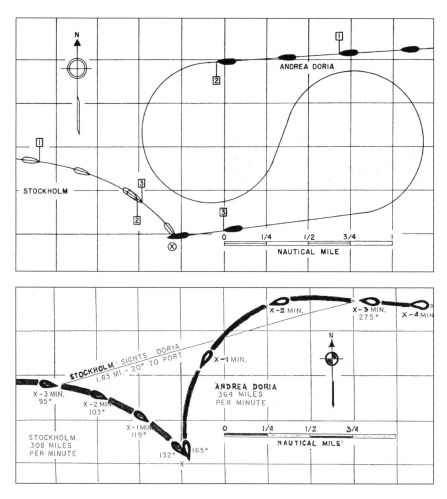

Top, Figure 2: An enlarged illustration of the testimony of the *Stockholm*'s third officer. Above, Figure 3: The diagram illustrates Swedish American Line attorney Charles Haight's contention that the accident must have happened at the end of a long port turn, initiated three minutes before the collision. (Courtesy of John Carrothers)

The absurdity of this conclusion provoked Carrothers to write another article for *Proceedings,* whose title—"There Must Have Been a Third Ship!"—was meant as a "tongue-in-cheek" explanation of the *Stockholm* testimony:

> In analyzing the testimony it is plain to see that, barring perjury, there is only one possible conclusion: The original lights sighted by the *Stockholm* were not those of the *Andrea Doria!* If the *Stockholm's* navigational watch was correct in seeing lights over the *Stockholm's* port bow three minutes before the collision, then these lights were being displayed from a ship other than the *Andrea Doria.* And, in turning away from these lights, the *Stockholm* plunged directly into the *Andrea Doria* coming up on the *Stockholm's* starboard side. The course recorder graphs confirm this theory.[36]

Captain Richard A. Cahill, fellow of the British Royal Institute of Navigation, assesses the collision by giving equal blame to both vessels for traveling at excessive speeds in fog conditions:

> It was not the practice of transatlantic liners, particularly since the advent of radar, to slow in fog. Skill and vigilance were felt to be enough protection against the threat posed by approaching traffic and these ships could not have remained in competition had they slowed appreciably when visibility closed in. Speed was judged an acceptable risk as long as it did not lead to an accident.

But after reviewing all the testimony and doing his own studies, he concludes:

> What the reconstruction surprisingly reveals is that it was not the port turn of the *Andrea Doria* that caused the collision, but the starboard turn of the *Stockholm.* Once that maneuver was executed the collision was all but inevitable.[37]

In his book *Watchstanding Guide for the Merchant Officer,*[38] Meurn states:

In more than 90 percent of the groundings and 75 percent of the collisions and fires/explosions, human error is present. Accidents attributable to human error derive from two major sources: failure to navigate safely and failure to use available equipment correctly.

After studying dozens of maritime disasters, Meurn saw a dire need for better training to improve the skills of maritime watchstanders (officers of the watch). He programmed a virtual-reality simulator that re-created the *Andrea Doria-Stockholm* collision. It is located at the Merchant Marine Academy in Kings Point, New York. Built in 1976, this sophisticated Computer Assisted Operational Research Facility (CAORF) was originally built by Grumman and Sperry at a cost of $15 million. Meurn says:

It is designed for training and research, which will help to prevent accidents like the *Stockholm-Andrea Doria* collision and the grounding of the *Exxon Valdez*. By altering the visual field, our cadets experience what it's like to be on bridge watch . . . thereby enhancing the third mate's decision-making skills as they apply to traffic and voyage planning situations.[39]

Referring to the benefits of the simulator in explaining the *Doria-Stockholm* collision, Meurn states:

We can put to the test human memory as challenged and explained via nautical science. Forty years after the collision, the inquiry gives nautical experts the raw material to reconstruct the collision and display it on a computer simulation. The collision can be dissected and pieced back together, entertaining various scenarios and their viability. We are not at the mercy of the testimony alone.

In fact, testimony can be traced on computer screens to display every aspect. Then experts analyze whether the subjective words given under oath match the objective analyses of the computer.

Using this lengthy scientific process, Meurn draws these conclusions about the *Andrea Doria-Stockholm* collision:

The author visits the CAORF and receives an explanation of the simulation from Captain Robert Meurn. (David A. Bright Collection)

1. It appears that Third Officer Carstens erred in the reading of his radar.
2. The helmsman's yawing caused inaccuracy in the radar reading.
3. Carstens's claim that he saw a red port light at two miles' distance is not viable. Visibility was only at 0.3 mile.
4. The *Andrea Doria*'s fog whistle should have alerted Carstens that the *Andrea Doria* was not six miles away but only two miles. The whistle is generally not audible beyond two miles.
5. If Carstens heard the fog whistle, as he stated, he should have known that there were fog conditions . . . put the ship on "stand-by" conditions, slowed his speed, and expected the motorman to be at the throttle. Instead, the motorman was working three decks away from the throttle. When the *Doria* was sighted (from the bridge of the *Stockholm*, thirty seconds before the collision), and the throttle was finally placed on "full astern" (reverse), it was too late.

Having had years of experience in training cadets, Meurn sympathizes with Third Officer Carstens's challenging circumstances—his inexperience, being faced with too many responsibilities, and working with a demanding captain:

> In Carstens's defense, if I put myself in the same situation, I could see myself making the same mistake. In those days, you couldn't see what range scale you were on (they were not illuminated). Besides, his captain should have been on the bridge with him, considering all the circumstances—fog, traffic, and inexperience. I met Nordenson on the *Stockholm* when I was a teen and I found him very intimidating. If I had been Carstens, I would have been afraid to call him to the bridge, too.

Cahill asserts: "Carstens probably fell into the most common trap of all. He let his pride override his judgment. That is one of the frequent and serious mistakes made by watch officers . . . to call the master seems an admission of inadequacy."

And Bright adds: "Carstens was in way over his head. He was overworked . . . running all around, on the telephone communicating with the lookout, watching over a careless helmsman, taking fixes, watching the radar . . . all with limited experience. He should have had more help."

IN SPITE OF ALL THE RESEARCH and documentation provided by nautical experts, there is still an indelible impression that the accident must have been the fault of the *Andrea Doria*, for two reasons: (1) the *Doria* should not have made a left turn at the point of collision, and (2) the *Doria* should have provided logbooks to prove its alleged maneuvers.

Under normal circumstances, the rules state that ships are to pass each other port-to-port (left-to-left) when an approach is expected to be bow-to-bow. The captains of these two ships did not expect a bow-to-bow passage. (They expected a passing distance of about one mile.) Therefore, the rule did not apply in the *Doria-Stockholm* situation. Even if it had applied, when conditions are "in extremis," such as in a collision situation, the rules allow for any maneuver to "avoid immediate danger." Since the *Doria*'s captain saw at a glance that his only and last chance was to try to get across the *Stockholm*'s bow, he opted for preventing a collision. We could imagine a parallel scenario. Let's assume that a bus driver is traveling in his lane, when suddenly he sees a pickup truck coming at him from the right, at full speed, seemingly about to collide with the bus at a 90-degree angle. Would the bus driver turn into the small truck or move into the left lane where there is no oncoming traffic? It seems only logical that he would head for the left lane to avoid a collision.

Naval architect Francesco Scotto explains the gamble that Captain Calamai had to take:

> Captain Calamai, realizing that he had no time to turn right (it was calculated later that would have needed eleven more seconds to clear the other bow), made a permissible decision to turn left. A right turn would most likely have split the *Stockholm* in half, since the *Doria* was twice the size of the *Stockholm*.

As for the importance of the logbooks during the trial, a competent attorney with the opportunity to address this subject could easily demonstrate that entries in logbooks are made after completing the watch; hence, entries are subjective. Third Officer Carstens produced his logbooks, but his alleged entries had been erased. On the other hand, Captain Calamai admitted to his crew's error in leaving the logbooks on board, but it must be considered that this was an oversight made under life-threatening conditions. Should the logbooks be an issue at all in a court of law? When asked this question, Meurn responds, "The logbook is written after the watch, not as an event happens. The fact that the logs were lost is not that relevant. I think the lawyers made this a bigger issue than it was. What is relevant is the information stored on the course recorder graph."

In judging a calamity of such proportions, it is easy for the public to read about it and draw conclusions, sometimes based on facts and sometimes based on social bigotry. It is undeniable that public perception during the 1950s assigned certain unfavorable

traits to Italian comportment: loud, emotional, irrational, unedu-
cated, to name a few. Scandinavians, on the other hand, were
stereotyped as levelheaded, logical, and educated. Could the
Andrea Doria-Stockholm tragedy have an analogy to the infamous
Sacco and Vanzetti trial of the 1920s? All of the testimony during
the trial of the two Italian merchants indicated that neither Sacco
nor Vanzetti was present at the shooting of two bank robbers. Nevertheless, both were sent to the electric chair and to this day are the
scapegoats for the real murderers of the bank guards. Sociologists
have concluded that the crime for which Sacco and Vanzetti were
punished was that of being Italian immigrants.

This analogy in no way implies that there was murder on the
night of July 25, 1956, only that there was cultural bias in the way
the public perceived the event. However, no one can deny these
facts: the *Stockholm* was traveling at full speed, in an unassigned
lane, in a fog-laden corridor that was crowded with sea traffic, and
its watch officer was young and inexperienced.

The findings outlined here are still only an intelligent apprais-
al of the tragic event. As Meurn reflects:

> With these facts and theories, the layman, the man of the sea, and
> the maritime experts can reach an informed judgment as to
> whether the ships were port-to-port or starboard-to-starboard
> prior to the collision. But it will only be an opinion, for in the final
> analysis, only a court of law can make a conclusive and binding
> determination on so controversial a matter. And this case, one of
> the most complex and yet most swiftly handled in admiralty law,
> never did reach such a final judgment; for in January 1957, short-
> ly before the engineering officers of the *Andrea Doria* were sched-
> uled to take the witness stand, the case was settled out of court.

Amid the anger and despair, the injustice and disappoint-
ments, a sparkle of gratification has surfaced. Much has been
learned about safety at sea as a result of the *Andrea Doria-Stockholm*
tragedy. Because of this knowledge, travelers on cruise ships are
acting out a new maritime script; the stage is set for romance, com-
edy, and adventure—without the risks. They are the beneficiaries

of new navigational rules and equipment that provide for safe travel:

- Inbound and outbound ships are required to use prescribed sea-lanes; this is regardless of whether they are within a major port or on constricted waterways, such as the English Channel and the Singapore Straits.
- On most passenger and cruise ships, there must be two officers on watch, instead of just one.
- Merchant Marine officers must be certified in the use of radar and must obtain radar endorsement updates every five years.
- Every vessel must be equipped with VHF (very high frequency) radio sets for bridge-to-bridge (ship-to-ship) radio-telephone communications. This facilitates the exchange of maneuvering intentions between ships.
- Range scales on radar are illuminated so that the watch officers using them can easily distinguish which scale is in use. This is to prevent misreading of distance between ships.
- Global positioning systems (GPS) have replaced the radio direction finder and loran as navigational aids.

CHAPTER 11

The Sinking of the Unsinkable

The wonder is not that the Andrea Doria *sank,*
but that she stayed afloat so long.
—Leonard J. Matteson
United States Maritime Law Association

O N THE MORNING OF JULY 26, 1956, CBS Evening News correspondent Douglas Edwards reported what he witnessed from a plane dipping 500 feet above the water:

There below, on glasslike water, water strewn with wreckage and oil, was the *Andrea Doria*, listing at a 45-degree angle and taking water by the minute . . . the ugly gash in her side covered by the Atlantic. . . . Her three swimming pools were empty of water, emptied the hard way, spilled into the ocean. . . . A few minutes past ten o'clock . . . the ship's list was at 50 degrees. Her funnels were taking water . . . the boiling green foam increasing. . . . Three minutes later the *Andrea Doria* settled gracefully below the smooth Atlantic—a terrible sight to see. A Navy commander had tears in his eyes. Nobody felt anything but an awful helplessness. There was one thing to be thankful for: the loss of life was not nearly, not nearly as great as it might have been. At 10:09 it was all over, the *Andrea Doria* was gone.[1]

As with the "unsinkable" *Titanic*, there is tragic irony in the "unsinkable" *Andrea Doria* account. We all know too well what caused the demise of the former: the hull breached by the ripping damage of a gigantic iceberg. But how and why did a newer ship, sailing warm waters and built to withstand a powerful impact, meet its end?

Built in Sestri, Italy, by the Ansaldo Shipyard, the *Andrea Doria* was modern in every respect. For safety, it was equipped with all of the most recent navigational aids that were specified in the 1948 Convention for the Safety of Life at Sea (SOLAS). This included two radar sets, instruments that became heavily relied upon in the 1950s.

As for the *Doria*'s nautical specifications, it was described as 697 feet long, with a beam of 90 feet, with eleven decks, and with a gross tonnage of 29,100. Its top speed of 26 knots was achieved by steam turbines developing 35,000 horsepower.

In order to understand the sinking or capsizing of any vessel, one must take into account certain standard issues. Among them are ballasting, weather, speed, location, and the type and extent of damage.

First, it must be noted that, technically, the *Andrea Doria* did not sink—it capsized. In responding to the issue of proper ballasting, marine surveyor Maurizio Eliseo[2] states:

> The *Andrea Doria* met not only the SOLAS 48 requirement of a minimum metacentric height of 0.5 foot, but a higher requirement imposed by the Italian flag authorities of no less than 1.0 foot. When it sank, its metacentric height was more than 3.3 feet. The ballasting plan and record, saved by the engine crew, were among the papers sent to the court of New York for the crew's interrogation—which, unfortunately, never took place.
>
> The ballasting record clearly confirms that the vessel still had 1,907 tons of fuel oil (more than sufficient to complete the return leg of its voyage); therefore, it didn't need to fuel in New York to be properly ballasted and safe, as has been suggested elsewhere. Yes, the *Doria*'s fuel tanks were half empty at the time of the sinking, but it was built to return safely to Genova on the remaining fuel. This was demonstrated by the ship's previous 100 trips and those of its sister ship, the *Cristoforo Colombo*.
>
> So, why did the ship capsize? Because until SOLAS amendments entered in force in 1990, the shipbuilding industry did not consider leaks above the watertight deck as a possibility—as in the case of the *Andrea Doria*. Therefore, the sudden flooding of some 500 tons of water into the ruptured tanks caused the ship to list some 20 degrees[3] to starboard during the first minute. Fortunately, its heavy cargo was fastened securely; otherwise, there

would have been a sharper list, and the capsizing would have been swifter. All of these facts have been verified by the latest computer technology.

All experts agree: the *Andrea Doria* was doomed the moment it was hit; the damage occurred in its most vulnerable area. Moreover, the American Bureau of Shipping, which studied collisions, learned that previous ones of this type showed that the maximum penetration was usually less than 15 percent of the beam of the ship, whereas in the case of the *Doria*, penetration was closer to 25 percent. This difference is considerable. The excessive breach, in conjunction with its location between two watertight compartments, caused an excessive list which allowed water to cascade over the tops of the watertight bulkheads that extended up to A Deck. As the adjacent watertight compartments flooded, the list continued to increase, until the ship finally capsized, its fate sealed, nearly eleven hours later. Robert T. Young, a naval architect, classified surveyor, and former president of the board of the American Shipping Bureau, explains the flooding in detail:

> The actual point of impact occurred between two watertight bulkheads. Located between the two bulkheads, immediately above the double-bottom of the ship, there was a battery of fuel oil tanks known as deep tanks, which extended across the full breadth of the ship with a longitudinal oil tight and watertight bulkhead on the centerline of the ship. The *Stockholm*'s bow penetrated all the starboard deep tanks, thereby flooding them. An effort was made to counteract the list by pumping ballast water into the port tanks; unfortunately, it had the opposite effect, because, due to the initial list, the center of gravity of the port tanks was higher than that of the starboard ones, a fact which only aggravated the condition.
>
> The space containing the main electric generators was located between transverse bulkheads. It was in a compartment of its own, separated from the main engine room by a watertight bulkhead. The transverse bulkhead was penetrated, which flooded this generator space and short-circuited the generators and switchboards, putting them all out of action. The emergency diesel generator, which was located in its own compartment at a

much higher level in the ship, started up and supplied the necessary power for the emergency lighting and bilge and ballast
pumps; the emergency generator was still running when the last
lifeboat left the ship.[4]

The *Andrea Doria* was built as a "two-compartment ship"; this
denotes its ability to stay afloat when only two compartments are
damaged.[5] But as a result of the ripping-type damage, which tore
open an arc of 90 degrees along the *Doria*'s hull (see Chapter 10),
more than three compartments were compromised; in fact, many
more were flooded because of longitudinal and transverse damage

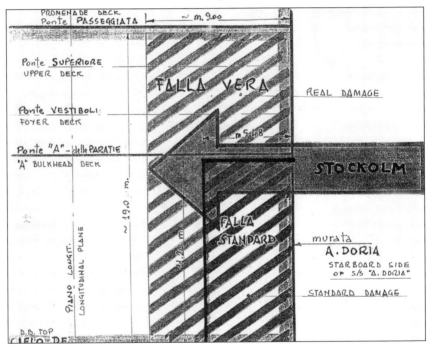

The *Stockholm* penetrated through one-third of the *Andrea Doria*. This
compares with the collision norm of one-fifth. The amount of flooding
was four times the norm. There was "continous-type flooding" not
only from the penetration but also from the ripping damage. This
affected more than the two allowable compartments. (Courtesy of
Francesco Scotto and the Round Table)

to the main bulkhead. It must be noted that the average penetration in a collision does not exceed one-fifth of the ship. In the case of the *Doria*, it was one-third.[6] Therefore, when taking into account the ripping damage that caused continual and irregular flooding, it is clear to see why the list was on a continuum toward doom.

Naval architect Francesco Scotto responds to anyone who questions whether there was a missing door going to the watertight compartments or whether these doors were closed: "The watertight doors were closed perfectly at the moment in which the measures for navigating in fog were taken."[7]

Another factor that must be considered regarding the watertight compartments is that the two ships were traveling at high speeds: the *Stockholm* at its maximum 18.0 knots and the *Doria* at a slightly reduced speed of 21.8 knots. Additionally, the *Stockholm* hit the *Doria* just under the bridge wing with its steel-reinforced, ice-breaking bow. Because the *Stockholm* was riding lower than its target—being half its size—it had the effect of pushing the *Doria* to its left. In addition, since the *Doria* was speeding "hard to port" as ordered by its captain (in order to avoid the collision with the approaching *Stockholm* on its starboard side), this also caused it to lean onto its left side, further exposing the keel. Under these conditions, the keel became vulnerable to a blow from the *Stockholm*.

David Bright explains how he and other divers have seen evidence of the breached keel during their expeditions to the *Doria*:

> Peter Gimbel[8] was the first to notice the fracture in the keel on his last expedition. During this dive in 1981, he was able to go into the gift shop located in the foyer; he cut a hole into one of the ventilator shafts, which provide a passageway into the generator room; then he swam through the generator room, which led him to a large hole and directly into the ocean. So he theorized that more than three compartments had been damaged; therefore, whether there was a missing door between the watertight compartments or not wasn't a factor in the sinking—the ship was already doomed.

Not only was the structural integrity of the starboard side breached, but because the ships were going so fast and the *Stock-*

Facing page, top: In the earliest hours of daylight, *Ile de France* lifeboats transport passengers away from the sinking Italian liner. Middle: At daybreak, rescue vessels *Cape Ann* and the Coast Guard's *Private William H. Thomas* witness the *Doria* listing precariously on its starboard side. Bottom: The *Andrea Doria* capsizes on its starboard side and clearly shows all port-side lifeboats still steadfast on their davits.

Above: The stern of the *Andrea Doria* with its port-side propeller was the last section of the luxury liner to sink. (David A. Bright Collection)

holm was so much lower,[9] in the process of pushing the *Doria* up into that 20-degree list, it actually exposed the keel.

When I dove the *Doria* in the '80s, I saw the physical proof: from the port side, I saw a large hole that extended through to the starboard side; it was about five feet wide and even longer. Perhaps [at the time of the collision] it just started out as a hairline crack, but today this fissure has expanded throughout the hull to the point where the bow is separating from the rest of the hull.[10]

Nautical scientists who have studied the sinking are amazed at some of the circumstances after the collision: no fires broke out, there were no explosions in spite of the fact that fuel tanks were smashed, and the emergency generators lit the disaster scene right up to the capsizing.

Scotto adds:

> It would be ridiculous to attribute only luck to these [aforementioned] facts. . . . We must discuss the solid construction and, above all, note the care and management of the machinists that prevented the generators, the furnaces, and the electric stations from creating problems and harming people and property.[11]

The greatest testament to the worthiness of the *Andrea Doria* as a well-constructed vessel is the reputation of its sister ship, the *Cristoforo Colombo*. It was also built by the Ansaldo Shipyard, with an identical design for safety, and it operated under the same standards. After the *Doria*'s sinking, many nautical agencies investigated the construction of the *Colombo*, including the U.S. Safety Commission of the House of Representatives and the U.S. Coast Guard. No one ever disputed the safety and stability of the sister ship, which continued to sail across the Atlantic Ocean for many years.

CHAPTER 12
Diving the *Doria*

Shipwrecks are time capsules of human civilization.
Underwater archaeology gives us the tools to rediscover
mankind's monuments that were forfeited
before their rightful time.
—David Bright

PROFESSIONAL SHIPWRECK DIVER David Bright explains, "Diving on the wreck of the *Andrea Doria* is a very hazardous adventure. It's one of the most difficult dives in the world." Having made 120 dives to the wreck, he speaks from personal experience. "The many bodies that I have seen recovered are a testament to the challenges the wreck poses, even to the most expert diver."

Death lurks around every corner and can manifest itself in many ways: being trapped by heavy objects, fishing nets, or hanging wires that wind around equipment; getting lost and running out of air; succumbing to air toxicity, resulting in poor decisions, convulsions, falling asleep, or even suffering a stroke or a heart attack; panicking and forgetting to decompress; equipment malfunction; strong currents; and sharks. At least thirteen divers have taken their last breaths while attempting to penetrate the *Doria*'s hull, decks, and corridors—often to retrieve that forbidden artifact that becomes their trophy.

Because the wreckage lies in waters 265 feet deep, twice the 130-foot limit of recreational sports diving, it is called the "Mount Everest" of diving. "Climbing Mount Everest and diving the *Doria* both offer the exhilaration of extreme sport," says Bright. "But for me, the allure is the ability to dive a very historic shipwreck and to become part of its legacy. Experiencing the *Andrea Doria* as a time capsule that has been buried under the sea is especially thrilling."

The corpse of this once-great liner lies 45 miles southwest of Nantucket. During the summer months, the area is famous for its fog banks, which can start to creep in from around 8:00 p.m. until the next morning. "We feel lucky if we even leave the boat dock," Bright says. The fog is very dense and makes visibility beyond 10 feet very difficult. The water south of the Nantucket shoals is very turbulent, being tossed by high winds. And the weather can change faster than you can say "Nantucket."

Expert scuba diver Kevin McMurray describes in his book *Deep Descent*[1] the ten-hour ordeal of reaching the *Doria* dive site:

> "Getting beat up" on the trip out is a rite of passage for *Doria* divers. It isn't just the mercurial Atlantic that conspires against you. The sleeping quarters aboard the speedy fiberglass *Wahoo*[2] are laughingly referred to as "spice racks." The *Wahoo*'s bunks are stacked like trays below the decks, and diesel fumes mingle with the odor of dozens of sweating bodies in the claustrophobic space. The smell of fear pervades belowdecks preceding any *Doria* dive. The common belief is that if you are not scared about doing the dive, you are either lying or stupid. Few get much sleep before the dive, and the fatigue adds to the likelihood of a mishap.

THE BEST TIME FOR A DIVING EXPEDITION is within a two-month weather window, from the last two weeks in June until the first two weeks in August. Out on the dive site, watch is posted twenty-four hours a day to make sure that huge oceangoing vessels do not run the divers over. Even though a dive boat is more than 50 feet long, it is very easy for a huge tanker or freighter on automatic pilot to be oblivious to it. Once moored over the wreck site, there is no guarantee for a dive. If the currents are more than 2.5 knots, the risks are too great, and the dive is aborted.

Divers go through many different layers of water as they descend to the wreck. At first, the water is a mesmerizing aqua blue and warm to the touch. The sun's rays refract, revealing an array of jellyfish drifting like silk scarves in various colors. But at 50 feet, the water turns sharply colder; everything is seen in hues of bluish green. As more layers of water are penetrated in this state, visibility can be as little as 5 feet; the only way to see is with a powerful light. Bright describes the scene:

This nondimensional environment can strike terror in the mind of an inexperienced diver; there's no point of reference except the dive line you're gripping and the air bubbles from divers below you. After several minutes, the light beam reflects upon the wreck at 170 feet down. It's eerie seeing the *Andrea Doria* where it was never meant to be. She's lying with her starboard side buried in the sand as if she wants to hide the mortal wound. The first divers in the '50s described the wreck as a sunken city, since it was longer than two football fields. But time has reduced it to a huge, dark, murky piece of steel covered with anemones, sea growth, and mineral deposits. But what's really beautiful is when I shine my light on it, a whole community of sea life makes it look like a reef. There's a lot of fish down there: pollock, bergalls, blackfish, and cod, not to mention our "friends," the sharks. The *Doria* is teeming with life!

The gruesome cadaver is a deeper dive now than when it first hit the ocean's bottom. The first dive by Peter Gimbel and his team measured a depth of 220 feet. However, North Atlantic currents, which converge to create an epicenter of turbulence, have swirled around the hull, burying the carcass deeper into silt and sand. Strong currents have caused swift and extensive decay over the past ten years. All of the top deck levels above the hull have collapsed and lie on the ocean floor like a huge junk pile—looking not unlike the remains of New York's Twin Towers just after September 11, 2001. "The famed Gimbel's Hole in the Foyer Deck[3] has twisted upon itself, and the entire bow is threatening to fall off," Bright remarks. "Even the *Titanic* is in much better shape compared with this once-beautiful superstructure."[4]

Exploring the deep is as challenging as exploring another planet when dealing with air supply. At the depth of the *Doria*, pressure increases by about six or seven times; the partial pressures of gases increase to a point that the body cannot handle, and air becomes toxic. Nitrogen can have a menacing side effect. Bright explains: "It can act as a narcotic and can severely impair one's abilities to dive safely. This is known as nitrogen narcosis or 'getting narced.' Sea explorer Jacques Cousteau called it 'raptures of the deep.' Imagine that every 50 feet you descend underwater is

Exploration of the First Class bar by David Bright reveals some Oriental-patterned fine porcelain china by famed Italian manufacturer Richard Ginori. (Nautical Research Group)

comparable to one dry martini on an empty stomach. It's called Martini's Law." Oxygen, too, becomes toxic at depths of more than 216 feet. The physiological effect is called oxygen toxicity; seizures, convulsions, and blackout can occur with little or no warning symptoms. Bright says, "The scary thing about oxygen toxicity is that one breath you could be totally fine, and the next breath you could be dead. It's very important to use special gas mixtures that will reduce the amounts of nitrogen and oxygen. As these gases are reduced, some other gas must be used to make up the difference. In almost all cases, this gas is helium—it will prevent the effects of nitrogen narcosis."

"For many years, the most conventional procedure is the use of scuba tanks," Bright says. Divers have been known to bring five tanks of various sizes. Combining this with all the other diving equipment could mean that a diver is loaded with 300 pounds of gear as he or she plunges into the water. Other required technical gear are a dry-suit, several underwater flashlights, diving reels, knives, a lift bag, and spare gas cylinders. The dry-suit will keep the body dry and warm since normal bottom temperatures are in the mid-40s Fahrenheit during the summer, even with a surface temperature of about 60 degrees Fahrenheit. With the advent of new diving technologies, closed-circuit rebreathers are replacing scuba tanks as the preferred method for diving the *Doria.*

In spite of the aid of the latest technology, every visit to this grande dame of the sea has its own drama. McMurray describes the hazards of the deep in this gripping episode:

Sally was shoulder to shoulder with Gary[5] when they started digging through the muck for the precious artifact. While she was concentrating on digging through the now billowing silt, something big suddenly slammed into Sally Wahrmann.

"At the time I didn't know what it was," she said. "Whatever it was, it really whacked me hard, it was all over me. It was almost like I got socked in the jaw. My regulator got knocked out of my mouth, my mask flooded, I lost my buoyancy, and I went barreling down to the bottom of the corridor coming to rest in a pile of rotting wood and debris."

Stunned, Sally was still able to get her regulator back in her mouth, then she cleared her mask of the invading seawater. . . . Had she not had the mask under her hood, she would probably have lost her mask, her underwater vision—and any hope of escaping death from deep inside the ship. . . .

Sally swam up and out of the hole, "faster than I should have," and thought about heading right for the anchor upline and to the surface. She hesitated and thought that whatever had slammed into her might have got her buddy. Without giving it another thought, Sally reentered Gimbel's Hole. Almost immediately she saw a bright beam from a diving light coming up at her. Sally held her breath, and Gary Gilligan emerged from the darkness.

[Realizing another member of the dive had not reported back to the anchor line, Billy Deans decided to return to the hole to take a peek in.] He immediately saw a light. Dropping down deeper into the hole, he then saw Ormsby,[6] and that he was in trouble.

Ormsby, floating face up, was tangled in cables. His regulator gave off intermittent trails of bubbles, and his eyes were shut. . . . Seeing the amount of cable wrapped around Ormsby's body reminded Deans of a fork that had been stuck in a plate of spaghetti and twisted. [After making a quick ascent without decompressing, in hopes of getting help,] Deans was back at John's side in minutes, but he saw no more air bubbling from the exhaust ports of the regulator. John Ormsby was not going to make it out alive.

Although actual "bottom time" on the *Andrea Doria* is fairly lit-

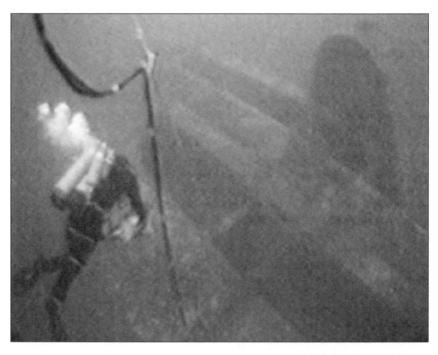

tle, twenty to forty-five minutes, the amount of decompression time can run into a few hours. Because nitrogen under pressure dissolves from the lungs into the blood and soft tissues, a diver must allow time for the nitrogen to transfer slowly back into the lungs. Without decompression, nitrogen bubbles would block flow to the heart, brain, and central nervous system causing gas embolisms, which could be crippling or lethal.

"To decompress sufficiently, divers stop at intervals on their way to the surface. This can lure curious sharks," says Bright. "These sharks are crafty and can swim at you from various angles. Your normal field of view is obscured by the diving mask, and we have found that hanging on the diving line back-to-back helps to increase our field of vision. Occasionally our tanks bang together creating a sound that temporarily repels these sharks."

UNTIL THE LAST FEW YEARS, before the superstructure collapsed, the penetration of the *Andrea Doria* wreck was a site where divers challenged themselves to explore the interior—whether for treasures or for adventure. This was bravura, a show of skill and physical strength. "It was very difficult to identify structures inside; they were dislocated from their normal horizontal plane," Bright explains. "I would have to memorize the layout of the ship and imagine that what used to be ceilings and walls had become floors. They were usually twisted or turned into an unrecognizable mass." If a diver is still in search of souvenirs today with the collapsed superstructure lying on the ocean floor, says Bright, "he might as well treat it as an archaeological dig. The new challenge is raking through the treasure buried among sand." But for Bright, the wreck's allure is based on research, scientific exploration, and historical documentation. "As part of marking the fiftieth anniversary of the collision, I will dive the *Andrea Doria* utilizing a digital video camera to document the morphological decay of the shipwreck."

Facing page, top: A diver descends to the submerged stern section of the *Doria* in the late 1980s. Bottom: Diver Steve Gatto recovered the stern steering helm on the dive boat *Seeker*. (David A. Bright Collection)

Bright, who has made two diving expeditions to the *Titanic* in a submersible, says, "A recent dive to the *Titanic* has located an undiscovered debris field that may indeed be the keel section. With further study, we may be able to determine the reasons the ship sank so fast. This information may provide us with many facts that will help us understand the capsizing of the *Doria* as well."

One fascinating "casualty" of the *Andrea Doria* sinking was a beautiful, one-of-a-kind automobile called the Norseman. This special prototype, with an unusual cantilevered roof and no side pillars, was designed by Chrysler and built by the Italian company Ghia. The estimated cost was $150,000 (in 1956 dollars). It was on its way to New York on the *Doria,* intended for the 1957 auto show circuit. But sadly, it would never be seen by the public.

Bright was one of the last people to pay homage to the Norseman. He describes its crypt as one of his most frightening explorations: "I visited cargo hold number 2, where the Norseman was specially packed in a crate—unlike the other passenger cars, which were parked in the garage and positioned strategically for stability. It was pretty scary in the cargo hold, because the ship is lying on its side." Once, while Bright was looking for a lost diver, he had an opportunity to see the Norseman for himself: "The crate had disintegrated, and the car was in very, very poor condition. The ocean's salt water had invaded the Norseman's metal, and most of the car was rust, corrosion, and a heap of indistinguishable junk. The tires were still there and have helped with its identification."

Bright has not been back to the cargo site since 1994, and, he says, "with all the decay that the wreck has had over the past ten years, it is doubtful if I (or anyone else) will ever get a chance to see the remains of the Norseman again."

THE PASSING OF TIME and the intrusion of divers have expunged traces of what were once the most beautiful spaces of interior design in the world: delicate fabrics, paints, lacquers, and teak are long gone; precious china and gold service sets are now in private collections; the undersea-life motifs that adorned muraled

**One of the *Doria*'s "passengers," the Chrysler Norseman, was a unique and innovative prototype bound for the U.S. auto show circuit. It would never be seen by the public.
(Courtesy of DaimlerChrysler Corporation)**

walls, mirrored panels, bas-reliefs, and the statue of Admiral Doria are mostly exhibited in museums. Perhaps the "dig" will provide small artifacts to deep-sea explorers for many more years, but the giant structure itself is nearly gone, the corpse claimed as a trophy by the fury of the sea. One day, the *Andrea Doria* will become an enormous lump, undistinguishable from the sea bottom. But for now, one explorer admits, "Divers continue to be obsessed by her dismal loneliness and her unexplored mysteries."

After all, only physical evidence has been washed away. In this sarcophagus sealed by the sea and wrapped in silence, what remains are memories. Along with the rhythmic hiss of his regulator, the diver recalls how—on that last night on board—the revelers danced to the joyful strains of "Arrivederci Roma."

AND BACK ON THE SURFACE, mankind fathoms the passage of half a century . . .

Captain John Turner and Glenn Garvin, on the dive boat *Top Cat*, retrieved the bronze statue of Admiral Andrea Doria from the First Class lounge in 1965. (Nautical Research Group)

Passages

Challenge is the core and the mainspring of all human activity.
If there's an ocean, we cross it; if there's a disease, we cure it;
if there's a wrong, we right it; if there's a record, we break it;
and finally, if there's a mountain, we climb it.
—James Ramsey Ullman

AS THE REST OF THE WORLD gazed at the pageantry surrounding Grace Kelly's marriage to Prince Rainier of Monaco, spectators gawked at the descent of the queen of the Italian Line to the kingdom of Neptune—delivering exquisite art panels of the same powerful sea god.[1] The *Andrea Doria* also sank with its icon—a statue of Admiral Doria,[2] the military hero for whom the ship was named. The admiral had lived to a remarkably old age for his time, while his namesake was being prematurely interred at the age of four.

The passing of the *Andrea Doria* symbolized the end of an era. Opulent sea travel was being dominated by the swiftness of airplanes, immigration en masse became a closely streamlined process with stricter laws, and Italy, in its resurgence from the ashes of World War II, was glowing with renewed optimism.

The three ocean liners involved in the *Andrea Doria* tragedy, once having traced a routine path from the Old World to the New World, now headed toward three distinct destinies. The *Andrea Doria* began it subservience to nature's fury. Currents from several oceans now systematically converge on its gravesite, swirling and strangling all that lies at its epicenter. Tenacious tentacles of the deep embrace every surface of the once-pristine hull, extracting life from the mortal remains.

The *Ile de France* continued its transatlantic service for many years before being sold to various owners. Eventually, its passage ended under the direction of Japanese filmmakers whose mission was to satisfy thrill-seeking moviegoers. For their grand finale, they exploded and sank France's grande dame.

The severely damaged *Stockholm* was repaired and resumed its service in the spring of 1957. Although it did slightly alter its former sea-lane, it once again found itself on a collision course with another vessel. Author Alvin Moscow, who was traveling on the *Stockholm* that spring, reported in his book *Collision Course* that the passengers had a déjà vu sensation as the ship suddenly began to wobble and rumble while braking and switching to full speed astern. Years later, the *Stockholm* sailed from the same pier once assigned to the *Andrea Doria*—ironically calling itself the *Italia Prima*. In 1994, it was completely rebuilt from the hull upward. It subsequently sailed under several names and various owners. Today, the *Stockholm* is sailing the Mediterranean and the Caribbean for Arcalia's Classic International Cruises. Its name is *Athena*.

The passages of these once-vital liners can be surpassed in curiosity only by the destinies of their masters. After the *Ile de France*'s participation in the rescue of the *Andrea Doria*, Captain Raoul de Beaudéan was given full command of his ship. Recognizing his heroism, France decorated him as an Officier de la Légion d'Honneur, the highest honor bestowed on a French citizen.

The Swedish Line, wishing to demonstrate its confidence in the two major officers of the *Stockholm*, swiftly assigned Captain Harry Gunnar Nordenson and Third Officer Ernst Carstens-Johannsen to the new flagship of the White Viking Fleet, the *Gripsholm*, which had been built in Italy.

The Italian Line took a different approach with the handling of its captain. In spite of the fact that the Italian government had declared its full support of Piero Calamai's comportment regarding the collision—and that culpability had never been established—the captain never sailed again. Although Calamai was offered the command of another great vessel, the *Cristoforo Colombo*,[3] the official assignment never arrived. Those who knew Captain Calamai well described the *Doria*'s master as a man of impeccable integrity but also as a proud man who would not offer resistance by defending himself during the inquiries in New York and, later, in Italy. In interviews with both American and Italian media, Calamai's answer was often a stoic "No comment." In a gesture of surrender—and perhaps disgust—Calamai announced his retirement within one year after the collision.

American naval engineer John Carrothers asserts that this could have been avoided:

> Less than six months after the *Andrea Doria* tragedy . . . the case was finalized in the Federal Court of the United States without benefit of trial. Seafaring men who followed the official inquiry into this accident were convinced that the case was settled in a conspiracy to obstruct justice. This apparently was done to limit the financial responsibilities of the steamship companies in the settlement of the third-party claims for death and injury and the loss of personal effects and cargo.[4]

Additional commentaries about this tragic passage of a brilliant career offer further insight. Retired naval architect and executive for the Italian Line Francesco Scotto[5] explains:

> Captain Calamai returned to Genova hoping to be recognized for doing his duty, and doing it well. He had participated in a successful sea rescue. Then he had suffered through a grueling ordeal during the court depositions; he was incredulous about what the Swedes had testified during the hearings. Even though he knew the collision was not his fault, he assumed the responsibility for forty-six casualties. This was a lot for any person to endure. He expected to be welcomed back by the Italian Line. Instead, he received a cool reception.[6]

Second Officer Guido Badano's recollections of his visit with the captain reveal that he felt "alone, unsupported, and wronged by the media and his people. He had been promised another ship, but Italian maritime law required that he be interrogated for another year. This exhausted his pride. He became depressed and unwilling to confront unreasonable questioning."[7]

Captain Robert Meurn, maritime professor and author, feels that Calamai's downfall can be explained by analyzing the man and the politics surrounding him:

A sea captain represents his nation; he does not have the resources at his disposal to defy his government or his employer. He was an easy target because of this and because of his stoic nature. He was the perfect candidate to become the "scapegoat captain" [a term used also by Carrothers]. Calamai chose to shoulder any blame that might have been aimed at the Italian Line; this is the kind of man he was. Had the Coast Guard conducted the official inquiry, justice would have prevailed. The reason the Coast Guard did not investigate it is that the accident involved foreign ships in international waters.[8]

The *Titanic* case is a perfect parallel of how the public and the major institutions concerned with a collision resort to scapegoating to avoid scrutiny. Captain Stanley Lord of the *California* was blamed for not coming to the rescue of desperate passengers. But the *California* was too far away and was unaware of the sinking. Officers on the *Titanic* who had seen a vessel nearby mistook it for the *California*, but it was really a Norwegian seal-poaching boat. This was not revealed so as not to cause international disputes.

The real problem was that there were not enough lifeboats on board the *Titanic*. The Board of Trade, the British institution in charge of authorizing the number of lifeboats, didn't do its job. Coincidentally, they were also the ones who held the trial after the accident. Since they could not blame themselves, they blamed Captain Lord of the *California*. The media publicized this, and so Captain Lord became the scapegoat for the loss of life. In implication of guilt, he was spat upon on the streets of London. This deflected the blame away from the Board of Trade to Captain Lord.

In the *Andrea Doria* case, Lloyd's of London was the insurer for both the *Doria* and the *Stockholm*. It didn't matter to them who was really at fault—the insurance payments would be the same. If neither ship was found guilty, the case would be settled as "limited liability," there would be no reason to go to trial, and the insurer would avoid a lengthy trial that would have become extremely costly. Besides, having a scapegoat shifted the blame away from the two lines, and Calamai was the easiest target—he was honest, he offered no resistance, and he was Italian! Besides, it's easier to blame a person than an organization. As a result, the

Coast Guard was never called in to testify about the misinterpretation of the course recorders. So the case was settled as one of the most expedient in maritime history.

Because of the limited-liability settlement, Lloyd's of London used the value of the two ships (the *Andrea Doria* and the *Stockholm* combined) for determining compensation to the third parties. Therefore, when passengers sued for loss of life, loss of property, and injuries, their total of $85 million in claims was settled for a mere $6 million.[9]

According to Italian Line executive Scotto, his former employer was also an accomplice to this injustice:

The Italians used silence as a public relations tactic—both during the inquiry and in the media. [The Italian Line] even refused an interview by *Life* magazine. . . . For the U.S. press and public opinion, silence, caution, fear of the public are a symptom of guilt.[10]

This tactic is documented in correspondence between the Italian Line manager and curious mariners or laypersons asking for information about the collision. The response was that "realizing that endeavors to fight our case in the newspapers at that time would not be beneficial to us but merely prolong the controversy, we chose dignified silence."

Scotto adds facetiously:

Even giving technical support to Captain Calamai . . . was considered dangerous. . . . On the second of August 1956, the Italian Line's New York office declined the request to send a naval architect from Genova [at the conclusion of the official inquiry]. Everyone officially concerned with the matter was silenced after the inquiry.[11] But defamatory voices[12] obviously . . . were allowed over the past thirty years to say whatever they wished on the subject without any official voice being heard to challenge what was said.

Third Officer Eugenio Giannini concurs with Scotto's view of the Italian Line's poor public relations: "The prize for the worst marketing concerning the *Doria* affair should be awarded to the Italian Line's press office."

According to *Andrea Doria* historian and educator David Bright, the first book about the disaster, 1959's *Collision Course* by Alvin Moscow, sealed the public's opinion:

> The public believed Moscow's portrayal of Nordic seamen behaving in a cool and levelheaded manner, while the Italians were confused and out of control. He says that Captain Nordenson left his cabin and assumed levelheaded command of his ship while Calamai shied away from duty by not giving information to his passengers. This implies that the Italians were cowards, having deserted the passengers and abandoned the ship.

Psychiatrists Paul Friedman and Louis Linn maintain that the public easily believed that the collision had to be the Italians' fault. In interviews with several *Ile de France* passengers,[13] it was apparent to them that stereotype thinking was still prevalent:

> dramatizing its capacity to dominate opinion during periods of crisis and its influence in distorting perception and judgment. . . . Expressions of prejudice were not confined to fixing the blame for the accident on the *Andrea Doria*, but also manifested themselves in the contempt voiced by some toward the Italian immigrant survivors because of their uncontrolled demonstrations of despair.[14]

Friedman and Linn also refer to the transcripts from the *Titanic* trial, where the word *Italian* was used freely as a synonym for *coward*. They suggest that the belief in the superiority of Anglo-Saxon courage was still pervasive during the *Andrea Doria* affair. Friedman and Linn explain that Italian passengers who "blamed the *Andrea Doria* for their misery derived their feelings [from the idea] of having been failed." In other words, they had been promised safe passage on an unsinkable ship—and this they were denied.

Psychiatry describes the assigning of a scapegoat as a device often used to turn aggression outward. It also explains that facts are distorted when tainted by prejudice. It's not surprising, then, that an Italian captain, who, by implication, was cowardly in assuming his duties—thereby betraying his passengers and losing his ship on the open seas—would become the target of scapegoatism.

Carrothers felt deep empathy for Calamai. In a letter sent to the captain in the winter of 1972, Carrothers conveyed a message of vindication:

> Those of us who watched you suffer through the disgraceful official inquiry in New York have nothing but sympathy, admiration, and respect for you. Sympathy because of the brutal treatment you were subjected to in the Federal Court of the United States, admiration for your absolute integrity and loyalty to your owners, and respect for the manner in which you conducted yourself since the accident. Rest assured, Captain Calamai, there are many of us who would be more than willing to serve under your command at any time.

IN AN EFFORT TO FURTHER EXONERATE Captain Calamai, Meurn and Carrothers headed for Italy in June 1972. They carried with them the technical evidence that they believed would relieve Calamai of culpability. But they arrived too late. Calamai had begun feeling ill during the winter. His daughter Marina recalls, "On April 9, my father checked himself into the hospital. Before any diagnosis was made, he passed away." In the hills of Genova, which overlook the Mediterranean and the pier that once housed his beloved *Doria*, Captain Calamai exhaled his last breath, muttering, "Are the passengers safe?"

At the time of Calamai's death, the *New York Times* quoted Carrothers in an obituary, dated April 10, 1972:

> The most tragic figure to come out of this disaster is Captain Piero Calamai, master of the *Andrea Doria*. A victim of circumstances, he sits alone, brokenhearted, unable to defend himself. . . . Of all the principals involved, companies and individuals, Captain Calamai is the least responsible.

The captain's friends alleged that he died of *crepacuore,* a broken heart. And as *Andrea Doria* historian Bright says, "It's a shame that a man of such impeccable character would have to shoulder all the load of a disastrous event."

JUST LIKE THAT OF A SEAFARING VESSEL, the journey to truth's destination is not always pleasant. My thirst for truth led me to a spring that satisfies the senses yet leaves a trace of unpleasant taste. I feel that my own questions about the tragedy of July 25, 1956, have been answered—I now know what caused the horrific collision. Nevertheless, truth does not glisten like spring water. It is tainted with particles of distortion, silence, threat, misinterpretation, expense, and expedience. I am saddened not only by the loss of life but also by the aftermath of the tragedy; by the fact that *Andrea Doria* passengers initially blamed their captain and crew without knowing a single fact; that the Italians were later stereotyped as incompetent at sea, thus tainting the image created by master mariners Christopher Columbus and Amerigo Vespucci; that the hearings in the Federal Court in New York came abruptly to an end without a trial; that the Italian Line and its government did not stand up and speak loudly on its own behalf. But most of all, I feel remorse for having participated in assigning blame to the *Doria's* crew for many years. My opinion was based on hearsay, media inaccuracies, and lack of information.

But now, my research and writing have led me to exonerate the captain and the crew by acknowledging their innocence in the collision and their participation in history's greatest sea rescue. My work has also led me to a transitional phase in my own life: feeling quenched with satisfaction in knowing the truth and fulfilled for feeling proudly reconnected to my Italian roots. It is my hope that this work will result in changing public attitudes toward what transpired on July 25 and 26, 1956.

Captain Piero Calamai of the *Andrea Doria*.

Passengers and Crew
on the *Andrea Doria*

Because of the loss of the ship's manifest, names were retrieved from various sources, leading to some questions about spelling. Suggested alternative spellings are given here in parentheses.

First Class

Andrews, Marian

Badalamenti
  (Badalamenta),
  Emmanuel
Bain, Emmanuel
Barton, Gay
Bequillard, Alfredo
Bifulco, Dora
Bifulco, Vittorio
Bissette, Elsie
Bissette, Joseph
Bliss, Barbara
Boggs, Barbara
Boggs, Robert B.
Boggs, Robert B., Jr.
Bollinger, Dorothy C.
Bollinger, Eleanor
Boyer, Malcolm
Boyer, Marion W.
Burks, Harry G., Jr.
Burks, Katherine

Cafiero, Frances
Carlin, Jeanette
Carlin, Col. Walter G.
Castillon, Aurora
Chevalier, Adrian
Cianfarra, Camille
Cianfarra, Jane
Cianfarra, Joan
Clemen, Maria
Clifton, William Frank
Coleman, Jane

Coleman, Margaret
Coleman, Nancy
Coleman, Stewart
Collani, Joseph
Cornelli, Ethel A.
Costantini, Aurelio
Costantini, P. Giuseppa
Crespi, Franco
Crespi, Giuliana

Davidson, Walter
De Perrot, Yvonne H.
Della Manna, Angelo
Della Manna, Ernesta
Di Mare, Emilia
Di Mare, Joyce
Di Mare, Lillian (Libera)
Di Mare, Paul
Di Mare, Thomas
Dilworth, Ann
Dilworth, Richardson
Doliciamore, Rev. John
Drake, Betsy Grant
Dunne, Margaret
Dwight, Margaret

Edmonds, Dean
Edwards, Annie (Amy) J.
Ellis, Mary
Els, Grace
Evans, Lt. Col. Robert F.

Felix, Harold
Fornaro, Josephine

Gifford, Charles

Gifford, Clarence
Gifford, John
Gifford, Priscilla
Goll, Josephine
Green, Alfred
Green, Beverly
Grigg, Ernest
Grigg, Ernest III
Grigg, Margaret
Guellen (Guillen), Jose
Gustin, Henry
Gustin, Monique

Hall, Richard
Hazel, Jaspar
Hicks, Berta Valles
Hicks, Blanca Valles
Hicks, Frederico
  Rodriquez, M.D
Hicks, Isaura de Valle
Hicks, Maria Elena Rojo
  de Rodriquez
Hutchens (Hutchins),
  Morris L.
Hutchens (Hutchins),
  Velma J.

Jackson, Barbara
Jackson, Richard

Kazazdan (Kazazean),
  Angelina
Kazazdan (Kazazean),
  Arthur
Kazazdan (Kazazean),
  Astrid

Keil, Andree
Keil, Marguerite
Keil, Morris
Kerr, George Patrick
Kerr, Margaret (Matheson)
Kerr, Valkyrie (Kyrie)
Kovach, Nora

La Brucherie, Ennis
La Brucherie, John
Lambert, Rev. Paul
Lamp, Annie
Lampert, Dr. Herbert
Lampert, Darlene
Lavoratti, Arturo
Lavoratti, Marie
Latour, Antonio
Latour, Marta Elizadle
Lee, Al
Lee, Elenor
Levy, Joseph Bruno
Levy, Susana Rosa
Luedike (Luedke), Anita
    (August)

Mackerell, Alexander
Mackerell, Bessie
Markham, Father Daniel
Markham, Margaret
Massue, Alexandrine G.
Massue, Josette
Massue, Nicholas
Mayer de Berncastle, John
Mc Ado, Mc Ado
Mc Ado, Mary
Merlin, Josephine
Merlin, Kenneth F.
Monterastelli, Erminia
Monterastelli, Rudolph
Moore, Lester
Moore, Marie
Morey (More), Sarah
    (Sadie)
Morey (More), Sigmund
Morgan, Linda

Novik (Novak), Manya
Novik (Novak), Morris S.

Oppitz, Rev. Joseph W.
Orr, Mildred
Orr, Robert W.
Orr, Ronnie

Palazzola (Palazzolo),
    Salvatore (Sam)
Parker, Edward Leroy
Parker, Virginia (Inez)
Passante, Max Louis
Passante, Theresa R.
Perellis, Esther
Perellis, Irving
Peterson, Martha
Peterson, Thure
Piacenza, Emilia
Piacenza, Giuseppina
Post, Donald J.

Quinn, Elizabeth
    McMillan

Rabovsky, Istvan
Reinert, Jerome Stanley
Roces, Armando
Roces, Georgina
Roman, Ruth
Ruth, Donald
Ruth, Jean

Sagner, Helen L.
Sagner, Stanley
Santana, Annabel
Santana, Isa
Schiff, Anne
Schiff, Stanley
Schneider, Aldred
Schwab, Robert H.
Schwartz, Regina
Sertorio (Seorio), Regina
Sferra, Enrico
Sparrer (Siarrer), Dorothy
Stevens, Archie
Stevens, Herminia
Stevens, Sigmund
Stewart, Janet
Straube, Alfred H.
Strelitz, Judy

Strelitz, Julia Marie
Stroh, Morris

Thieriot, Ferdinand M.
Thieriot, Frances
Thieriot, Peter
Tumin, I. Rupert
Trachtenburg, Arline
    (Adrianne)
Trachtenburg, Philip

Van Sciver, Myrtle M.

Wojcik, Father Richard J.
Wright, Bessie M.
Wyatt, Alice Smith

Young, David T.
Young, Madge H.
Young, Robert T.
Young, Virginia

Cabin Class

Abatti, Rosa Angela
    Freddi
Adragna, Olivia
Adragna, Rose
Aidinoff, Celia
Aidinoff, M. Bernard
Aljinovic, Frances
Angelico, Armando
Angelico, Loraine
Angelico, Mary
Annino, Charles
Annino, George
Annino, Lilliana
Annino, Sandra
Arnsby, Sister Callistus

Babic, Milan
Baker, Sister Marie
    Raymond
Banducci, Casimiro
Barba, Lucio
Bartolo, Bernardo
Belardo, Angelo
Belluomini, Adele

Belluomini, Angelo
Belt, Christine Felicia
Belt, Judith Ann
Belt, Linda Mae
Belt, William
Berotti (Berutti), Pietro
    (Peter)
Buehler, Hans Herman
    Cadorin, Delfina

Cadorin, Dina
Caia, Ada Louise
Caia, Pasquale
Camboni, Antonio
Camboni, Rose
Canto, Carlos
Cattani, Delfina
Chidiac, George
Ciotti, Luigi
Conti, Anna Maria
Conti, Lucia
Corda, Alfred
Corda, Evelyn
Corda, Giuseppe
Corosu, Giovanna
Coscia, Mary
Crudele, Carlo

D'Agostine (D'Agostino),
    Annie
D'Agostine (D'Agostino),
    John
Damiano, Immacolata
Dassetto, Dante
De Francesco, Gennaro
De Francesco, Guy
    (Gaetano)
Delbourg, Eugenie
De Sane, Angelina
De Santis, Giulio
Dier, Joan M.
Di Francesco, Giuseppe
Di Fusco, Pasquale
Di Meo, Anna
Di Meo, Rigoletto
Di Prospero, Felice
Donza, Nora
D'Urzo, Erasmo

Ellis, Antonina
Errante, Antonina

Ferrano, Maria Assunta
Ferrarelli, Dr. Luigi
Fisher, Arthur
Frank, Clarence C.
Frank, Dorothy B.
Frank, Marty
Franetovitch, Nick
Franetovitch, Vinca
Frassino-Prato, Pietrina
Fratto, Giovanni
Frederico, Jennie
Freeman, Henrietta
Frlekin, Dana
Frlekin, Sam

Galasso, Josephine
Galipo, Maria
Gasperi, Luigi
Gasperi, Severina
Gerhardt, Helen
Gerhardt, Neil H.
Gentile (Gentle), Viola
Gladstone, Eugene W.
Gladstone, Frieda
Glaudia, Amelia
Goedert, Rev. Raymond
Goldfarb, Samuel
Goldfarb, Sylvia
Greco (Grego), Julia
Gressier, Christine
Griffin, John W.
Griffith, Joseph Chastain
Grillo, Angela
Grillo, Anthony
Grossi, Mariano

Hall, Frances E.
Hall, Margaret
Harvey, Constance
Harvey, Harold
Haywood, Dorothy
Hendler, Sylvan
Hill, Clara
Hill, Ellis D.
Hill, Eric

Hill, Jeffery
Hill, Nancy
Hill, Thomas
Hill, Timothy
Hollinger, Harvey
Hollinger, Lois
Hollyer, David
Hollyer, Louise
Holt, David George
Holt, Delagneau Bianca
    Maria
Holt, Richard Stephen
Holt, Robert Sterling

Ippolito, Charles
    (Calogero)

Jacobs, Ann Jeanette
Jacobs, Milton
Joyce, Martin
Joyce, Mary Louise

Kelly, Rev. Thomas M.
Korelich, Maria
Korelich, Peter
Krendell, George J.

La Capria, Michelle
La Capria, Santa
Lalli, Romolo
Lalli, Rosina
Lapides, Dorothy
    (Rhonda)
Lapides, Irving
La Porte, Joseph M.
La Porte, Sidonia
La Quaglia, Amabile
    (Mabel)
La Quaglia, Charles
Lattaro Tocci, Amelia
Lederle, Madeline
Lederle, Neal
Lilley, Marguerite
Lippi, Onorato
Losita (Locito),
    Giuseppina
Lucas, Thelma
Luder (Luber), Ruth

Lynch, Olive

Macera, Silvestro
MacKenzie, Ann
MacKenzie, Ruby B.
Magana, Dr. Alvaro
Magana, Alvaro, Jr.
Magana, Concha
Magana, Maria Elena
Magana, Mario
Mainiero, Josephine
Mainiero, Leonard
Mainiero, Leonard, Jr.
Mangarelli, Aniello
Mangels, Conrad
Mangels, Vera B.
Manello, Adele
Manello, Mario
Marek (Marik), Pietro
Marek (Marik), Irma
Marino, Dario
Marsich, Mary
Marturano, Ignazio
Masucci, Dr. Italo
Matteri, Bessie
Mazzu, Francesca
McLean, Grace
McLean, Julianne
McLean, Mr.
McLean, Mrs.
Mc Whinny, John
Mc Whinny, Lois
Medcalfe, Gordon N.
Medcalfe, Katherine
Messina, Justine
Micciolo (Micciola),
    Adeline
Micciolo (Micciola), Grace
Micciolo (Micciola),
    Lorenzo
Miller, Richard R.
Milligan, Carolyn M.
Montepaone (Montepone),
    Francesco
Morea, Vincenzo
Morelli, Angelo N.
Morgan, Chester
Morgan, Lida Belle

Moulton, Bernice
Moulton, William S.
Myerscough,
    Sister Angelita

Olive (Olivio), Sam
    (Salvatore)
O'Ryan, Edith

Palmeri, Baldassare
Palmeri, Giovanna
Palmeri, James
Panelli, Angelo
Paolinelli (Paolinetti), Bert
Paolinelli (Paolinetti),
    Selena
Paparone, Gaetano
Paparone, Maria
Patrito, Giovanni
Paxton, Marion Pat
Peri, Mario
Peterson, Helen
Peterson, Warren C.
Pick, Cecilia
Pick, John
Prata, Enrico
Prata, Margherita

Raimengia, Alda
Raimengia, Frank
Ranieri, Leonieda
Rapp, Arthur
Rapp, Paula
Ricci, Antonio
Riccio, Silvio
Riggi, Antonio
Riggi, Giuseppe
Riggi, Pietro
Riggi, Seirica Maria
Rigby, Gordon
Rigby, Olga
Ritter, Pearl D.
Ritter, Dr. Saul A. (Leo)
Rocklin, Carlyn L.
Rocklin, Julius Paul

Sager, Lettie
Salcetti, Helen
San Felice, Dorothy

Schoenborn, Frank
Scianimanico, Lena M.
Scirica, Anna
Scirica, Antonino
Scirica, Matteo
Scirica, Paolo Giovanni
Sciulli, Nicola
Sejda, Dolores
Sejda, Dr. Martin B., Jr.
Sejda, Martin Robert
Sejda, Mary E.
Silenzi, Agnes
Sinnott, R. A.
Sinnott, Mrs. R.A.
Sortino, Giuseppa
Sortino, Giuseppe
Sortino, Libora Maria
Staidohar (Stagdohar),
    George
Stegin (Skegin), Ann
Stevens, Marie
Stevens, William B.
Stoller, Meryl
Stoller, Mike
Swanson, June

Talierco, Giuseppina
Tosi, Patricia
Trabucco, Domenico
Trabucco, Maria
Treat, Charlotte
Treat, Stella H.
Treglia, Domenico
Treglia, Giovanni
Tysk (Tysh), Robert J.

Urban, Mary

Vulpis, Gaetano

Watres, Carl E.
Watres, Lillian
White (Weite), Adelaide
White (Weite), Cheryl

Zamparo, Giovanna
    Palumbo

Tourist Class

Agnoletti, Teresa
Agrusa, Francesco
Agrusa, Girolama
Agrusa, Vita
Albanese, Dino
Alben, Guido
Alfano, Calgero (Charles)
Alfieri, Antonietta
Altobelli, Giovanna
Ambrose, Cosimo
  Damiano
Anchini, Ida
Andreini (Andrini),
  Gelsomino (James)
Andreini (Andrini),
  Angelina
Angelone, Alfredo
Angelone, Domenico
Angelone, Ida
Angelone, Silvana
Angelone, Silvana
Angelone, Vincenza
Anponaco, Marguerite
Ansuini, Domenico
Ansuini, Giulia
Ansuini, Fillipo
Ansuini, Melania
Ansuini, Pasquale
Antonacci, Margherita
Anveo, Mari
Armstrong, Janette
Armstrong, Jean
Arnone, Michela
Ashjian, Anahid
Ashjian, Ara
Ashjian, Hagop Nousa
Ashjian, Stella
Aveni, Tranzana Carmelo

Bacchelli, Olga Bei
Balboni, Alfred
Balzarini, Laura
Banchio, Michele
Baratta, Agnes
Baratta, Margherita
  Pontecorvi

Barca, Angelo
Bartoli, Rev. Giuseppe
  (Joseph)
Bellomo, Frank
Bellomo, Joseph
Bellomo, Louis
Bellomo, Maria Collette
Bellomo, Mattia Manzari
Bendrihem, Alegria
Bendrihem, Isidor
Bendrihem, Joseph
Benedict, Brother Simon
Benvenuti, Livia
Berardinelli, Camillo
Berrutti, Pietro
Biffoli, Gastone
Bifulco, Francesco
Bisio (Bisle) (Bision),
  Beatrice Anna
Boccarossa, Ugo
Boito, Arrigo
Bollinger, Hugh H
Bolzano, Gaetano
Bonaventura, Liliana V.
Bonaventura, Saveria
Bossalini (Bonalini),
  Caterina
Bellomo, Mattia Manzari
Bottini, Savina
Boubli, Albert
Brandolino, Lucas James
Bravo, Gerolama
Bremermann, Laura Pittau
Breschia, Rosa
Brocchetelli, Gino
Brunoli, Alfredo
Bucci, Beatrice Jean
Buehler, Hanns Hermann
Burrows (Barrows), Ann
Burzio, Domenica
Burzio, Piera Domenica
Burzio, Pietro

Caira, Antonio
Caira, Piera
Calamai, Mario
Caliendo, Alfonso
Caluori, Elenore Mary

Capasso, Annunziata
Capasso, Sanita
Cappello, Pasquale
Cappello, Tommaso
Capponi, Valda
Caputo, Aniballe
Caputo, Celestina
Caputo, Eugenio
Caranci, Nicandro
Carbone, Carmelo
Carboni, Liviano
Carboni, Mario
Carboni, Patrizia
Carboni, Renata
Cardazzo, Giuseppe
Cardazzo, Maria
Carlin, Matteo
Carola, Luigi
Carola, Margaret
Carola, Rosa
Carola, Teresa
Caronna, Maria Donata
Casadei, Anna Marina
Cascio, Francesco
Cascio, M. Giuseppa
Castagna, John
Castaneda, Carlos
Castelli, Raffaele
Cataldo, Gaetana
Cataldo, Salvatore
Cataldo, Vito
Cavalli, Antonia
Cavolina, Sadie
Cavolina, Salvatore
Censale, Angelo
Cerolini, Enzo
Chiaradia, Eufemia
  Garzone
Chidiac, George M.
Chiesa, Luigi
Ciallella, Domenica
Ciarlo, Carmelo
Ciarlo, Lucia Longo
Ciccone, Corrado Nicolo
Cinque, Assunta
Cioffari, Anita
Cirelli, Martin J.
Cirincione, Giuseppe

Cirincione, Rosalia
Colagrande, Ezio
Colavito, Gaetano
Colavito, Giuseppe
Colavito, Lina
Colavito, Nicola
Colavito, Teresa
Colella, Elio
Colistra (Colitra), Carmel
Colistra (Colitra), John
Colombo, Salvatore
Colosi, Giuseppina
Colosi, Nicola
Conigliaro, Joseph
Conigliaro, Joseph L.
    (Pippo)
Conigliaro, Pasqua
Contecorvi, Margherita
Contento (Contenti,
    Contente), Rev.
    Antonio
Cooper, Helen Evans
Coppola, Anna
Coppola, Filippo
Coppola, Francesco
Coppola, Luigi
Corrado (Corrao),
    Theodore
Corrado, Salvatore
Costantini, Anselmo
Costantini, Maria Theresa
Costanzo, Antonino
Covino, Christina
Cristillo, Amedeo
Cucchi, Rafaelle
Curcio, Benito
Cusumano, Caterina

D'Addario, Antonietta
Dahan, Miriam
D'Alessio (D'Alessandro),
    Francesco
D'Alessio (D'Alessandro),
    Nedda
D'Aloia, Sister Barbara
D'Amico, Giorgio Croce
D'Angelo, Vincenzo
Daro, Giuseppe

Dazzo, Carmela
Dazzo, Giovanni (John)
Dean, Ellen
De Angelis, Marcello
DeBartolomeis, Achille
De Capite-Macini
    (Mancini), Mario
De Francesco, Joseph
De Francesco, Rosa
De George, Anthony
De George, Vince
De Giovanni, Masino
De Girolamo, Anna
De Girolamo, Antonio
De Girolamo, Biagio
De Girolamo, Francesco
De Girolamo, Maria
    Rosaria
De Girolamo, Mario
De Girolamo, Nicola
De Grandi, Giuseppe
De Grandi, Giuseppe (son)
De Grandi, Lucia
Del Bosque, Alfredo
Del Gaudio, Teresa Maria
D'Elia, Anna
D'Elia, Antonio
D'Elia, Carmela
D'Elia, Francesco (with
    wife and 5 children)
D'Elia, Giovanni
D'Elia, Rocco
D'Elia, Salvatore
D'Elia, Vincenzo
Della Valle, Giuseppe
Della Valle, Lorenzo
Delleo (Dalleo), Assunta
Delleo (Dalleo), Frank
Del Monaco, Amelia
Del Monaco, Nicola
Del Monaco, Pasqaule
Del Monaco, Silvana
Del Toro, Louis
De Luca, Ludovico
De Luca, Teresa
Del Vecchio, Francesco
Del Vecchio, Maria (Mary)
Demasi, Maria

De Michele, Benedetta
De Michele, Pio
Deo, Nicholas Joseph
De Rubeis, Antonio
De Rubeis, Federico
De Vecchis, Gino
De Vecchis, Leonida
De Vermilio, Peter
Diana, Biaggio
Diana, Victoria
Diener, Rosina
Di Fabio, Adalgisa
Di Fiore, Nicola
Di Fiore, Nicola (cousin)
Di Giacomo, Giovina
Di Giacomo, Maria
Di Giovanni, Beatrice
Di Giovanni , Maria
Di Ioia, Michele
Di Leo (De Leo), Attilio
Di Luzio, Angelo (Angela)
Di Luzio, Maria
Di Michele, Antonio
Di Paola, Cecilia
Di Michele, Concetta
Di Paola, Bruno
Di Paola, Enrico
Di Paola, Maria
Di Pego, Gino
Di Pego, Maria
Di Sandro, Filomena
Di Sandro, Norma
Di Sandro, Tullio
Di Schino, Alessandrina
Di Schino, Damiano
Di Schino, Elisa
Di Schino, Maria Pia
Di Sipio, Giovanni
Di Vincenzo, Angiolina
Donato, Antonio
D'Onofrio, Germaine
    (Germina)
Dooner, Liliana
Dooner, Maria
Doran (Dorin), Kathleen
Dorneich, Klaus C.

Edwards, Helen A.

Fabbri, Amelio
Faiola, Vincenza Marini
Fais, Andrea
Famularo, Domenico
Famularo, Gaetano
Famularo, Maria
Farinella, Maria
Ferlore, Sergio
Ferrara, Salvatore
Ferraro, Josephina
Finia (Femia), Francesco
Fiocca, Raffaello
Fiocca, Vincenzina
Fiorucci, Adelaide
Fiorucci, Amato
Fitzpatrick, Larry
Fontini (Fantini),
    Giuseppe
Forte, Rosina Zumbo
Forte, Vincenzo
Forza, Alessandro
Franciscucci, Antonia
Fratarcangeli, Margherita
Fratarcangeli, Pasquale
Fusco, Adolfo
Fusco, Franco A.
Fushi, Domenico

Gaberlian, Sarkis
Gaetano, L.
Gallerani, Ettore
Galliano (Galleano),
    Porfilio
Gallinari, Dante
Gallinari, Elsa
Gallo, Armando
Garonci, Micandro
Garzone, Maria
Genilla, Alberto
Gentile, Albert
Gentile, Celestino
Giannobile, Alberto
Giannobile, Felice
Giannobile, Franco
Giannobile, Ida
Giannobile, Marianna
Gianonne, Carmelo
Giordano, Camillo Frank

Giralomo, Bravo
Giuliano, Gerardino
Giuvintano (Giurintano),
    Salvatore
Gonzales, Angelina C.
Gonzales, Raymond
Graf, Elisa A.
Graf, Marilyn J.
Gramigni (Gramioni),
    Dolores
Gramigni (Gramioni),
    Lena
Gramigni (Gramioni),
    Ottavio
Gramigni (Gramioni),
    Taormino
Gramigni, Thomas
Grammatica, Nicola
Grasia, Marie C.
Grassi, Francesco
Grechi, Maria
Grego, Angelina
Grillo, Luciano
Grossi, Louis
Grossi, Lucie
Grubenman, Adolf
Grubenman, Jacob (Jack)
Grubenman, Violet
Guarneri, Mrs.
Guerrera, Mario
Guerrera, Michele
Guzzi, Antonietta
Guzzi, Giuseppe

Hamparian, John
Hamparian, Mary
Hanson, Andrew
Hanson, Ardith
Hanson, Donald
Hanson, Elizabeth M.
Holzbauer, Wilhelm
Hudson, Robert Lee

Iacobacci, Amelia
Iacobacci, Elena
Iacobacci, Lorencina
    (Lorenzina)
Iacobelli, Annunziata

Ianni, Giuseppa
Ianni, Giuseppe
Ianni, Netta
Ianni, Teresa
Iazzetta, Amelia
Iazzetta, Benvenuto
Imberlone, Giacomo
Imberlone, Giuseppe
Imberlone, Maria
    Theresina
Ippolito, Alogers
    (Calogero)

Juliano, Antonio

Kerbow, Catherine
Kimmelman, Beatrice

La Ferrara, Giuseppa
    Saporito
La Flamme, Theresa
La Font (La Fonte), Rev.
    Ernest
La Font (La Fonte), Jeosine
La Font (La Fonte),
    Leyland
La Laina, Antonio
Lamari, Venera
Lambert, Jean
Lamp, Walter
Landino, Amelia
Lanz, Irwin (Irving)
La Rocca, Felice
La Rosa, Bruno
La Vigna, Alessandro
Leo (Lee), Nancy
Leo, Nunziata
Leone, Vita
Leoni, Anita Arrigoni
Liseo, Salvatore
Lodal, Inger
Lombardi, Antonio
Longo, M. Annetta
Lopez, Maria
Lopez Duranona, Ramon
Loprete, Virginia
Lore (Lo Re), Antonio
    (Antonia)

Lozzi, Albert
Lozzi, Francesca
Lucchesi, Anna
Lucchesi, Guido

Maccherani, Maria
   Antonietta
Macchiona, Caterina
Macchiona, Francesco
Macchiona, Giulia
Mac Donald, Robert E.
Madonna, Nicola
Maggio, Giuseppe
Magro, Loreto
Mancino, Arturo
Mancuso, Joseph
Mancuso, Maria
Mandella, Giuseppe
Manicuccio, Angelo
Manolini (Mannolini),
   Agata
Marano, Armando
Marchetti, Aurelio
Marchetti, Nella
Marconi, Caterina
Marconi, Giulia
Margiotta, Rosa
Margo, Larto
Mariani, Alfonso
Marinella, Ossola
Marinelli, Mirello
Marinelli, Natalina
Marra, Riziere
Marrazzo, Ettore
Marrinos, Geraldin
Martina, Anthony
Martinelli, Francisco
Martini, Angela M.
Martini, Cesidio
Martini, Rosa
Masarenti, Giuseppi
Massa, Paolina
Massa (Masso), Anella
   (Onella)
Massa, Edoardo
Massarella, Domenico
   Antonio
Mastrincola, Arlene

Mastrincola, Pasquale
Mastrincola, Rosa
Matteo, Serafino (Serafina)
Maximi, Vincenta
McGowan (MacGowan),
   Beulah
McGowan (MacGowan),
   Edgar
McKee, Peter
Medaglia, Alfredo
Merlin, Josephine
Meruzzi (Miruzzi), Arthur
Micalef, Lawrence
Migliorini, Francesco
Migliorini, Maria
Milillo, Michele
Minicucci, Amadio
Minniti, Angelo
Miriello, Chiaromonte
Miraglia, Nicolina
   (Margaret)
Miraglia, Peter
Mittica (Mitica), Antonio
Mittica (Mitica), Domenico
Mocchi, Giuseppe
Molino, Salvatore
Monestera, Valerio
Monasterio, Aurelio
Monteleone, Maggio
Morelli, Antonio
Morelli, Lena
Morgan, Chiarina
Mormile, Vincenza
Morrone, Giovanni
Morrone, Mario
Morrone, Vincenza
Moscatiello, Angela
Moscatiello, Luigi
Moscatiello, Michael
Muccino, Camillo
Murgia, Antonio
Muscara, Giuseppa
Musico (Muscio), Luigi

Napoleone, Gianpietro
Napoletano, Mauro
Napoli, Mr.
Napoli, Mrs.

Napoli, Angelina
Napoli, Giuseppe (Joseph)
Napoli, Rosa
Napolitano, Assunta
Narvas (Navas), Carlos
   (Charles)
Narvas (Navas), Carlos Jr.
   (Charles)
Navarro, Eduardo
Nesci, Antonio
Neylo, Carmen
Neylo, Maria
Neylo, Mrs.
Nocera (Noceroa), Rosario
Nogatino, Virgilio
Notaro, Francesco
Notaro, Rafaelle
Novi, Graziano

Occhiogrosso, Maria
Occhiogrosso, Tomasso
Odehnal, Eva
Onder, Joseph
Onder, Marie

Pacchiano, Antonio
Pacchiano, Felice
Pacchiano, Francesca
Pacchiano, Francesca
   (daughter)
Pacchiano, Giuseppina
Pacchiano, Grazia
Pacchiano, Lucia
Pagella, Giustina
Paladino, Antonia
Paladino, Felicia
Paladino, Giovanna
   Simone
Paladino, Leonardo
Paladino, Maria
Paladino, Rocco
Palaia (Palsia), Franceso
Palermo, Santo
Palmeri, Benjamin
Palmeri, Domenico
Palmeri, Francesca Maria
Palumbo, Anna Maria
Paneccione, Elmorinda

Buonaccorsi, Alfredo
Buono, Giuseppe
Busco, Mario
Bussi, Officer Carlo

Cacace, Luciano
Calamai, Superior Captain
  Piero
Callegari, Fernando
Calligaris, Menotti
Cama, Officer Emanuele
Campo, Giuseppe
Campodonico, Giuseppe
Camporeale, Vincenzo
Canale, Eduardo
Canale, Mario
Cantore, Stefano
Cappai, Antonio
Cappai, Nicola
Carabellese, Nicola
Carotenuto, Gennaro
Carpenetti, Ferruccio
Carro, Jacopo
Caser, Renzo
Castellano, Salvatore
Caviglia, Luigi
Cecchini, Giuseppe
Ceresa, Luigi
Cervivi, Guarina
Cesco, Alberto
Chernigoi, Adriano
Chersevani, Giuseppe
Chert, Silvano
Chiappori, Engineer
  Dalciso
Chicco, Mario
Chiussi, Fabio D.
Ciaravolo, Raffaele
Ciarlatani, Officer
  Umberto
Cimoli, Officer Umberto
Cirillo, Vincenzo
Ciulinni, Manola
Coelli, Egidio
Cogliolo, Cadet Valerio
Colace, Salvatore
Colantonio, Ciro
Colantonio, Gaetano

Colli, Albino
Collu, Adriana
Colombo, Officer Mario
Colotto, Almo
Comici, Officer Antonio
Consalvo, Bruno
Conte, Giovanni
Coppa, Officer Luigi
Coppa, Raffaele
Coppola, Salvatore
Cordera, Officer Giovanni
Coretti, Antonia
Corosu, Leonardo
Cortotto-Cravetto, Carlo
Coschetti, Oscar
Cosimo, Luciano
Costa, Benedetto
Costa, Francesco
Costa, Leonardo
Costantini, Arnaldo
Costantini, Luigi
Crovetto, Filippo
Cuomo, Giuseppe
Cuttica, Mario

D'Alessandro, Egidio
Dal Pino, Luigi
Dalvise, Santo
Danesi, Enrico
Dapelo, Cadet Felice
D'Arrigo, Giacomo
Dascola, Giuseppe
De Angelis, Luigi
De Biasi, Aldo
De Cristo, Luigi
De Cristofaro, Rodolfo
De Domenico, Rocco
De Fonte, Vito
De Franchi, Leo
De Giovanni, Marino
Degola, Giuseppe
Del Carlo, Giampaolo
Del Corso, Giacomo
Del Gatto, Luigi
Del Gaudio, Legantino
Dello Strologo, Arnaldo
De Luca, Francesco
De Luca, Mario

De Marco, Teodoro
De Martino, Gennaro
De Paoli, Lucia
De Pasquale, Salvatore
De Pompeis, Gaetano
Derchi, Gianbattista
De Robertis, Carlo
De Sario, Giovanni
Desenibus, Giovanni
Desenibus, Giulio
Devescovi, Aldo
De Vincenzi, Sergio
Diamant, Erminio
Di Bono, Michele
Di Camillo, Ferdinando
Di Donato, Antonio
Di Donna, Ciro
Di Donna, Giuseppe
Di Donna, Luigi
Di Donna, Luigi
Di Martino, Giovanni
Di Martino, Luigi
D'Istria, Raffaelle
Domenichini, Carlo
Donato, Officer Antonio
Donato, Antonino
Donato, Domenico
Dossola, Leone
Drago, Giuseppe
D'Urzo, Crescenzo
D'Urzo, Luigi

Ercolano, Natale
Errico, Guiseppe
Esposito, Luigi
Esposito, Maria
Esposito, Pasquale

Fama, Pasquale
Fama, Roberto
Fancellu, Paolo
Fantini, Giuseppe
Farella, Ciro
Favilla, Giovanni
Fegio, Giuseppina
Feliciotti, Antonio
Felluga, Mariano
Femiano, Carmen

Ferlora, Sergio
Ferrara, Giuseppe
Ferrari, Giuseppina
Ferro, Salvatore
Filippis, Francesco
Filipponi, Giuseppe
Fillini, Giordano
Fonda, Andrea
Fonda, Ezio
Fonda, Francesco
Fonda, Giorgio
Formisano, Renato
Forti, Giorgio
Foschi, Pier Mario
Fragomeno, Antonio
Fragomeno, Francesco
Francese, Silvestro
Franchini, Officer Curzio
Francia, Luigi
Francioni, Giovanni
Francisosi, Franca
Freti, Alberico
Frisone, Andrea

Gallo, Armando
Gallo, Officer Dario
Gamberini, Salvatore
Garbarini, Giulio
Garbato, Michele
Garofalo, Leopoldo
Garre, Giuseppe
Garrone, Officer Felice
Gasparini, Angelo
Gasparini, Giovanni
Gasparini, Guglielmo
Gasparini, Luigi
Gasparini, Ruggiero
Gatto Ronchieri, Antonio
Gentilli, Alberto
Gerbi, Albino
Germiniasi, Carlo
Geromella, Vittorio
Gesmundo, Michele
Ghiggini, Giuseppe
Giacco, Michele
Giadrossi, Alfredo
Gianni, Ezio
Giannini, Officer Eugenio

Giannini, Dr. Renzo
Giannotti, Ettore
Giglio, Pietro
Gilberti, Angelo
Ginanni, Corradini
Ginanni, Costantino
Gnetti, Marco
Goretta, Lidio
Gormarino, Giuseppe
Grasso, Francesco
Graziano, Luigi
Greco, Attilio
Greco, Engineer Giovanni
Grisan, Gaetano
Grisan, Nicolo
Guarino, Cesare
Guida, Giuseppe
Guidi, Officer Francesco

Iannacore, Carmine
Iannelli, Domenico
Iardino, Fedele
Ignaro, Luigi
Infantino, Paolo
Ingenito, Natale
Ingianni, Officer Francesco
Iosso, Gennaro
Iviani, Francesco

Kirn, Officer Carlo

La Camera, Paolo
Lami, Anna Maria
La Motta, Salvatore
Langella, Aniello
Langella, Salvatore
Lanzilli, Preziosa
La Rosa, Sebastiano
Lettich, Gasparo
Libardo, Domenico
Licastro, Domenico
Lippi, Anna Maria
Loiacono, Raffaele
Lombardi, Pier Giorgio
Lombardo, Giuseppe
Lombardo, Salvatore
Lovazzano, Bianca
Luccisano, Umberto

Lugnan, Antonio
Lugnan, Bernardo
Luminato, Giuseppe
Lunanova, Mauro
Lussi, Galliano
Luxardo, Giulio

Macri, Paolo
Macri, Vittorio
Madonna, Giuseppe
Magagnini, Captain
  Osvaldo
Maggiolo, Giacomo
Magnani, Flavio
Maiella, Felice
Maiuolo, Antonio
Malissa, Pietro
Manfredi, Federico
Mantero, Officer Oscar
Maracci, Cadet Mario
Marazzo, Vincenzo
Maremonti, Umberto
Mari, Arveo
Marini, Francesco
Marino, Michele
Marmorato, Francesco
Marrazzo, Augusto
Marrollo, Emiliano
Marsala, Francesco
Martellani, Bruno
Martinelli, Francesco
Martini, Giovanni
Martuccelli, Pasquale
Massa, Dino
Massa, Giovanni
Massarenti, Elide
Masotti, Maria
Mastellone, Giovanni
Maurel, Elide
Mauri, Vincenzo
Mazzitelli, Francesco
Mazzoni, Elmo
Mazzotti, Officer Antonio
Mellone, Ciro
Melloni, Officer Otello
Mennella, Francesco
Mennella, Giuseppe
Mennella, Michele

Mian, Angelo
Micera, Ciro
Micheli, Alessandro
Mignone, Domenico
Milovich, Marcello
Minetti, Giobatta
Minotauro, Gaetano
Mocca, Cadet Giuseppe
Moggi, Galileo
Molica, Francesco
Molinaro, Salvatore
Mollero, Marianna
Monaro, Alberto
Mondini, Officer Giuseppe
Montanari, Tito
Montefusco, Salvatore
Montello, Nicola
Montevergine, Vincenzo
Morabito, Giorgio
Morandi, Carmelo
Morelli, Ciro
Morieri, Antonino
Moroni, Emilio
Moroni, Franco
Morvillo, Michele
Motta, Michele
Murgia, Antonio
Musi, Antonio
Musico, Officer Luigi

Nanni, Ercole
Napoli, Giovanni
Nappi, Leonardo
Naso, Gaetano
Natta, Monsignor
  Sebastiano
Nebiacolombo, Giuseppe
Nesbeda, Carlo
Nicelli, Alfredo
Nicoli, Salvatore
Nicolich, Giuseppe
Nicora, Emilio
Nocentino, Virgilio
Nocerino, Domenico
Norma, Franco
Nosari, Santa

Oldano, Innocenzo

Olivieri, Andrea
Oliviero, Raffaele
Oliviero, Vincenzo
Oneto, Captain Luigi

Pagani, Carlo
Pagnin, Giovanni
Pagnini, Arrigo
Paino, Office Biagio
Palmieri, Pietro
Palomba, Aniello
Palomba, Michele
Palumbo, Giuseppe
Paniate, Giuseppe
Paoletti, Maria
Paolini, Officer Pasquale
Papaccio, Giuseppe
Parisi, Giovanni
Parlati, Guglielmo
Passalacqua, Nilo
Pazzaglia, Officer Luigi
Pecunia, Attilo
Pecunia, Gio Batta
Pecunia, Libero
Pellino, Francesco
Pensante, Tito
Perez, Vincenzo
Perla, Renato
Pernice, Luigi
Pernice, Michele
Perruchon, Maria
Pesce, Andrea
Petronio, Giuliano
Piaggio, Giovanni
Piano, Ermmano
Piccardi, Luigi
Piccardo, Carlo
Pierattoni, Italo
Piergallino, Vincenzo
Pieroni, Mario
Pirelli, Giuliano
Piro, Giuseppe
Pirozzi, Giuseppe
Pitacco, Giuseppe
Pizzorno, Stefano
Pletersek, Augusto
Poeti, Livio
Poggi, Ferrucio

Polese, Amalia
Pompei, Enrico
Poppi, Pietro
Predonzan, Odorico
Presetnik, Aldo
Puntelli, Aroldo
Prisco, Alfonso
Puzio, Vincenzo

Quaretti, Ivano

Raffellini, Giobatta
Raimondi, Tullio
Rainato, Italo
Raiola, Francesco
Rak, Giovanni
Ramagli, Giziano
Ramaglia, Mario
Rando, Salvatore
Ravasio, Officer Natalino
Realino, Bruno
Regnicoli, Nello
Repetti, Fedele
Repetto, Luigi
Resasco, Marcantonio
Ricca, Giacomo
Ricciardi, Salvatore
Ricevuto, Leonardo
Rima, Raffaele
Rivieccio, Nicola
Rizzotto, Letterio
Robbiano, Pietro
Rocco, Giovanni
Rocco, Mario
Rocco, Renato
Rolla, Germano
Romanelli, Antonino
Romano, Francesco
Romeo, Giovanni
Romeo, Giuseppe
Rosin, Valentino
Rossetti, Marcello
Rossi, Mario
Rovelli, Giovanni
Roy, Giulio
Rozzi, Rino
Ruello, Nicolo
Ruggiero, Girolamo

Russo, Giuseppa
Russo, Maria
Rutigliano, Ettore

Saccani, Nino
Salerno, Raffaele
Saluzzo, Amedeo
Salvagno, Luigi
Salvo, Elio
Salvo, Giulia
Sannino, Giuseppe
Santoro, Filippo
Sarno, Vincenzo
Savastano, Mario
Scala, Isidoro
Scala, Rafaelle
Scala, Salvatore
Scandurra, Sebastiano
Scarfi, Antonino
Scarpati, Alfonso
Scarpati, Francesco
Scatti, Ferruccio
Schiano, Pasquale
Sciacchitano, Antonio
Scotti, Armando
Scotto di Covella,
    Vincenzo
Scotto di Vettimo, Michele
Sedmak, Mario
Semprevivo, Ciro
Seremedi, Stefano
Sergi, Giorgio
Serpe, Amedeo
Serpe, Ciro
Serpe, Giuseppe
Serra, Italo

Sfettina, Domenico
Sila, Mario
Silvestri, Cesare
Silvetti, Faus
Simani, Ino
Simonini, Michele
Sivestri, Luigi
Skerl, Giacomo
Solari, Marco
Soncini, Guglielmo
Soriana, Nicolo
Sorrentino, Ferdinando
Sorrentino, Raffaele
Spagnolo, Attilio
Spina, Fortunato
Sporti, Antonio
Stagnaro, Giacomo
Steffe, Francesco
Stenni, Anteo
Stingi, Pasquale
Stossi, Giuseppe
Subriano, Gaetano
Sulfaro, Antonio

Tamberi, Pietro
Tarantino, Natale
Tartarini, Pia
Tassistro, Itala
Teolis, Giovanni
Tigano, Nicola
Toldo, Carlo
Torino, Orlando
Tortori-Donati, Dr. Bruno
Tosto, Francesco
Traverso, Ilio
Trevissoi, Officer Glauco

Turco, Officer Glauco

Ugalia, Giacomo
Ursino, Gaetano

Vacatello, Giuseppe
Valle, Armando
Valore, Giulio
Varriale, Armando
Vascotto, Luigi
Verdecchia, Bruno
Verrusio, Tommaso
Vidali, Giuseppe
Vidrini, Pietro
Vigano, Giovanni
Vignes, Ciro
Virgilio, Salvatore
Visciano, Giulio
Vitale, Benvenuto
Vitellozzi, Carlo
Vitiello, Antonio
Vitiello, Giuseppe
Vitiello, Stanislao

Zaccaro, Officer Mario
Zaina, Mario
Zampieri, Luciana
Zanella, Carlo
Zanghi, Eugenio
Zennaro, Sergio
Zillio, Simeone
Zincchinolfi, Giovanni
Zoppi, Vincenzo
Zotter, Tulio

In Memoriam

Of the 1,706 people aboard the *Andrea Doria*, 46 perished in the collision or shortly afterward. On the *Stockholm*, 5 crewmen lost their lives.

Andrea Doria

Paul Anderson
Agnese Baratta
Margherita Pontecorvi Baratta
Laura Bremmerman
Jeanette Carlin
Margaret Carola
Camille Cianfarra
Joan Cianfarra
Giuseppe Cirincione
Rosalia Cirincione
Christina Covina
Giuseppe DeGrandi, Jr.
Lucia DeGrandi
Theresa Del Guadio
Angelina Diana
Biaggio Diana
Victoria Diana
Maria Di Luzio
Concetta Di Miche
Norma Di Sandro
Josephine Ferraro
Angelina Gonzales
Marie Grechi
Antoinette Guzzi
Giuseppe Guzzi
Amelia Iazzetta

Marie Imbelloni
Anita Leoni
Domenico Palmeri
Francesca Palmeri
Martha Peterson
Giovanina Russo
Maria Russo
Michael Russo
Vincenza Russo
Anna Maria Sergio
Domenica Sergio
Giuseppe Sergio
Maria Sergio
Rocco Sergio
Michelina Suozzi
Ferdinand Thieriot
Frances Thieriot
Carl Watres
Rose Zumbo
Vincenzo Zumbo

Stockholm

Alf Johannson
Carl Jonasson
Karl Osterberg
Sune Steen
Evert Svensson

NOTES

PART ONE   Stories of Survival

CHAPTER 1   Autobiography of a Survivor

1. A small farming village in the Piedmont region, at the foot of the Italian Alps, bordering France and Switzerland.
2. *Nonno* is "Grandpa," and *Nonna* is "Grandma" in Italian.
3. Pedrin and China (pronounced "Keena") are nicknames in the dialect of Piemontese. Their real names are Pietro and Domenica.
4. A diminutive nickname for Piera—a name the townspeople still call me now.
5. A slang word for "fellow countrymen."
6. A classification company that approves a ship's safety for insurance purposes. ABS had ascertained that the Italian Line built the *Andrea Doria* in compliance with the 1948 Convention for Safety of Life at Sea.
7. The resistance party working against the Fascists of Mussolini.

CHAPTER 2   Officers and Gentlemen

1. *Collisione Andrea Doria-Stockholm—The Round Table.* Genova, Italy, 1988. Research document by a working group of nautical experts, Francesco Scotto, coordinator.

CHAPTER 5   When Her Watch Stopped

1. The address is www.andreadoria.org.

CHAPTER 7   Sisters and Priests: Saving Spirits

1. Dr. Peterson had been hurled into the priests' cabin, which adjoined his. He would awaken later to assist his wife and Jane Cianfarra, who herself had been thrown into the Petersons' cabin.
2. This telegram inspired author William Hoffer to use *Saved!* as the title of his book on the *Andrea Doria: Saved! The Story of the Andrea Doria* (New York: Summit, 1979).
3. "O Mary, Star of the Sea, watch kindly over us on this voyage. You, who are help of Christians, obtain for us from the Lord who is mas-

ter of winds and hearts, that every storm and every other danger to soul and body be kept far from us. May God's grace accompany us on this trip, and may the remembrance of God's presence never be far from our minds, nor the image of our family be far from our eyes, nor a longing for our country be far from our hearts. Grant that we may reach our destination happily. Strengthened in body and spirit may we embrace our dear ones, and then together with them sing a hymn of thanksgiving to you, as a prelude to the song we shall sing when we have reached the port of our eternal salvation."

4. Maria de Mattias was canonized as a saint in May 2003. She was born near Rome and lived from 1805 to 1866. Her life was dedicated to working as an educator and to helping the poor.

5. She later earned a Ph.D. in theology and biblical studies.

CHAPTER 8   **The Rich and the Famous**

1. On board was the Chrysler prototype, the Norseman. See pages 262-263.

2. "What I Learned from the People of the *Andrea Doria*," reprinted from *Parade Magazine,* September 9, 1956.

3. Rhythm-and-blues singer Big Mama Thornton first recorded "Hound Dog" in 1952.

4. 1985, Songwriters Hall of Fame; 1987, Rock and Roll Hall of Fame; 1991, ASCAP's Founder's Award; 2000, Johnny Mercer Award for for wonderful and lasting contributions to our musical culture; 2000, Britain's Ivor Novello Award; 2006, lifetime achievement award, Flanders Film Festival, Belgium.

5. The oldest engineering institution in the United States. Reinert later earned a master's degree in finance and did doctoral research in corporate and money market finance at New York University.

6. The entry was made in September 1956.

7. Robert Young's article, "Collision in the Night: The End of the Andrea Doria," was published in *USA Today* in July 1981.

8. Young was in charge of Western European operations for the American Bureau of Shipping (ABS), a company that puts its seal of approval on a ship; the ship is then "classed." Young, a naval architect and marine engineer, was trained as a classification surveyor for ABS.

9. It appears that this was Father Paul Lambert.

10. Edward P. Morgan delivered a popular nightly broadcast for the ABC Radio Network.
11. Linda's book already had autographs from Cary Grant, Betsy Drake, Gregory Peck, and John Steinbeck.
12. All of the officers on duty were expected to remain on the bridge that night.
13. Linda was found at the very top of the *Stockholm* bow, at the edge of the mangled ice-breaking steel. She lay amid girders, timbers, and furniture. Within minutes, the same part of the bow would fall into the ocean.
14. Sixty-four-year-old Jeanette Carlin had also been catapulted onto the *Stockholm*. (Earlier, she had been reading in bed next to her husband, in cabin 46.) Her body dropped off the bow and into the ocean.
15. Amazingly, he was the only Spanish-speaking sailor on board the Swedish liner.
16. The sailors had been painting when the crash occurred.
17. Miraculously, Linda had no internal injuries.
18. García went back to the bow a short time after finding Linda, where he discovered the red autograph book. Shortly after, the entire bow, where Linda had lain and the other woman (later identified as Jeanette Carlin) had cried, fell into the sea.
19. As excerpted in Hoffer, *Saved!* Courtesy of ABC Radio Network.
20. This number included Camille Cianfarra and his daughter Joan.
21. Dr. Thure Peterson, who freed Linda's mother, Jane, from the wreckage, claimed he saw the bodies of the two girls in the rubble of their cabin.
22. As excerpted in Hoffer, *Saved!* Courtesy of ABC Radio Network.

CHAPTER 9   **History's Greatest Sea Rescue**

1. The purpose of these compartments is to protect the ship from sinking when water enters. The *Doria* was built to withstand the impact of two compartments.
2. United States Naval Institute magazine, *Proceedings*.
3. Richard Goldstein, *Desperate Hours: The Epic Rescue of the Andrea Doria* (New York: John Wiley & Sons, 2001), pp. 80-81.
4. The *Stockholm*'s safety drill was scheduled for the following day, so passengers had not been informed of their assigned muster stations.
5. Measurements taken in dry dock reveal that the *Stockholm*'s bow

had been ripped back 75 feet, 300 tons of steels had fallen into the sea, and damage extended 55 feet along the waterline and about 40 feet along the keel. Goldstein, *Desperate Hours.*

6. Captain Nordenson had established by then that his ship would not sink.

7. The davits, constructed according to the regulations of the 1945 International SOLAS convention, allowed for a launching with a list of up to a maximum of 15 degrees.

8. Eight crew members were assigned to each *Doria* lifeboat.

9. It is important to note that the *Andrea Doria-Stockholm* collision took place where there was an abundance of traffic.

10. All vessels arrived on July 26, except for the *Stockholm*, which arrived on July 27.

11. It remained afloat for eleven hours.

12. Scotto was the founder and coordinator of the Working Group.

13. Published in October 1988, with a second edition in process.

14. Ibid.

15. Ibid.

16. Ibid.

17. Ibid.

18. Young was in charge of the Western European operations for his company.

19. Young, "Collision in the Night."

20. *American Journal of Psychiatry* 114, no. 5 (November 1957): 427-28.

21. Officer Giannini was in charge of Stoller's muster station. He remained on the bridge with the captain until 2:30 a.m. The crew admits to giving precedence to the starboard side, since it was impossible to lower the lifeboats on the port side and it was decided they would be more needed there, where the evacuation was taking place.

22. *Collisione Andrea Doria-Stockholm—The Round Table.*

PART TWO   **Stories of the Ship**

CHAPTER 10   **Anatomy of a Collision**

1. This was unlawful because the Swedish Royal Decree n. 581 of 18 July 1952, entered in force on 5 February 1953 by order of the Royal Swedish Ministry of Commerce, obliged to follow the 1953 the

North Atlantic Track Agreement. It states: "Ships belonging to the following shipping companies must follow the recommended routes marked in the Pilot Charts of the North Atlantic Ocean and published by the US Hydrographic Office; Svenska Amerika Linje. . . ."

2. Nautical miles per hour are referred to as knots.

3. Because of the high concentration of traffic to and from Europe, the area between the Nantucket Lightship and the Ambrose Lightship was dubbed in maritime circles "the Times Square of the Atlantic." Ships used one or the other as their first or last contact with New York.

4. The *Andrea Doria* stopped in Cannes, Naples, and Gibraltar before reaching the open seas.

5. In relation to the *Andrea Doria*, the *Stockholm* was in an inbound lane, ahead and slightly on the *Doria*'s starboard bow.

6. Officers Franchini and Giannini both held master's licenses, qualifying them as captains.

7. This is to enable the vessel to maneuver swiftly, if necessary, in the presence of restricted visibility.

8. The Nantucket Lightship was broadcasting its meteorological report of fog, reporting visibility at 15 feet. It also was continuously sounding a fog-alert signal.

9. All traffic in the area is normally east and west.

10. *Collisione Andrea Doria-Stockholm—The Round Table.*

11. The position obtained by looking straight ahead and 90 degrees to the right or left.

12. This indicates viewing the starboard side of the *Stockholm*; hence a starboard-to-starboard passing.

13. It was calculated by naval engineer Francesco Scotto that Calamai would have needed 11 more seconds to cross ahead of the *Stockholm*'s bow and avoid the collision.

14. Carstens, age twenty-six, was given command of the *Stockholm* for the first time, after three month's experience on the ship. He did not hold a master's license.

15. RDF is used to take two or more bearings of RDF stations. Each station emits different sound signals to determine bearings, which are then plotted on a chart. The intersection of these bearing lines is the vessel's position.

16. The average age of crew members on the bridge watch was twenty-two.

17. *Collisione Andrea Doria-Stockholm—The Round Table.*
18. It is surprising that no fires broke out.
19. Watertight compartments make a ship stable. A ship can be a two- or three-compartment ship, indicating the number of belowdeck compartments that can be penetrated by water before a vessel is no longer stable. The *Andrea Doria* was a two-compartment vessel. Since more than two of its compartments were compromised, it was no longer seaworthy.
20. The *Doria's* builders had never estimated more than a 15-degree list.
21. These estimates reflect a total penetration of 28 meters: 9 within the *Doria*, plus 22 off the *Stockholm*, minus 3 from compressed material.
22. Captain Robert Meurn recalls: "I was serving as a deck cadet on the *Excambion* when we received the SOS from the *Andrea Doria*. I remember continuous dense fog all along the coastline on July 25."
23. Meurn maintains that by drawing grease-pencil marks every three minutes on the radarscope, the target's course and closest point of approach are evident.
24. It was not common practice for transatlantic liners, especially since the advent of radar, to slow down in fog conditions.
25. Meurn maintains that a safe passing distance, with the use of radar, is about one mile.
26. According to Meurn, Scotto, and others, by interpreting the two ships' course recorders, a correct conclusion about the events would have been easily reached. This is standard procedure when the Coast Guard analyzes data for collision cases. But it was not done in this case.
27. In a limited-liability case, reimbursement is made according to the value of the vessels involved.
28. Several of them gave their accounts to the Round Table.
29. Official pretrial transcripts, as cited in Hoffer, *Saved!*
30. After the collision, the captain of the *Stockholm* waited one hour before giving his vessel's actual position. One can only assume that Captain Nordenson was not fully aware of his position.
31. The gyrocompass course repeater did not have input to radar.
32. Alvin Moscow, *Collision Course: The Classic Story of the Collision of the Andrea Doria and the Stockholm* (Guilford, Connecticut: Lyons Press, 2004).
33. Based on taking the two course recorder graph readings and working out the data mathematically.

34. This is a calculation made by naval architects, based on the relative position and distance between the two vessels.
35. Meurn had originally believed that the *Stockholm* was not at fault.
36. This was only a hypothetical scenario, but some people didn't understand it, which further confused the issue.
37. Richard A. Cahill, *Collisions and Their Causes* (London: Fairplay Publications, 1983).
38. Robert Meurn, *Watchstanding Guide for the Merchant Officer* (Centreville, Maryland: Cornell Maritime Press, 1990).
39. The simulator provides a variety of sea and weather conditions with actual visibility, night and day vision, 300-degree peripheral vision, various signals (fog, traffic, etc.), and the presence of other ships, planes, helicopters, etc. It also prepares the student on methods to avoid collisions and groundings.

CHAPTER 11   The Sinking of the Unsinkable

1. Courtesy of www.andreadoria.org.
2. Maurizio Eliseo is an inspector of cruise ships, naval historian, university lecturer, and author.
3. The maximum list foreseen and stipulated by SOLAS was 15 degrees.
4. Young, "Collision in the Night."
5. The entire ship was divided into watertight compartments for protection from flooding.
6. Approximately 30 feet or more of the *Doria*.
7. *Collisione Andrea Doria-Stockholm—The Round Table.*
8. The department-store magnate was the first person to dive the *Doria* after the collision in 1956.
9. The *Stockholm* was the smallest transatlantic passenger liner.
10. Bright plans to dive the *Andrea Doria* again in July 2006.
11. *Collisione Andrea Doria-Stockholm—The Round Table.*

CHAPTER 12   Diving the *Doria*

1. New York: Simon & Schuster/Touchstone, 2001.
2. Dive boat R.V. *Wahoo.*
3. The location where Gimbel found the Bank of Rome safe in 1980.
4. In comparison, the *Titanic*, which sank in 1912, lies at a depth of 12,500 feet, or 2.5 miles. Bright has dived the *Titanic* wreck in a submersible as part of a research team.

5. Expert shipwreck divers Sally Wahrmann and Gary Gilligan.
6. Veteran diver John Ormsby.

EPILOGUE   **Passages**

1. Painter Pietro Zuffi graced a wall of the First Class ballroom with a cubist-surrealist-style mural. His work depicting Neptune holding court at the banquet table was called *Neptune's Banquet.*
2. Admiral Andrea Doria, who protected Genova from foreign invaders during the seventeenth century, died at the age of ninety-three. His bronze statue was displayed in an alcove of the First Class lounge.
3. Sister ship of the *Andrea Doria.*
4. Letter to the Editor, *Norfolk Ledger-Star,* October 17, 1975.
5. From Genova, he was an executive for the Italian Line from 1963 to 1974.
6. Interview, July 2004.
7. Ibid.
8. The same law applies today.
9. Interview, October 2005.
10. *Collisione Andrea Doria-Stockholm—The Round Table.*
11. By law, parties involved in the deposition process were required not to speak about it publicly.
12. The media and the public.
13. The psychiatrists were traveling on the *Ile de France*. Interviews took place on board.
14. "Some Psychiatric Notes on the *Andrea Doria* Disaster," *American Journal of Psychiatry* 114, no. 5 (November 1957): 427.

GLOSSARY

aft. The direction toward the stern of the ship.

astern. Behind, or a backward direction in the line of a vessel's fore-and-aft line. When a vessel moves backward, it is said to move astern.

ballast. Any weight or weights used to keep the ship from becoming top-heavy or to increase its draft and/or trim.

boat deck. The deck on which the lifeboats are kept.

bow. The forward part of a ship.

bridge. The location from which a vessel is steered and its speed controlled.

bridge deck. The deck upon which the bridge is located.

bulkhead. A vertical steel partition corresponding to the wall of a room, extending either athwart ship (crosswise) or fore and aft.

buoyancy. The ability to float; the upward force of water pressure, equal to the weight of the displaced liquid.

chart. A map for use by navigators.

crow's nest. An elevated lookout station located forward, usually on the masthead.

davit. Crane arm that when lowered can project over the side of the ship in order to lower or raise boats to or from the water.

dead ahead. Directly ahead on the extension of the ship's fore-and-aft line.

deck. A platform extending horizontally from one side of a ship to the other.

displacement. The weight of water displaced by a floating vessel; thus, a ship's weight in terms of long tons (2,240 pounds equal 1 long ton).

double-bottom. Compartments at the bottom of the ship between inner and outer bottoms, used for ballast tanks, oil, water, fuel, etc.

draft. The distance from the surface of the water to the ship's keel (how deep the ship is into the water).

fathom. A measure of length, equivalent to 6 linear feet, used for depths of water and lengths of rope or chain.

helm. Used as the steering wheel of the ship, it is a tiller or a wheel generally installed in the bridge or wheelhouse to turn the rudder in order to change course during maneuvering and navigation.

hull. The main body of a vessel, including shell plating, framing, decks, and bulkheads.

inclinometer. An instrument for determining ocular inclination, angles, and directions of the visual axes.

in extremis. In grave or extreme circumstances. A situation so perilous that both approaching vessels must change course in order to avoid a collision.

Jacob's ladder. A rope ladder suspended from the side of a vessel and used for boarding.

keel. The chief structural member of a ship that extends longitudinally along the center of its bottom and often projects from the bottom.

knot. Speed at sea (1 nautical mile per hour equals 1 knot).

lightship. A stationary vessel (at anchor), carrying a light used for navigation, serving the same purpose as a lighthouse.

list. An inclination to one side.

lookout. A member of the crew stationed on the bridge or on the crow's nest at the top of one of the main masts. His duty is to watch for any dangerous objects or for other vessels approaching.

loran. A long-range aid to navigational systems in which position is determined by an analysis involving the time intervals between pulsed signals from two or more pairs of ground stations of known position.

muster station. A place on a ship where passengers or crew must gather in case of emergency.

nautical mile. One minute of latitude, approximately 6076 feet; about one-eighth longer than the statute mile of 5280 feet.

navigation rules. The regulations governing the movement of vessels in relation to one another, generally called steering and sailing rules or the rules of the road.

pilot house. The enclosed deckhouse on the navigating bridge from which a ship is controlled when under way.

piloting. Navigation by use of visible references.

porthole. A round opening in the side of a ship, normally kept weather- and watertight by a transparent glass cover.

port side. The left-hand side of a ship when facing forward. The port side of a ship during darkness is indicated by a red sidelight.

seaworthiness. The condition of a ship, its sufficiency in terms of materials, construction, equipment, crew, and outfit for the trade in which it is employed. Any sort of damage to the vessel by which the cargo may suffer may cause it to become not seaworthy.

ship's log. A journal used to record any event that may have occurred on board; there may be, for example, an engine room log, a deck log, etc.

stability. The tendency of a ship to return to its upright position when inclined away from that position.

starboard side. The right-hand side of a ship when facing forward. The starboard side of a ship during darkness is indicated by a green sidelight.

stem. The forwardmost part of the bow.

stern. The rearmost section of the ship.

watchstanding. The duties performed by an officer who assists the captain in surveillance and data handling.

winch. A machine for lifting and lowering cargo and for other purposes that cannot be handled by manual power; it consists of a drum or a barrel around which a rope or a cable is wound to achieve either a lifting or lowering motion.

windlass. A machine used to hoist the anchor.

yaw. To swing or steer off course.

SOURCES

Books

Badano, Guido. *Ricordi di un Capitano (A Captain's Memoirs)*. Genova, Italy: Galleria Mazzini, 1992.

Ballard, Robert D., with Rick Archbold. *Lost Liners: From the Titanic to the Andrea Doria, the Ocean Floor Reveals Its Greatest Lost Ships*. New York: Hyperion, 1997.

Benziger, Barbara. *The Prisoner of My Mind*. New York: Walker and Company, 1969.

Cahill, Richard A. *Collisions and Their Causes*. London: Fairplay Publications, 1983.

Cunningham, Anthony. *The Titanic Diaries*. London: Nostalgia, 2005.

Gentile, Gary. *Andrea Doria: Dive to an Era*. Philadelphia: Gary Gentile Productions, 1989.

Goldstein, Richard. *Desperate Hours*. New York: John Wiley & Sons, Inc., 2001

Haberstroh, Joe. *Fatal Depth: Deep Sea Diving, China Fever, and the Wreck of the Andrea Doria*. Guilford, Connecticut: Lyons Press, 2004.

Hoffer, William. *Saved! The Story of the Andrea Doria, the Greatest Sea Rescue in History*. New York: Summit Books, 1979.

Lord, Walter. *A Night to Remember*. New York: Holt, Reinhart & Winston, 1991.

McMurray, Kevin. *Deep Descent: Adventure and Death Diving the Andrea Doria*. New York: Touchstone, 2001.

Mattsson, Algot. *Out of the Fog: The Sinking of the Andrea Doria*. Centreville, Maryland: Cornell Maritime Press, 1986.

Meurn, Robert J. *Survival Guide for the Mariner*. Centreville, Maryland: Cornell Maritime Press, 1993.

_____. *Watchstanding Guide for the Merchant Officer*. Centreville, Maryland: Cornell Maritime Press, 1990.

_____. *Marine Cargo Operations—A Guide to Stowage*. Centreville, Maryland: Cornell Maritime Press, 2004.

Miller, William H., Jr. *Picture History of the Italian Line*. New York: Dover Publications, 1999.

Moscow, Alvin. *Collision Course*. Guilford, Connecticut: Lyons Press, 2004.

Scotto, Francesco. *Collisione A. Doria-Stockholm—Tavola Rotonda (Round Table)*. Genova: Sala Garibaldi, 1988.

_____. *Andrea Doria 1956-2006 Per Non Dimenticare (Grupo di Lavoro Stockholm-Andrea Doria)*. Genova: Frilli, 2006

Interviews and Correspondence

Charlotte Adelsperger
Guido Badano
Frank Braynard
David Bright
Marina Calamai
Celeste Caputo
Mario Cassiano
Gino Chiesa
Catherine Coppola
Giovanni Cordera
Anthony DiGirolamo
Father John Dolciamore
Maurizio Eliseo
Leonardo Faccenda
Eugenio Giannini
Father Raymond Goedert
Angela Grillo
Anthony Grillo
Carmelo Grillo
Luciano Grillo
Donald Hanson
David Hollyer
Louise Hollyer
Father Thomas Kelly

Chris Kolh
Julianne McLean
Pat Mahoney
Vivian Massa
Pat Mastrincola
Linda Morgan
Captain Robert Meurn
Linda Morgan
Sister Angelita Myerscough
Giovanna Paladino
Leonardo Paladino
Alfred Pearson
Fabio Pozzo
Jerome Reinert
Franco Ricci
Francesco Scotto
Carla Silvestri
Meryl Stoller
Mike Stoller
Germaine Donofrio-Strobel
Father Richard Wojcik
Madge Young
Friends and family in Pranzalito,
    Italy

Videos, Documentaries, and Radio Broadcasts

Commentaries: ABC Radio Network. July 26 and 27, 1956.
Andrea Doria: Spirit of Survival. Discovery Channel. 1995.
Caught on Film. The History Channel.
Fatal Collision. Discovery Channel. 1998.
The Sinking of the Andrea Doria. Arts and Entertainment Channel. 1997.
Andrea Doria: The Final Chapter. Independent United Distributors. 1986.

Newspapers

U.S.A.: *New York Times, Chicago Sun-Times (Parade), San Antonio Express-News, New York World-Telegram, U.S. News and World Report, Grand Rapids CIO News, Detroit News, Detroit Free Press, Detroit Times, New York Post, New York Daily News, Daily Mirror, Oregonian, Il Progresso Italo-Americano, Herald Tribune, South Florida Sun-Sentinel, Houston Post.*

Italy: *La Stampa, L'Italia E La Voce Del Popolo, Oggi, Visto, L'Automazione Navale, Quotidiano Nazionale, Corriere Mercantile, Il Nuovo Corriere Della Sera, Il Giornale, La Nuova Stampa, Il Popolo Nuovo.*

France: *Le Soir.*

Magazines, Newsletters, Journals

Life, Nautical Institute: Safety At Sea International, U.S. Naval Institute Proceedings, Kings Pointer, Friends of the Andrea Doria Newsletter, Shipping & Psychology Newsletter, American Journal of Psychiatry, Shipwrecks, Collier's, Saturday Review.

Letters and Memoranda

Italian Line Inter-Office letters and press releases; Elizabeth Quinn, "The Last Night of the Last Voyage of the Andrea Doria"; Chris Guitaut; James T. Shirley, Jr.; Italian Broadcasting & Advertising Company.

Internet

http://home.planet.nl/~denne073
http://www.andreadoria.org
http://www.lostliners.com
http://www.michelangelo-raffaello.com
http://www.nauticalresearch.com
http://www.shipwreck.blogs.com
http://www.titanic.bizhosting.com

INDEX

ABC Radio, 179, 293

Addario, Carmelo, 129

Admiral Nakimov, 209

Adorers of the Precious Blood of Christ, 136-37, 141, 142-43, 145-51

Ambrose Lightship, 112, 176, 218, 295

America, 170

American Bureau of Shipping, 35, 153, 178, 206, 249, 291, 292

Ansaldo Shipyard, 169, 247, 254

Arcalia's Classic International Cruises, 266

Arnsby, Sister Callistus, 138

Athena, 266

Badano, Guido, 53-58, 60-64, 65, 67-70, 72, 73, 74-75, 190, 203, 204-5, 267

Baker, Sister Marie Raymond, 138

Barton, Gay, 163, 165

Benvenuti, Livia, 194

Bjorkman, Ingemar, 222

Bollinger, Dorothy, 169, 172, 175

Bright, David, 235, 243, 251-54, 255-58, 261-62, 270, 272

British Royal Institute of Navigation, 240

Burzio, Domenica, 21-51, 291

Burzio, Piera (Pierette Domenica Simpson), 21-51, 83, 104, 242

Burzio, Pietro, 21-51, 291

Burzio, Vivina, 21, 22, 25, 26-27, 44, 45-50

Cahill, Captain Richard A., 240, 243

Calamai, Marina, 271

Calamai, Oreste, 56

Calamai, Paolo, 56

Calamai, Captain Piero, 17, 53-65, 67-75, 118-19, 125, 150, 179, 180, 188, 189-90, 193, 196, 197, 200, 202, 203, 204, 205, 206, 208, 218, 219-22, 226, 243-44, 266-73, 295

California, 268

Calma, Officer, 61

Campbell,189

Cape Ann, 60, 65, 87, 118, 160, 189, 190, 193, 196-97, 198, 200, 253

Caputo, Celeste, 93-95, 97-101, 104

Carlin, Jeanette, 139-40, 293

Carrothers, John C., 235-40, 249, 267, 268, 271

Carstens-Johannsen, Ernst, 191-92, 222-23, 224, 225, 226, 231-39, 242-43, 244, 266, 295

CBS Evening News, 247

Chiappori, Dalciso, 205

Chiesa, Gino, 33-34, 42

Chopin, Frederic, "The Butter-
    fly," 118, 119, 120, 129
Chrysler Norseman, 262-63, 292
Cianfarra, Camille, 177, 178, 179-
    80, 181, 183, 293
Cianfarra, Jane, 59, 65-67, 178-80,
    183, 291, 293
Cianfarra, Joan, 176, 177, 179,
    180, 293
Cianfarra, Linda. *See* Linda Mor-
    gan
Coast Guard, 65, 72, 112, 188-89,
    198, 238, 253, 254, 268, 296
Cogliolo, Officer, 61
Coleridge, Samuel Taylor, *The
    Rime of the Ancient Mariner,*
    41, 69, 70
Collision, description and analy-
    sis, 216-46
Colombo, Officer, 61
Columbus, Christopher, 17, 272
Computer Assisted Operational
    Research Facility (CAORF),
    237, 241, 242
Conte Biancamano, 105
Cordera, Giovanni, 61, 204, 205-
    6
Council of American Master
    Mariners, 237
Cousteau, Jacques, 257
Crew members (list), 284-88
Cristoforo Colombo, 103, 254, 266

De Beaudéan, Captain Raoul, 64,
    124, 125, 126, 167, 189-90,
    199, 218, 266
De Berc, Guy, 164-67, 168, 190

De Girolamo family (Francesco,
    Gino, Mario, Antonio, Nico-
    la),195
De Mattias, Saint Maria, 148,
    149, 150, 292
Deans, Billy, 259
Di Meo family (Rigoletto, Anna),
    109
DiPaola, Cecilia, 188, 194
Di Sandro family (Tullio, Filom-
    ena, Norma), 83, 87, 89-90,
    196, 198
Diving. *See* Shipwreck
Dolciamore, Father John, 133-34,
    145, 151-52
Donato, Third Officer, 204, 205
D'Onofrio, Antonietta, 93, 102-4
D'Onofrio, Germina, 93-104
D'Onofrio, Giuseppe, 101-4
Dooner, Liliana, 188, 194
Dooner, Maria, 188, 194
Doria, Admiral Andrea, 262, 264,
    265, 298

Eagle, 189
Edward H. Allen, 65, 73, 74, 87,
    189
Edwards, Douglas, 247
Els, Grace, 155-56
Emergency Position Indicating
    Rapid Beacons (EPIRBS), 209
Empress of Ireland, 209
Enestrom, Lars, 222
Erdmann, Lieutenant Roger, 72
Evergreen, 62, 189
Exxon Valdez, 241

Fatalities (list), 289
Federal Court of New York, 218, 225, 271, 272
Fischer, Arthur, 160
Fitzpatrick, Lawrence, 210
Fornasetti, Piero, 214
Foxfire (movie), 79, 93
Franchini, Curzio, 56, 204, 219, 295
Francis, Arlene, 128
French Line, 164
Friedman, Paul, 207, 270

Gallo, Officer, 61
Gambone wall panels, 211
García, Barnabé Polanco, 180-81, 184, 293
Garvin, Glenn, 264
Gatto, Steve, 261
Geisen, William, 165-66, 168
Ghia, 262
Giannini, Eugenio, 52, 53, 64, 68, 203-4, 205, 219-22, 227, 269-70, 294, 295
Gilligan, Gary, 259
Gimbel, Peter, 251, 257, 297
Ginori, Richard, 258
Global Maritime Distress and Safety System (GMDSS), 209
Goedert, Father Raymond, 131, 133, 138-40, 145, 151
Graziosi, Esther, 145
Grillo, Angela, 105-16
Grillo, Anthony, 83, 105, 106, 107, 108-16
Grillo, Carmelo, 105-7, 112-13, 114-16

Grillo, Luciano, 33, 207
Gripsholm, 266
Gronchi, Giovanni, 73
Guitaut, Chris, 208
Gulinelli, Luigi, 105-6

Haight, Charles S., 238-38
Hall, Richard (Dickie) Roman, 154-56
Hanson family (Elizabeth, Andy, Ardith, Donnie), 195-96
Heyliger, 189
Hoffer, William, *Saved!* 291, 293
Hollyer, David, 195
Hollyer, Louise, 195
Hornbeam, 71-72, 73, 189, 197, 200

Ile de France, 39, 41, 43, 64-65, 82, 84-86, 111-13, 115, 118, 122-26, 136, 140-41, 147, 149, 151, 156, 159-60, 163, 166-67, 168, 172, 174, 175, 176, 177, 182, 183, 189, 197, 198, 200, 201, 206, 207, 208, 218, 225, 253, 265, 266, 270
Italia Prima, 266
Italian Line, 54, 59, 67, 71, 73, 85, 105, 106, 112, 115, 119, 169, 217, 225, 227, 232, 265, 266, 267, 268, 269, 270, 272, 291
J. L. Hudson Company, 101
Jonah E. Kelly, 189, 198

Kallback, Gustav Herbert, 192
Kelly, Grace, 265
Kelly, Father Thomas, 131-32, 138-39, 143-44, 145, 148, 151

Kirn, Carlo, 68, 204, 205

Lambert, Father Paul, 133, 292
Larsen, Peder, 222
Lawsuits, 225-27, 245, 267, 268-69
Legare, 189
Leiber, Jerry, 157, 160-62
Linn, Louis, 207, 270
Lloyd's of London, 91, 226-27, 268-69
Lord, Captain Stanley, 268
Lusitania, 209

McDonald, Robert, 210
McKee, Peter, 210
McLean, Julianne, 117-30
McLean, Mr. and Mrs., 117-18, 120
McMurray, Kevin, *Deep Descent*, 256, 258-59
Macy's, 142
Magagnini, Osvaldo, 64, 68, 69-70, 202, 204, 205
Manaqui, 65, 197
Mantero, Officer, 61
Manzotti, Officer, 61
Maracci, Mario, 60, 63
Marine Safety Commission, 210
Maritime Association of the Port of New York, 166
Mastrincola family (Mrs., Pat, Arlene), 31-33, 34, 38, 41, 42, 50-51, 83
Maze, Harry, 167
Menu, First Class, 212-13

Meurn, Captain Robert, 217, 231-32, 233-36, 240-43, 244, 245, 267-69, 271, 296, 297
Morgan, Edward P., 153, 179, 181-83, 184-86, 293
Morgan, Linda, 153, 178-86, 169, 175, 176, 177
Moscow, Alvin, *Collision Course*, 233-35, 238, 266, 270
Moss, Lewellyn, 126-27
Myerscough, Sister Angelita, 131-32, 134-38, 140-43, 145-51

Nantucket Lightship, 60, 190, 218, 219, 222, 223, 295
Natta, Monsignor Sebastian, 68, 132-33, 138, 143, 148, 150, 203
New York Times, 178, 179, 183, 231, 271
Nordenson, Captain Harry Gunnar, 191-92, 193, 217-18, 222, 223, 226, 266, 270, 294, 295, 296
Norseman. *See* Chrysler Norseman

Oneto, Luigi, 63, 64
Ormsby, John, 259
Owasco, 189

Paladino family (Leonardo, Giovanna, Maria, Felicia, Antonia), 76-92
Paladino, Rocco, 80
Passengers (lists), 275-84

Pazzaglia, Luigi, 61, 205
Peterson, Martha, 59, 65-67, 68, 121, 124, 204, 291
Peterson, Dr. Thure, 59, 65-67, 68, 72, 121, 124, 134, 204, 291, 293
Pino, Officer, 61
Pius XII, 73, 129
Presley, Elvis, 157, 161, 162
Private William H. Thomas, 87, 189, 196-97, 200, 253

Quinn, Elizabeth, 208

Raffaello, 150, 204
Rainier, Prince, 265
Ravasio, Officer, 61
Red Cross, 88-89, 90
Regina, Antonio, 89
Reinert, Jerome, 153, 162-69
Renda, Pietro, 34
Rescue, description and analysis, 187-210
Riggs, Ruth, 126-27
Robert E. Hopkins, 189
Roman, Ruth, 153, 154-56, 165
Rovelli, Giovanni, 65-67, 68, 121

Sacco and Vanzetti trial, 245
Safety of Life at Sea Convention (SOLAS), 178, 248, 291, 294, 297
Scotto, Francesco, 200-203, 244, 251, 254, 267, 269, 294, 295, 296
Seeker, 261

Shipwreck, diving on, 251-54, 255-64
Shirley, James, 236-37
Sinking, description and analysis, 247-54
Stephens, Captain Hugh M., 237
Stereotyping, ethnic, 244-45, 270-71
Stingi, Pasquale, 70
Stockholm, 15, 52, 54, 59, 60, 62, 98-101, 125, 127, 138-40, 143-44, 150, 166, 175, 177, 181, 182, 183, 185, 187, 189, 191-93, 196-97, 200, 201, 202, 203, 218, 219, 220, 221, 222-25, 226, 228-45, 248, 249-50, 251, 261, 266, 268, 269, 293, 294, 295, 296, 297
Stoller, Corky Hale, 162
Stoller, Meryl, 156-61, 207-8
Stoller, Mike, 153, 156-62
Strike It Rich (TV), 90-91
Svensson, Evert, 187
Swedish-American Line, 217, 225, 227, 236, 238, 239, 266, 294

Tamaroa, 189
Thierot, Peter, 169, 175, 195
Thomas E. Hopkins, 65
Thornton, Big Mama, 161, 292
Titanic, 15, 60, 89, 95, 99, 127, 159, 204, 209, 247, 257, 262, 268, 297
Today Show, 128
Top Cat, 264

Tortori-Donati, Dr. Bruno, 68, 203
Toscanini, Arturo, 118
Turner, Captain John, 264

Underwood, Eugene, 232-33
U.S. Merchant Marine Academy, 130, 231, 241
U.S. Naval Institute, *Proceedings*, 236

Vespucci, Amerigo, 272
Vestris, 209
Visciano, Giulio, 53

Wahoo, 256
Wahrmann, Sally, 259
Web site, 116, 297

White Viking Fleet, 266
Wichita Eagle, 128
Wojcik, Father Richard, 133-34, 141, 145, 152

Yakutat, 189
Young, David, 169-78
Young, Madge, 153, 169-78, 179, 182
Young, Robert T., 35, 169-78, 206-7, 249-50, 292, 294
Young, Virginia, 169-78, 182

Zamparo, Giovanna, 135, 136, 137
Zodiac Room, 214
Zuffi, Pietro, 297

Purple Mountain Press, established in 1973, acquired Harbor Hill books in 1990. In addition to New York State regional books, Purple Mountain Press publishes books of colonial military history and, under the Harbor Hill imprint, maritime books. It also distributes the maritime books of Carmania Press (London) in North America. Recently published titles of interest include *Death Passage on the Hudson: The Wreck of the Henry Clay*, *Thomas Cornell and the Cornell Steamboat Company*, *Queen of Sea Routes: The Merchants and Miners Transportation Company*, *The Ocean Steamship Company of Savannah: The Savannah Line*, and *SS Independence SS Constitution: Great American Ocean Liners* (the last three were co-published with the Steamship Historical Society of America). For a free catalog, write Purple Mountain Press, PO Box 309, Fleischmanns, NY 12430-0309, or call 800-325-2665, or fax 845-254-4476, or email purple@catskill.net. Visit us on the web at www.catskill.net/purple.

Half Hollow Hills Community Library
55 Vanderbilt Parkway
Dix Hills, New York

21 DAY LOAN